MINNESOTA VIKINGS
The Complete Illustrated History

StarTribune

MINNESOTA VIKINGS

The Complete Illustrated History

by Patrick Reusse

Contributions by Judd Zulgad and Jim Souhan

Foreword by Bill Brown
Afterword by Senator Amy Klobuchar

Voyageur Press

First published in 2008 by Voyageur Press, an imprint of MBI
Publishing Company and the Quayside Publishing Group, 400
First Avenue N, Suite 300, Minneapolis, MN 55401 USA

Voyageur Press titles are also available at discounts in bulk quan-
tity for industrial or sales-promotional use. For details write
to Special Sales Manager at MBI Publishing Company, 400 First
Avenue N, Suite 300, Minneapolis, MN 55401 USA.

Library of Congress Cataloging-in-Publication Data

Reusse, Patrick.
  Minnesota Vikings : the complete illustrated history / Patrick
Reusse.
     p. cm.
  Includes index.
  ISBN 978-0-7603-3232-0 (hb w/ jkt)
  1. Minnesota Vikings (Football team)--History. I. Title.
  GV956.M5R48 2008
  796.332'6409776579--dc22

                                        2008008740

Editor: Josh Leventhal
Designed by Greg Nettles

Printed in Hong Kong

On the frontispiece: Cris Carter, 1999.
Brian Peterson/Star Tribune

On the title page: Adrian Peterson, 2007.
Carlos Gonzales/Star Tribune

On the back cover: (top, left to right) Matt Birk, 1999; Bud
Grant, 1980; John Randle, 1997; (middle, left to right) Ahmad
Rashad, 1979; Vikings fans, 2001; Chuck Foreman and Ed White,
1975; (bottom, left to right) Adrian Peterson, 2007; Carl Eller,
1977; Randy Moss, 1999. *Star Tribune*

CONTENTS

PREFACE

Professional football first came to Minnesota in 1961, and heavy winter snowfall was a regular presence during the two decades in which the Vikings played in the open-air Metropolitan Stadium. Here the players trudge through mounds of snow at the team's practice facility at Midway Stadium in December 1961. *John Croft/Star Tribune*

My father, Richard Reusse, was the undertaker in Fulda, Minnesota, until 1962, when he sold the business and we moved to Prior Lake. One advantage of this move was that we could decide to attend Twins games at the spur of the moment, rather than having to plan ahead for the three-and-a-half-hour journey.

Richard was a devoted follower of Minnesota sports, particularly the football Gophers and all things baseball. We were fans of the Minneapolis Millers down there in southwest Minnesota, before the Twins came to the region for the 1961 season.

He was enthusiastic about the arrival of the National Football League and the Minnesota Vikings that same year, although this was also the period when the Gophers went to back-to-back Rose Bowls. The transition from Gophers fanatic to Vikings fanatic took some time for Richard, as it did for many Minnesotans.

The change was consummated in 1968, when Coach Bud Grant took the Vikings to the playoffs for the first time. A year later, the Vikings posted a 12-2 record, and the anticipation was gargantuan leading up to the first NFL playoff game at Met Stadium, to be played on December 27, 1969. The opponents were the Los Angeles Rams, and much was being made of how a team from Southern California could handle playing in the middle of winter in Minnesota.

Over the years, Richard had kept numerous photos showing his children and their pals standing in front of huge snowdrifts after blizzards swept across the prairie. He also had a couple of shoeboxes filled with newspaper headlines and photos describing and displaying Minnesota snowfalls, including the notorious Armistice Day Blizzard of November 1940.

Richard decided it was his duty to taunt Roman Gabriel, the Rams quarterback, with some of his Minnesota wintertime memorabilia. He mailed envelopes filled with these photos and clippings and sent several addressed to "Roman Gabriel, Los Angeles Rams, Los Angeles, Calif." It seemed unlikely to Richard's offspring that those envelopes ever made it to their intended target, particularly when Roman and the Rams came to Minnesota a few days before the game to practice in cold weather.

The Vikings defeated the Rams 23-20 in a wonderfully dramatic game, and then thumped the Cleveland Browns 27-7 a week later in the NFL title game to advance to their first Super Bowl.

Hardly anyone in Minnesota—including Richard—gave a thought to the idea that Joe Kapp's offense and the fabulous Purple People Eaters defense could lose that championship game to the AFL's Chiefs, but that's what happened: Kansas City 23, Vikings 7.

A few days after the Super Bowl, Richard received a letter with a return address of Southern California. Inside was a newspaper clipping that featured a photo of Kapp walking off the field late in the game, holding his shoul-

Minnesota fans have been enthusiastic and creative supporters of their beloved Vikings for nearly five decades, through good times and bad.
Brian Peterson/Star Tribune

der in agony. There was also a note that offered a simple message.

"Dear Richard: What happened to your Vikings?" The note was signed Suzanne Gabriel—Roman's wife.

All Purple followers have their favorite Vikings story from the team's five decades as a Minnesota institution, and that is mine—confirmation that my father didn't send all those winter scenes to the rival quarterback in vain, but they were received and accepted in good humor.

While doing the research for this celebration of the Vikings' unconventional, unpredictable history, we looked for all of these things—the humor, the glory, the agony, the heroic moments, and yes, the embarrassing moments. We scoured the archives of the *Minneapolis Tribune*, the *Minneapolis Star*, and the *Star Tribune*. The *Star Tribune* did not develop an electronic library until 1986, and the first quarter century of this team's existence was studied through clippings stuffed in envelopes. Many gems were found inside those yellowed envelopes.

What I have done here, for the most part, is look at this team's history in actual time, rather than in retrospect. I don't consider myself a Vikings historian, but more a follower and observer, and it was fascinating to be reminded of moments and stories long since forgotten.

The *Star Tribune*'s Judd Zulgad—one of the best, most tireless beat reporters covering an NFL team for any newspaper in the country—contributed several side stories and the recaps of the four Super Bowls.

Jim Souhan, my colleague as a *Star Tribune* sports columnist, wrote Chapter Eight, which covers the first six seasons (1992–1997) of the Dennis Green era. Souhan covered the Vikings at the start of Green's tenure. It was also during this time that Coach Green accused three local sports columnists of trying to run him out of town. Green never named names, but on the outside chance that I was on the list, I asked Jim to write this chapter as a bow to both his insight and his objectivity.

Joel Rippel from the *Star Tribune* sports staff helped greatly with the research. Chris Reusse, my son and also a member of the *Star Tribune* sports staff, provided a statistical look at the Vikings.

I want to pay tribute as well to the words written through the years by Jim Klobuchar, Dick Cullum, Dick Gordon, Charley Johnson, Merrill Swanson, Allan Holbert, Joe Soucheray, and yes, Sid Hartman—to name a few—for their contributions over the years in chronicling the adventures of the Minnesota Vikings for readers of the morning *Tribune*, the afternoon *Star*, and, since 1982, the *Star Tribune*.

The same goes for the photographers, from the great John Croft to today's masters of the craft, including Jerry Holt, Jeff Wheeler, Carlos Gonzalez, and others. And, of course, we must mention the brilliant Brian Peterson, who snapped the iconic "Weeping Blondes" image a few minutes after the Vikings' loss to Atlanta in January 1999 in the NFC title game. That picture is not worth a thousand words—it's worth a million.

FOREWORD
BY BILL BROWN

I was a rookie with the Chicago Bears and hanging out on the other sideline when the Vikings played their first game on September 17, 1961, at Metropolitan Stadium. We came to town expecting to handle the expansion team. Then Fran Tarkenton, their rookie quarterback, came in late in the first quarter, started running like a wild man, and lit up the Bears with a 37-13 victory.

Chicago had players like Doug Atkins—the huge, veteran defensive end—and seeing a quarterback scramble like Tarkenton was a whole new thing for him. To say the least, Big Doug was not real happy about trying to chase a quarterback from sideline to sideline.

Another guy who was not real happy was George Halas, who was both the Bears owner and the coach. Halas was embarrassed by what happened and called us some very unflattering names after the game.

A year later, I was traded to the Vikings. That first training camp in Bemidji is where I first got to spend quality time with Coach Norm Van Brocklin.

I had never been around a coach like the Dutchman in my life. Not even Halas in a bad mood could compare with Van Brocklin. He ran training camp like nothing I had experienced with Chicago. We were going hard and hitting hard for hours every day. And the Dutchman spiced up those practices with his foul language.

One of the hard things about Van Brocklin was that he was unpredictable. One day he would be telling jokes and treating people fairly. The next day he would fly off the handle and was not fair at all. On those days, you could be doing everything right, and you still couldn't do anything right in his eyes.

The film sessions with Van Brocklin were something too. We would be in this dark room, and only the light would be coming from the film projector. He would see someone make a mistake and just run it back over and over again.

Tommy Mason, who could have been a real star as a running back in the NFL if he had not hurt his knee early in his career, tells a story about a game in which he missed a block and allowed Tarkenton to get trampled by the defense.

A story had appeared in the Minneapolis newspaper a few days earlier about Mason and how he played the banjo and the guitar, owned a monkey (named "Dutch"), and drove a Cadillac.

Van Brocklin played the missed block over and over, and finally he said, "Mason, take that guitar, that monkey, that Cadillac, stick 'em you know where, and play some football!"

The first few seasons were up and down for Van Brocklin and the team. After he abruptly retired in the middle of the 1965 season and then just as abruptly returned a day later, the coach's relationship with the players took a difficult turn. When he came back, his attitude was beyond belief. He went berserk, screaming at people in practice and in the locker room. He was mad at everybody. Mostly, I think he was mad at himself. He was embarrassed that he had quit.

I wasn't around for the team's first year, but from the day I got here, you could see the problems between Tarkenton and Van Brocklin. Both of them wanted things their way. They really couldn't stand each other. By 1966 it was clear that both were on their way out. Van Brocklin wasn't talking to Tarkenton; he was hardly talking to anyone. No one was surprised when Tarkenton demanded a trade, and Van Brocklin resigned from the Vikings for good.

And then Jim Finks—who wasn't an easy general manager for the players to deal with, by the way—brought in this guy from Canada that not one of us had heard about.

The players who had been together, myself and Mick Tingelhoff and Grady Alderman, Bozo Sharockman and Paul Dickson, were all saying, "Who's Bud Grant?"

Then we got to Mankato (the new Vikings training camp site), and from the first day you knew that things were going to be different. By different, I mean, they were going to be better.

You could talk straight to Bud, and Bud talked straight to you. He took immediate control of the team, without ever having to yell at anyone. He knew exactly what he wanted. He would make sure that he got that across. If he saw any doubt, he would repeat it until he was sure things were going to be done his way.

I don't think I ever had one problem with Bud Grant. He didn't have the attitude that a coach had to be a tough guy. He didn't kill anybody in training camp. The greatest thing that happened to me as a player, and to the Minnesota Vikings as a team, was the hiring of Bud Grant as head coach.

Tarkenton had been traded to the New York Giants, so we needed a quarterback. Finks and Grant both had come from the Canadian Football League, and they liked a guy who was free agent up there: Joe Kapp.

What a piece of work he turned out to be! Everything the fans have heard about Joe was true. He let everything hang out on the field and off the field. He was definitely a crazy man in those years. Kapp was also perfect for that team. He gave the offense a fire to go with our great defense and helped get us to that first Super Bowl. He was a tremendous teammate.

When Joe departed following a contract dispute in 1970, we weren't the same team offensively. Then Tarkenton came back in 1972.

Some people have the impression that Fran was a bit aloof, but I never saw it that way—not at all. Fran and I were buddies. We picked on him and he took it well. And no one should ever forget that he was a great competitor. He took the Vikings to three Super Bowls. There's only a few quarterbacks who have done that.

We're always asked about that, of course—the four Super Bowl losses. It's been more than 30 years since the last one, and you know what? Those losses still hurt.

I have to say, we had a hard time understanding how the talented teams that we had could lose four Super Bowls. You look back, and those were all terrific teams from the AFL and AFC: Kansas City, Miami, Pittsburgh, Oakland. Those Miami and Pittsburgh outfits might be among the best teams ever.

That said, I still don't think we ever played our game in a Super Bowl. We played our game part of the time, but we never were at our best for four quarters.

The team had almost the same roster year after year. You would show up in Mankato and line up first offense against first defense, and there were Tarkenton and Dave Osborn and Mick Tingelhoff and Grady Alderman and Stu Voigt and Ron Yary on your side of the ball, and there were Carl Eller, Jim Marshall, Alan Page, Gary Larsen,

Wally Hilgenberg, Roy Winston, Bobby Bryant, and Paul Krause on the other side.

An amazing number of those Vikings moved to the Twin Cities, raised their families here, and are still here. We went to work together, we socialized together, our wives became best friends, and our kids knew each other growing up.

Free agency has brought a lot of great things for the players—in my day, every contract negotiation was like trying to get blood from a turnip—but the modern NFL teams will never have that same stability, that same sociability, that we had with Bud's Vikings.

And we still have it, by the way. Those same guys I went out with on that frozen dirt in December playoff games at the Met are still the best friends I have in the world.

The rugged fullback Bill "Boom Boom" Brown spent 13 seasons with the Vikings and played on three of Minnesota's Super Bowl teams. He ranks first in rushing attempts and third in rushing yardage on the franchise's all-time list. *Charles Bjorgen/Star Tribune*

INTRODUCTION
ECSTASY AND AGONY

In January 1970, the Minnesota Vikings became the last team to represent the National Football League in the Super Bowl against the rival American Football League. The upset 23-7 loss to the AFL's Kansas City Chiefs was the first true kick-in-the-stomach agony for the Vikings' faithful legions of fans. It would not be the last, of course.

For the 1970 regular season, the National Football League and the American Football League completed the full merger of the competing leagues, marking the beginning of the NFL's modern era. Teams from the newly established National Football Conference and American Football Conferences competed against each other during the regular season. The term "wild card" also became part of the national sports lexicon for the first time in 1970.

From 1933 through 1966, the NFL postseason consisted strictly of Eastern and Western Conference champions playing for the title. From 1967 through 1969, there were four four-team divisions, and the division winners met in a two-round playoff format to determine the league championship. Beginning in 1966, the NFL champ faced the champion team from the AFL in the Super Bowl

Then came the 1970 merger, and the NFL decreed that the playoffs would feature four teams from both the NFC and the AFC—three division winners and a wild-card team, the division runner-up with the best record.

The numbers of divisions and wild cards has changed through the years, but going back to 1970 is when we can make some valid comparisons between the Vikings and their NFL brethren. What you discover is that followers of the Purple have had it pretty good.

Consider this: In the 38 seasons from 1970 through 2007, the Vikings have the fifth-best overall record in the NFL, with 333 wins, 249 losses, and 2 ties, for a winning percentage of .572. They trail only the Miami Dolphins (354 wins, .608), Pittsburgh Steelers (351 wins, .603), Dallas Cowboys (347 wins, .594), and Denver Broncos (339 wins, .586).

As for their traditional division rivals, since 1970 the Vikings have had 40 more regular-season victories than the Green Bay Packers (293 wins, .509), 43 more victories than the Chicago Bears (290 wins, .497), and 87 more than the long-suffering Detroit Lions (246 wins, .425).

During this same era, the Vikings are third in the number of playoff seasons with 22. Dallas has 25 and Pittsburgh has 23; the Vikings are followed by Miami and the San Francisco 49ers, with 21 each. Further down the list, the Packers and the Bears each have 13 playoff seasons, and the Lions have 9.

The Vikings have 16 playoff victories in these 38 seasons, which puts them in a tie for eighth best. Still, it is three more than the Packers and the Bears (13 postseason wins apiece) and 15 more than those poor Lions, whose one and only playoff victory came after the 1991 season.

There is a downside to this success—and isn't there always a downside for our beloved Purple? It's the agony to go with the ecstasy: The Vikings have the maximum number of losses a team can have in 22 playoff seasons, with 22.

That number represents more postseason losses than any other NFL team since 1970. It's more losses than the Cowboys, who have five Super Bowl titles to go with 20 postseason losses; the Dolphins, who have two Super Bowl titles to go with their 19 disappointments; the Steelers who have five Super Bowl titles against 18 losses; and the Raiders who have three Super Bowl titles to go with their 18 bitter ends. The Packers and the Bears each have one Super Bowl title since 1970 to go with 12 postseason losses, and those lucky Lions have a mere nine playoff losses.

Sorry, folks. We couldn't chronicle the five decades that the Vikings have been in Minnesota's midst and on our minds without mentioning those two dreadful words—Super Bowl—and there will be reviews of the four distressing events in the pages that follow.

We wanted to start here, though, with a reminder that there has been substantial joy for followers of this team: victories in 57 percent of the games they have played in the post-merger schedule in a parity-loving NFL, and playoff berths in 58 percent of the 38 seasons from 1970 to 2007. Vikings fans have been able to enjoy Alan Page, Carl Eller, and later, the crazed, face-painted John Randle overrunning quarterbacks; Fran Tarkenton and Tommy Kramer throwing darts; Randy Moss and the Carter lads, Cris and Anthony, electrifying the atmosphere in the Metrodome with their hands, while Robert Smith did it with his legs; Randall McDaniel and Gary Zimmerman trampling defenders to the left; Ed White and Ron Yary doing the same to defenders on the right; and Bud Grant taking it in, steely-eyed on the sideline, and offering the emotional sendoff, "Thank you for not smoking," on the day he was honored at the Metrodome.

All this and plenty more has put smiles on the faces and cheers in the throats of the Purple faithful. As a reminder that all the best things are not in the past, we offer two words to renew those smiles and cheers: Adrian Peterson.

ECSTASY: NFC PLAYOFFS, DECEMBER 1973

The Minnesota Vikings had a roster of players in their prime and a defense for the ages when they went to the Super Bowl after the 1969 season. They had the look of such a powerhouse that the Detroit Lions lobbied to move the Vikings to a different conference when the NFL and AFL merged.

Yet the Vikings managed to go the next three seasons without winning a playoff game. They had first-round losses at Met Stadium to San Francisco and Dallas in 1970 and 1971, respectively. Then, in 1972, Fran Tarkenton was reacquired from the New York Giants, and his first season back in Bloomington turned into a 7-7 flop.

The veteran quarterback received considerable ridicule for this. The national NFL media—a much smaller group than it is today—suggested that mediocrity might be the best that could be expected from Tarkenton.

Then, in 1973, the Vikings cruised to a 12-2 record and returned to the playoffs as champions of the NFC Central Division after a one-year absence. Their opponents for the playoff opener at Met Stadium on December 22 were the Washington Redskins, the NFC's first wild-card team.

The game was played on a Saturday. Washington coach George Allen announced late Friday that Billy Kilmer was recovered from an intestinal ailment and would start at quarterback, rather than 39-year-old Sonny Jurgensen. This was a controversy that went on in Washington from 1971 to 1974: Billy or Sonny?

Defensive end Carl "Moose" Eller was worked up before the game about the four-year gap since the last playoff victory.

"This is the most important game we've ever played," Eller said. "This has been a big year, and we want to make it bigger by going to the Super Bowl. I can't remember a Viking team being more ready to play a game, both physically and mentally."

The Vikings weren't as ready as their Moose had detected. Washington had a 125-9 advantage in yards and an 8-0 edge in first downs in the first quarter. Fortunately for the home team, Washington kicker Curt Knight missed a field goal from 17 yards and then missed a 49-yarder early in the second quarter.

Jubilant fans tear down the goal posts at Metropolitan Stadium in Bloomington following the Vikings' 27-20 win over the Washington Redskins on December 22, 1973. The victory earned the team a trip to the conference championship game the following weekend.
John Croft/Star Tribune

Finally, Vikings running back Oscar Reed turned a short pass into a 50-yard gain to set up a chip-shot field goal by Fred Cox to give Minnesota a 3-0 lead.

That still was the score when Bobby Bryant fumbled a punt for the Vikings. The Redskins recovered at the Vikings' 21-yard line. Kilmer threw an 18-yard pass to Charley Taylor; then Larry Brown ran three yards for a touchdown.

The Vikings trailed 7-3 when they reached the locker room at halftime. The coaches had not yet gathered the players together when Eller's deep voice bellowed through the room and demanded attention.

"We've gone too damn far to play like this," he said. "We are so tight out there we are embarrassing ourselves. Let's play our game."

He walked over to wide receiver John Gilliam, who had dropped two Tarkenton passes in the first half, and said: "We know you can do the job. You're going to get the ball again."

Eller then went over to the blackboard that was available for the coaches to scribble plays. "Carl didn't write anything on it," Reed recalled. "He punched it, tossed it around, and kicked it."

Bob Lurtsema, the backup defensive lineman, told Dwayne Netland of the *Minneapolis Tribune*: "He kept getting madder and madder. He told us we had to go out and take charge of the game."

The Vikings received the second-half kickoff and proceeded to score in 3 minutes, 14 seconds, to take a 10-7 lead. Reed set up the touchdown with a 46-yard run to Washington's 2-yard line; Bill Brown plunged into the end zone for the score.

This did not result in the Vikings taking charge. Inexplicably, Washington's Knight made field goals from 52 yards (equaling the longest in NFL playoff history) and 42 yards to give the Redskins a 13-10 lead one play into the fourth quarter.

The Vikings needed a drive, and Tarkenton produced it with a series of short passes. Then, from the Washington 28, he hit Gilliam in the right corner of the end zone.

Minnesota cornerback Nate Wright quickly followed with an interception of a Kilmer pass and returned it 26 yards through heavy traffic to the Redskins' 8-yard line.

On the next series, Tarkenton was flushed from the pocket and took off on one of his trademark scrambles before again finding Gilliam in the end zone. The receiver

Against Dallas in the 1973 NFC title game, Chuck Foreman gained 104 total yards—76 on the ground and 28 on pass receptions. The Vikings defense, meanwhile, limited the Cowboys offense to a total of 153 yards. *Vernon Biever/WireImage.com/ Getty Images*

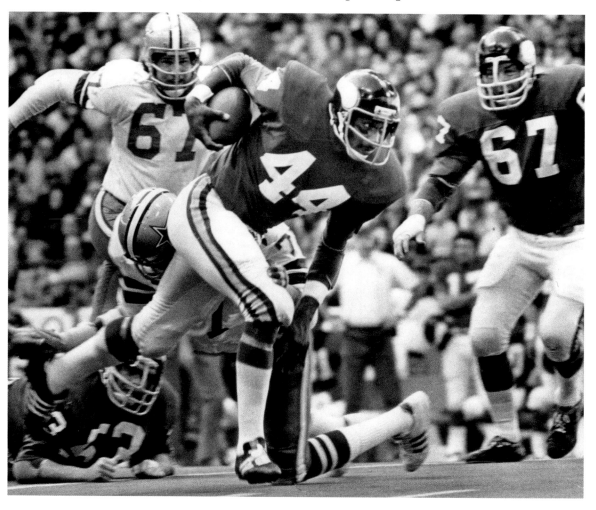

who had dropped one sure touchdown pass in the first half now had two TDs in the second half, and the Vikings were in front 24-13 with nine and a half minutes left.

The Met Stadium spectators were thumping their thermal mittens together and roaring madly. Then the Redskins pulled off a Vikings-style stunt: Ken Stone blocked a punt by Mike Eischeid. On the next play, Kilmer threw a 28-yard touchdown pass to Roy Jefferson.

Washington had cut Minnesota's lead to 24-20, and there still were five and a half minutes to play. The Vikings killed four minutes on the next possession, and Cox capped it with a 30-yard field goal with 1:40 remaining.

The Redskins reached the Vikings' 42. Eller knocked down a Kilmer pass. Two more incompletions and the Vikings had a 27-20 victory. All long-time Purple followers remember this victory as, "That's when Moose broke the blackboard at halftime."

The victory earned the Vikings a trip to Dallas for the NFC title game. These Cowboys would become the Vikings' rivals as the NFC's dominant team of the 1970s.

The Cowboys had eliminated the Vikings from the playoffs two seasons earlier at Met Stadium, which Dallas followed with its first Super Bowl victory, a 24-3 thumping of Miami in January 1972.

The Vikings spent three days practicing in Tulsa, Oklahoma. While there, Bud Grant made a point to laud Tarkenton, who had proved in his second season back in Minnesota that a team quarterbacked by him was not destined to be a non-contender.

"Fran is a stable person and a very intense man," Grant said. "He understands football as well as anyone I've been associated with.

"Fran, in the two years I've been working with him, has been an unselfish quarterback. He sets the stage for the team and gets his satisfaction from the way he leads the club on the field. He doesn't have to throw a touchdown pass to prove his value."

Quarterback Fran Tarkenton and receiver John Gilliam celebrate after completing a 54-yard touchdown pass against Dallas in the third quarter.
John Croft/Star Tribune

The Vikings arrived in Dallas as 6-point underdogs. One unexpected advantage for the Vikings was that Calvin Hill, the Cowboys' outstanding running back, was out with an injury.

The Vikings dominated the first half and took a 10-0 lead. The defensive front four put a big rush on Dallas quarterback Roger Staubach. Chuck Foreman rushed 12 times for 70 yards and scored the half's only touchdown.

The Vikings were taking it to the Cowboys with both front lines. Then came a wacked-out second half, when Dallas had six turnovers and the Vikings had four. For the Vikings, Bryant had two interceptions and Gary Larsen recovered two fumbles.

The first of those turnovers seemed to be huge: Bryant intercepted a Staubach pass at the Vikings' 2-yard line. The Cowboys' despondency over that missed opportunity didn't last long. The Vikings punted from their own end zone, and Golden Richards returned it 63 yards for a touchdown.

The score was 10-7, and the 60,272 spectators inside Texas Stadium were going bonkers. Then Tarkenton saw John Gilliam blow past Mel Renfroe, Dallas' star cornerback, and Tark hit him in stride at the Cowboys' 4-yard line for a 54-yard touchdown.

From there, the Vikings added a 63-yard interception return by Bryant for a touchdown and a 34-yard Cox field goal, both in the fourth quarter, to secure a 27-10 victory.

Grant gave credit to assistant coach Jerry Burns and the rest of the offensive coaching staff for the game plan they instituted during those three days in Tulsa.

"Game plans are no better than the players who execute them," the head coach said. "But our staff began their preparation with the conviction that Dallas plays a very predictable defense. They formulated the way we would go about attacking that defense."

Veterans Mick Tingelhoff (in his 12th season), Milt Sunde (10th), and Grady Alderman (14th) were part of an offensive line that allowed the Vikings to rush for 203 yards against Dallas' so-called Doomsday Defense.

"The old guys got tired of reading that they were old guys," Tingelhoff said. "We just reached down and came up with some gut football!"

For Tarkenton, it was his first trip to the playoffs in 13 seasons, and now he was headed to Houston, Texas, to take on the defending champions, the Miami Dolphins, in a Super Bowl.

Decades later, Fred Zamberletti, the Vikings' original trainer and an employee for life, would say: "When you're talking about great victories, it's hard to beat that one in Dallas in '73. No one on the outside thought we were going to win that game, and we kicked their butts."

Super Bowl bound! Upon arriving at Minneapolis-St. Paul International Airport following their NFC championship victory, Coach Bud Grant and the rest of the team are greeted by enthusiastic Vikings fans on December 30, 1973. *Regene Radniecki/Star Tribune*

AGONY: NFC TITLE GAME, JANUARY 17, 1999

The 1998 Vikings posted a 15-1 record in the regular season and set an NFL record with 556 points. They took a week off while the wild-card round of the playoffs was contested, then exploded again for a 41-21 victory over the Arizona Cardinals inside a rocking, roaring Metrodome.

The win advanced the Vikings to their first NFC title game in 11 years. The team coming to the Dome would be Atlanta. The Falcons had an impressive 14-2 record of their own, but few Vikings followers paid attention to that. The fans were too busy trying to figure out how to get to Miami to watch the Vikings in the Super Bowl on the last day of January.

The switchboards at both Winter Park, the team's complex in Eden Prairie, and the Dome's Vikings ticket office were overwhelmed with calls. Fans wanted information on Super Bowl tickets, on the availability of souvenir jerseys and shirts, and on how to secure hotel accommodations in Miami.

"It's crazy, but it's a good crazy," said Jeff Diamond, the Vikings vice president for football operations.

The arrival of Randy Moss, the emergence of Randall Cunningham, and the rest of the offensive machine created such a din in the Metrodome that Atlanta coach Dan Reeves was fretting the noise factor five days before the game.

Reeves was aware of previous complaints by Green Bay's Mike Holmgren about the proximity of speakers to the visitors' sideline. Reeves expressed his concern on Monday, and a day later, the Vikings received notice that the NFL was monitoring the situation.

Eventually, it was decided that the speakers should be moved from the 30-yard lines and closer to the end zones.

Every possible angle was covered in the Twin Cities media before this game, including the fact that Norm Van Brocklin coached the Vikings during their formative years and later coached the Falcons.

On the eve of the game, there was another odd attraction taking place in downtown Minneapolis: A crowd estimated at 14,000 showed up at Target Center for the "People's Celebration," the new governor's version of an inaugural ball. The new governor was former pro wrestler Jesse Ventura, which gave the visiting reporters who were covering the NFC Championship Game a chance to throw some ridicule at Minnesota.

Bob Ryan, a sports columnist from the *Boston Globe*, had another topic on his mind. He told a Minnesota reporter before the game: "The worst thing that has happened to the Vikings is that Gary Anderson hasn't missed a kick all season. You can't challenge fate like that. If the game's close, that's something that will haunt the Vikings."

Just out of reach. Receiver Cris Carter can't make the grab on a Randall Cunningham pass in the third quarter of the NFC championship game against the Atlanta Falcons on January 17, 1999. It was one of several near misses in the contest.
Jeff Wheeler/Star Tribune

Ryan would have had a tough time finding any horned-hat-wearing fan who shared his eerie prediction. The Vikings were 11½ point favorites, and Minnesotans sort of figured that number was kind to the Falcons.

The Vikings were leading 20-7 late in the first half. They had the ball on their 18-yard line when Cunningham threw two incompletions to make it third-and-10 with 1:08 remaining.

Again, Cunningham dropped to pass. This time, Atlanta end Chuck Smith came flying around the corner toward the quarterback. As Cunningham cocked his arm for that

Gary Anderson stares in disbelief as his field goal attempt sails wide in the fourth quarter of the NFC title game—his only missed kick of the entire season. *Jerry Holt/Star Tribune*

long throwing motion of his, Smith knocked the football away and teammate Travis Hall recovered at the Vikings 14.

On their first play, Falcons quarterback Chris Chandler threw a touchdown pass to Terance Mathis, and the Falcons were in the game, down 20-14 at halftime.

Atlanta's Morten Andersen made it 20-17 with a field goal early in the third quarter. The Vikings offense sputtered a bit, but then they went on a 15-play, 82-yard drive that consumed nearly seven minutes. Cunningham threw a 5-yard pass to backup receiver Matthew Hatchette for a touchdown. The score was now 27-17, with 79 seconds gone in the fourth quarter.

Inside the suite occupied by owner Red McCombs and his family, someone started to hand out white caps that read "Minnesota Vikings NFC Champions" on the front and "Miami Bound" on the back.

Among the people visiting the suite to offer congratulations to McCombs was Evander Holyfield, the legendary heavyweight boxer, who was also a Falcons fan.

The Metrodome was as loud as a stadium can get when the Falcons gained possession at their own 27, but all day, the veteran Chandler had operated with a silent count, and the Falcons had avoided false start and delay-of-game penalties.

They did it again—the Falcons drove nearly 70 yards before Andersen kicked a field goal to make it 27-20.

Jim Marshall, the Vikings great, took off the white hat that he had placed on his head a few minutes earlier in McCombs' suite.

The Vikings had one more drive in them. They reached the Falcons' 20-yard line with under 2-1/2 minutes remaining. Coach Dennis Green sent in Gary Anderson to attempt a field goal. The kicker had made 106 consecutive kicks since the start of the regular season, including 39 of 39 field goals.

The ball was put down at the Falcons' 28-yard line, making it a 38-yard kick. Anderson could use his smooth stroke from there, since there was no need to get a little extra on the kick to cover the distance.

The ball was snapped and the kick was on its way before the frantic Falcons rushers could do anything about it. The Metrodome crowd went into a frenzy, certain that Anderson had given the Vikings a 10-point lead with 2:07 remaining.

Then, something shocking happened. The official signaled that the ball was outside the left goal post. The Falcons players danced around madly. The Dome turned from bedlam to quiet.

Bob Ryan was right. Minnesota was wrong. Karma, fate, or whatever the cause meant that Anderson's only miss of the season came at the most critical time for the Vikings.

On their next possession, the Falcons moved 71 yards in a mere 1:18, and Chandler hit Mathis with a 16-yard pass for the game-tying touchdown.

The Vikings started with the ball at the 20-yard line after the kickoff. After two plays, they were third-and-3 at the 27, and there were 30 seconds left on the clock. That's when Coach Dennis Green made the decision that has select Vikings fans still referring to him as "Den-knee" a decade later. Rather than a take a shot downfield, Green instructed Cunningham to kneel down in order to run out the clock and send the game into overtime.

"When you're down to 30 seconds, then you need to take two good downs, and if you don't have a first down by then, then you better go and move the other way," said Green, with convoluted rapidity after the game.

The first three possessions of the overtime resulted in punts, two by the Vikings. Then, on the fourth posses-sion, the Falcons moved the ball downfield into position for their Andersen, Morten, to also try a 38-yard field goal. He kicked it down the middle of the uprights. The Falcons had a 30-27 victory—as well as a trip to the Super Bowl in Miami that all of Minnesota was so certain these high-powered Vikings were going to take.

Gary Anderson stood up and faced reporters after the game. Then he headed home, weary and still a bit shocked, to encounter his 9-year-old son Austin when he walked in the door.

"He came over and gave me a hug," Anderson said. "And reminded me of one of the lessons that I try to teach him. He said, 'All right, Dad. You tell me all the time that you can't make them all.'"

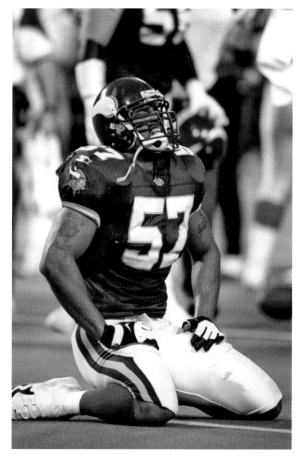

Linebacker Dwayne Rudd sits in anguish after the Falcons kicked the winning field goal in overtime to defeat the Vikings, 30-27, and deny Minnesota its first trip to the Super Bowl in more than two decades.
Brian Peterson/Star Tribune

The Weeping Blondes.
Brian Peterson/Star Tribune

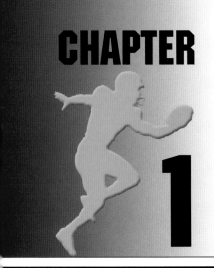

CHAPTER 1

GETTING STARTED
VIKINGS PREHISTORY AND THE FIRST SEASON

THE PURSUIT

Metropolitan Stadium opened in 1956 as the home to the Minneapolis Millers of baseball's Class AAA American Association. The real purpose of this new stadium was to allow the Twin Cities to bring a Major League Baseball team, a National Football League franchise, or preferably both to the Bloomington prairie.

The task force in charge of these pursuits was headed by Charles Johnson, the executive sports editor of the *Minneapolis Star and Morning Tribune*. Johnson was also the lead sports columnist for the afternoon *Star*. Obviously, there was no pretense a half-century ago about journalists taking an objective position when it came to local sports.

The 1961 Minnesota Vikings offensive squad (clockwise from top): Mel Triplett (#33), Fran Tarkenton (#10), Jerry Reichow (#89), Perry Richards (#85), Frank Youso (#72), Mike Rabold (#64), Bill Lapham (#52), Gerry Huth (#65), Grady Alderman (#67), Dave Middleton (#84), Hugh McElhenny (#39).
Eliot Elisofon/Time & Life Pictures/Getty Images

There was also little pretense that this was a united effort to acquire major league sports for the Twin Cities. The old jealousies between Minneapolis and St. Paul still were evident. The city of St. Paul built its own ballpark, Midway Stadium, and also had a group working to bring a major league baseball team to Minnesota.

The first indication that something resembling big-league sports actually was on the way to Bloomington came on August 14, 1959. There was an announcement in Chicago that a rival league to the NFL, the American Football League, would start play in 1960.

Six cities were named for prospective franchises: New York, Los Angeles, Houston, Dallas, Denver, and Minneapolis. Buffalo was added as the seventh franchise in October.

The Minneapolis owners were going to be Max Winter, former general manager of the Minneapolis Lakers, and local businessmen Bill Boyer and H. P. Skoglund.

This Minneapolis group was so strongly involved in those early weeks of the AFL that Winter was put in charge of setting the guidelines for the league's first draft. Plus, it was the Minneapolis group that pushed the idea of naming Joe Foss, the World War II flying ace and former South Dakota governor, as the AFL's first commissioner.

Many important AFL matters were planned for discussion at the organizational meeting that would start November 22 at the Pick-Nicollet Hotel in Minneapolis.

The league decided that its draft would allow for territorial selections—meaning that teams would have the first choice on players from the region in which they operated. This rule had worked for Winter in the National Basketball Association with the Lakers, and he brought it to the first AFL draft.

During the meeting, Foss was nominated as commissioner, and Boston was certified as the eighth (and final) city to receive a franchise for the 1960 season.

Yet, there was one big problem in all this: Johnson, the influential newspaperman and head of Minneapolis' major league task force. Charley was an irascible fellow and was dead-set against joining the AFL. He did not deem the AFL to be a real major league. Johnson and Sid Hartman, already an influential presence as a sports columnist with the *Minneapolis Morning Tribune*, were in frequent contact with George Halas, the owner of the NFL's Chicago Bears.

Halas was around when the NFL originated in 1920, and he maintained great clout in the league during the late 1950s. Halas told Johnson and Hartman to get to Winter and have him bail out on the AFL.

Halas' message: We're going to combat this new league with two expansion teams—Dallas will get one, and Minneapolis will get the other.

The Chicago Cardinals, suffering at the gate as the city's second team behind the Bears, had played three exhibitions and a regular-season game in Buffalo in 1958. Then, in 1959, the tryout of new cities continued with two Cardinals regular-season games in Bloomington.

The first game was played on October 25. The opponent was the Philadelphia Eagles, and the Cardinals lost by a score of 28-24. The crowd was announced at 20,112, which was 6,000 below the Met's capacity and not much better than what Cardinals owner Walter Wolfner was drawing for his team in Chicago.

Then, on November 22, the very day that the AFL began its organizational meeting in downtown Minneapolis, the New York Giants came to the Met to take on the Cardinals. The game drew a sellout crowd of 26,625. Pat Summerall kicked three field goals in the Giants' 30-20 victory.

The large crowd at an NFL game was not the big pro football story in the Twin Cities on Monday morning, however. Charley Johnson still was working diligently to head off the AFL, and he produced the information for a front-page story in the *Tribune* that ran under the headline: "Twin Cities May Get National Grid Team."

The lead to the story read: "Ten of the 12 National Football League owners have approved the request of Minneapolis-St. Paul for a franchise in the NFL starting with the 1960 season, according to Charles Johnson, executive sports editor of the *Minneapolis Star and Tribune*.

"At the same time, backers of the Twin City entry in the newly organized American league are considering withdrawal.

"Johnson spoke for Max Winter, E. W. Boyer, and H. P. Skoglund, the same group which has held the [AFL] franchise. Later, after a heated six-hour session, Lamar Hunt, president of the Dallas team in the new loop, said reports that the Twin Cities entry is pulling out of the American league to join the NFL are 'unfounded,' according to Associated Press."

Johnson said that his information on the approval of 10 NFL teams came in a telegram from Halas. It was a telegram that Johnson had requested, so he would have a basis for the front-page bombshell that threw the AFL organizational meeting into chaos.

Winter had left the meeting at 2 a.m., telling the AFL people that he was going forth with the pursuit of an NFL expansion franchise. In the next day's *Tribune*, he was quoted as saying, "I have withdrawn from the Minneapolis-St. Paul football picture as far as the American league is concerned."

Boyer and Skoglund hung in with the AFL for a time. The AFL draft was conducted with the inclusion of a Minneapolis franchise. The team's first selection was Dale Hackbart, a quarterback from the University of Wisconsin. (Hackbart ultimately signed with Green Bay, was converted to a defensive back, and ended up playing for the Vikings from 1966 to 1970.)

Johnson's campaign against the AFL franchise continued in Monday's *Star*. The top sports story, under a Johnson byline, carried the headline: "Stadium Commission Favors NFL Franchise."

The Metropolitan Sports Area Commission was the landlord for Met Stadium. Gerald Moore, chairman of the commission as well as of the Minneapolis Chamber of Commerce, released this statement as the AFL meetings continued in his city:

"[The commission] wants the best possible pro football for fans in the Upper Midwest. The National Football League is now providing the best football possible. Naturally, we prefer a franchise in this established league."

Foss was officially appointed as AFL commissioner on November 30. He was a main influence in the AFL's decision to allow Minneapolis-St. Paul to end its commitment to the new league. The AFL took no legal action against the Minneapolis-St. Paul group. In fact, Foss saw to it that the AFL returned a $25,000 deposit for the franchise that had been made by Winter, Boyer, and Skoglund.

NFL NOT A SLAM DUNK

As the Twin Cities group was working to cut its ties with the AFL, the NFL was in the midst of its own share of

chaos. Commissioner Bert Bell died unexpectedly in October 1959. Austin Gunsel, his assistant, took over as interim commissioner, and the decision for a full-time replacement was put off until the league meeting, which was scheduled to start on January 20, 1960, in Miami.

That league meeting is where Dallas and Minneapolis-St. Paul expected to receive approval as the 13th and 14th franchises in the NFL. However, Washington Redskins owner George Preston Marshall threatened to sue if the NFL expanded without a unanimous vote of the 12 current owners, and Foss threatened a $100 million antitrust suit by the AFL if the NFL placed a franchise in Dallas.

The price tag for an NFL expansion team was $600,000, plus $400,000 in startup costs. Winter, Boyer, and Skoglund represented Minneapolis and had committed $600,000. They took in Bernie Ridder, the owner of the St. Paul newspapers, and Ridder's official investment was $300,000. The fifth partner was Ole Haugsrud from Duluth, the owner of the long-ago Duluth Eskimos. Ridder was an old friend to Haugsrud from his Duluth days and helped to cover the remaining $100,000.

The arrangement was advertised as uniting the "entire state—Minneapolis, St. Paul, Duluth" in the NFL effort. In reality, Winter, Boyer, and Skoglund needed Ridder's money to make the deal.

Winter and a delegation from the Twin Cities went to Miami expecting to receive the expansion franchise within the first couple of days of the meeting. It took longer than that for the NFL owners just to settle on a new commissioner.

The leading candidate was Marshall Leahy, a San Francisco attorney. He had eight firm votes, but could not get the ninth vote necessary to be elected. Finally, out of nowhere and six days after the meeting started, Pete Rozelle, the 33-year-old general manager of the Los Angeles Rams, was elected as commissioner.

One of Rozelle's first acts was to get the owners to change the NFL constitution to allow expansion with a 10-2 vote, rather the unanimous vote previously required. The vote to change the constitution conveniently was 10-2, with Marshall of the Redskins and Wolfner of the Cardinals as the only opposition.

The Minnesota delegation had dwindled during the long debate over a commissioner. Winter stayed. He was a constant presence in the lobby of the Kenilworth Hotel for 10 days.

On January 28, the NFL got around to the expansion vote that had been expected a week earlier. It was a given that Dallas would be admitted. It already had a front office, a coach in Tom Landry, 30 players signed, and a nickname: the Rangers. The name soon would be changed to Cowboys, to avoid confusion with the Dallas-Ft. Worth Rangers, a minor league baseball team.

Max Winter (second from right), owner of the new Minnesota NFL franchise, stands with Chicago's George Halas (far left) and Dallas Rangers owners Bedford Wynne and Clint Murchison Jr. in Miami Beach, Florida, after the league voted to approve the two expansion teams in January 1960.
AP/Wide World Photos

"At noon when the league adjourned for lunch, I thought we were dead," Winter said. "From everything I could gather, they were going to vote in Dallas and forget about the Twin Cities."

Winter said that changed when Halas, Pittsburgh's Art Rooney, Cleveland's Paul Brown, and Washington's Marshall (of all people) "went to bat" for Minneapolis-St. Paul as a second expansion team.

Once Marshall lost the fight for no expansion, he decided the league was better off with two teams rather than just one.

Rozelle made the announcement early in the evening: Dallas would become the league's 13th team in 1960 and Minnesota would become the 14th team in 1961.

When asked by a *Washington Post* reporter if he was upset about being required to wait a year to field a team, Winter said: "As long as we're in the NFL, what else could I ask?"

Charley Johnson took no direct credit in his *Minneapolis Star* column, although it is clear that without his insistence that this area deserved the best (the NFL), there would have been an AFL team on the Bloomington prairie in the fall of 1960.

"Ten years of frustration, disappointments, delays, and silly excuses are at an end for the Twin Cities of Minneapolis and St. Paul," Johnson wrote in the *Star* on January 29, 1960. "After a decade of intensive efforts behind the scenes to get either major league baseball or football, the goal was reached in Miami Beach Thursday night.

"It was back in 1948 at Chicago that the first request for a gridiron franchise was made by enthusiasts in this community. Each year, it was the same old story—no expansion and wait until next year.

"Even though the Twin Cities will not get big league football until 1961, it is worth waiting for."

You can almost hear the sneer in Johnson's typewriter toward the AFL when he used "big league football" in that sentence. Anyone who had even brief encounters with Charley knows that he could sneer with the best of them.

As an interesting footnote, on March 13, 1960, six weeks after the Twin Cities received the expansion franchise, Walter Wolfner—married to the widow of Cardinals patriarch Charles Bidwill—announced he was moving Chicago's second team to St. Louis. The Cardinals are now in Arizona and still are owned by the Bidwill family. From 1949 through 2007, the Cardinals have one playoff victory.

Six decades, one playoff victory—Minnesota's football fans can be very grateful that Mr. Wolfner was not overly impressed by those Met Stadium crowds in 1959 and chose not to move the Cardinals to the Twin Cities.

SETTING UP AN ORGANIZATION

The new NFL team was incorporated as Minnesota Professional Football, and Bill Boyer was elected president. On August 5, 1960, it was announced that Bert Rose would be the team's general manager.

Rose was a promotions director for the Los Angeles Rams and also a close friend of Pete Rozelle. The new commissioner was influential in getting Rose the job in Minnesota.

Rozelle tried to explain to Sid Hartman the reason that a promotions director was a good choice to be the boss of football operations with the Minnesota franchise.

"[Rams owner] Dan Reeves always has been a believer in the complete utilization of his staff," Rozelle said. "For that reason, the publicity men always played a strong part in the entire Rams program.

"Bert helped us prepare for the draft, sign and scout players, and was active in most every department. He is an excellent organizer and will do a great job."

The Twin Cities had a chance to revel in its new NFL status on September 11, 1960, when the Green Bay Packers and Dallas' expansion team played an exhibition game at Met Stadium. The crowd was announced at 20,151.

Six days later, the Minnesota franchise finally had a nickname: the Vikings.

It would be another four months before the Vikings would have a coach. On January 18, 1961, Norm Van Brocklin went directly from being an NFL championship quarterback with the Philadelphia Eagles to coach of Minnesota's expansion team. Van Brocklin and the Eagles had defeated Green Bay in the NFL title game on December 26, 1960. "The Dutchman" was 34 years old and had played 12 pro seasons.

Newly named head coach Norm Van Brocklin is all smiles as he prepares to lead the Vikings into their first NFL season.
Star Tribune

Minnesota's top five draft choices in 1961 (left to right): Tommy Mason, Rip Hawkins, Fran Tarkenton, Chuck Lamson, and Ed Sharockman. *John Croft/Star Tribune*

When asked at his introductory news conference what worried him the most about going from the playing field directly to coaching, Van Brocklin offered the cocksure response that his Minnesota employers, players, media, and fans would come to expect: "I don't worry about anything."

Van Brocklin had been paid as a scout by the Eagles in the offseason to study film on college players.

"It's a tough transition for the average player to take over coaching an NFL team," Max Winter said. "But Van Brocklin has the background that makes him the exception. He has been famous for developing young players."

The Vikings had interviewed three other people for the job, although the interview with Northwestern's Ara Parseghian was more a courtesy to the team than an attempt to get the job. The other interviewees were Bud Grant from the Winnipeg Blue Bombers and Joe Thomas, who had been hired by Rose a few months earlier as the team's chief scout.

Grant was making as much money in Winnipeg as the $20,000 to $25,000 that the Vikings planned to pay. Plus, Bud—a man of legendary common sense—later pointed out that it's a good idea to be the second coach of an expansion team, not the first who would have take all those losses.

Thomas stayed on as the Vikings' chief scout before landing with Miami's AFL expansion franchise.

The NFL draft had been conducted on December 27, one day after the Eagles defeated the Packers and three weeks before Van Brocklin was named as the Vikings coach.

The Vikings had the first overall selection and took Tommy Mason, a running back from Tulane. He was followed in the second and third rounds by linebacker Rip Hawkins of North Carolina and quarterback Fran Tarkenton of Georgia.

"I had a chance to study movies of these players last year when I was helping the Eagles in scouting," Van Brocklin said on the day he was hired. "Bert Rose and Joe Thomas did a great job drafting."

Eventually, Van Brocklin would have a different view of Rose—not to mention Tarkenton—but it was all happiness on that mid-January day in 1961.

The football brain trust was in place with Van Brocklin, Rose, and Thomas, and the top rookies were on their way to Minnesota. Training camp in the northern pines of Bemidji was six months away, and that's when the aforementioned groups (employers, players, media, fans) would start to find out that the Dutchman was as cantankerous as he was confident.

NFL ON THE PRAIRIE

The Vikings' top three selections in their first draft were Southerners: Tulane's Tommy Mason, North Carolina's Rip Hawkins, and Georgia's Fran Tarkenton.

The team brought the trio to Minnesota in early February 1961 to formally sign contracts and to get some attention in the local media. There was much discussion on the weather they might face playing here in the Great White North.

"I played in 15-degree weather in Kentucky once," Tarkenton said. "That was cold enough."

A photo in the *Minneapolis Sunday Tribune* showed Mason and Tarkenton wearing military caps and saluting Van Brocklin.

When asked about his future as an NFL quarterback, Tarkenton nodded in the direction of Van Brocklin and said, "I've got a pretty good teacher sitting over there."

It was Van Brocklin who was the first face of the franchise. During that first winter, he traveled around the region and appeared in front of business clubs. He promised a team that would put up a fight every Sunday, and he also was selling season tickets.

One motivational ploy suggested to Van Brocklin was that he should show the Vikings a copy of the whopping check of $5,116.55 he had received as his winner's share with the Philadelphia Eagles in the 1960 NFL title game.

"I would like to be able to keep it and show it to the players at training camp, but it will be long gone," he said.

Coach Van Brocklin shows off his championship-caliber throwing arm for the first-year players at Vikings training camp in Bemidji, July 1961. *John Croft/Star Tribune*

Van Brocklin was influential in choosing Bemidji State University as the site for the Vikings' training camp. He wanted to get the players in an isolated location where the bright lights of the Twin Cities were only a distant rumor.

The Dutchman gathered his rookies and first-year Vikings in Bemidji on July 7. There were five exhibitions scheduled before the regular season opened on September 17, 1961. The Vikings delegation would be headquartered in the North Woods for seven weeks, until the end of August.

"I've been out to the practice field at least 15 times in the past two days," Van Brocklin said on the eve of the first rookies practice. "I can't wait to get going."

The coach also said: "I will tolerate nothing short of having every man thinking football every minute of the day that he is on his feet."

The orders from Van Brocklin also prohibited dalliances with coeds attending summer session at Bemidji State. "The penalty for fraternization is automatic expulsion [from training camp]," the *Minneapolis Tribune* reported.

The football-only discipline did not always carry over to Van Brocklin himself. He came to enjoy Jack's, a steakhouse outside Bemidji. The Dutchman liked his cocktails and was known to get ornery when over-served.

Minnesota rookies Fran Tarkenton (right) and Tommy Mason (center) report for duty with Coach Van Brocklin in February 1961. The two southern-born players are wearing Confederate military caps. *Chuck Brill/Star Tribune*

Jim Klobuchar was the first Vikings' beat writer for the *Minneapolis Tribune*. He was as mercurial and gifted at his craft as Van Brocklin was at football. One evening a couple of years later, the Dutchman threw a punch at Klobuchar.

This was the first season, though—the first camp, the first tangible site of the modern-day NFL—and everyone was on the Van Brocklin bandwagon.

Van Brocklin had more than 1,600 pounds of linemen to work with at his first training camp, including (top to bottom) right tackle Frank Youso, center Bill Lapham, left guard Gerry Huth, left tackle Grady Alderman, end Bob Schnelker, Gene Selawski, and Bill Kimber. (Selawski and Kimber did not make the squad.)
AP/Wide World Photos

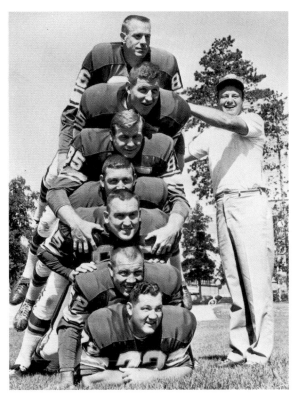

One irritant to Van Brocklin was the absence of rookies Mason and Hawkins. They were in attendance for the early days of rookie camp, but then left for Chicago to join the College All-Stars.

This team of seniors from the previous season would gather in Chicago in July and play the defending NFL champions. In this case, it was the Philadelphia Eagles, the team Van Brocklin had quarterbacked to the 1960 NFL title.

On the night before Mason left, Van Brocklin called him over to his table in the dining room, talked about the work that he should try to get done with the All-Stars, and then added with a wink: "If you score Tommy, flip that ball over your shoulder as you go into the end zone—and tell them you did it for the Dutchman."

When it came to national sports popularity, the early 1960s were a time when the NFL was a distant second to Major League Baseball. The College All-Star Game, which was played annually from 1934 to 1976, was the one event that brought national headlines to the NFL in midsummer. If a team's draft picks were selected for the game, they were allowed to participate, no questions asked.

"We got hurt when they took Tommy Mason and Rip Hawkins, when we needed them worked into our style of play," Van Brocklin said in late July. "But we got a break when they didn't take Tarkenton. We have him right here to move ahead step by step. He may be useful before the season is over."

The Vikings held their first public scrimmage on July 22, 1961. A crowd estimated at 2,000 was in attendance. The star was Don Ellersick, a former Los Angeles Rams defensive back who had been selected in the expansion draft. The Vikings converted him to a running back/receiver, and he caught five passes for 119 yards from Tarkenton in that first public scrimmage.

That performance proved to be Ellersick's highlight with the Vikings; he didn't make the team.

The first exhibition game was played on August 5 in Sioux Falls, South Dakota. The opponents were the Dallas Cowboys, the expansion team from a year earlier. Sioux Falls was a convenient location for the Cowboys, since they were conducting training camp at St. Olaf College in Northfield, Minnesota.

Van Brocklin was a native of South Dakota. His family had owned a farm near the tiny town of Parade. He was three years old when the Van Brocklins decided to escape the Dust Bowl and moved to California.

"There was nothing they could do when those winds started carrying the land away," Van Brocklin told a reporter on the plane ride from Bemidji to Sioux Falls.

It was also the first summer of Major League Baseball on the Bloomington prairie. The new Minnesota Twins were receiving lots of attention in the Upper Midwest, which was reflected in the sparse crowd of 4,954 that showed up for that first Vikings exhibition in Sioux Falls.

The Cowboys demonstrated that one extra year for an expansion team can make a large difference, as they cruised to a 38-13 victory. The Vikings made it easier for Dallas by giving up three fumbles that led to 17 Cowboys points.

The Vikings played their first four exhibitions on the road, all losses. The Vikings made their Met Stadium debut on September 10, 1961, and lost 21-17 to the Los Angeles Rams in the final exhibition. The attendance was 27,892.

The fourth exhibition loss had been a 30-7 defeat at the hands of the Chicago Bears in Cedar Rapids, Iowa, on September 2. Many assumed that this was a preview of the franchise's inaugural regular-season game, a Vikings-Bears contest to be held at Met Stadium on September 17.

That would prove to be an invalid assumption.

BEARS COME CALLING

George Halas was a founder of the National Football League. Forty-one years later, the 1961 season was opening, and he remained the owner, president, and coach of the Chicago Bears. Among NFL people, he had more to do than anyone with getting Minnesota an expansion team in the established league rather than a place as an original member of the fledgling AFL.

Halas was a menacing presence under his fedora and behind his tinted glasses. He was notorious for his cantankerous ways with players.

Years later, when he was long gone from the sideline and had turned over the day-to-day operation of the team to others, he was visited in his small office in downtown Chicago. Halas and another old-timer sold tickets to decades-long customers out of that office. It was only a tiny fraction of the Bears' ticket-selling business in the 1980s, but Halas still ran that office as if the NFL were the equivalent of a mom-and-pop store.

The visiting reporter spent several hours with Halas on that afternoon; he was able to look at his keepsakes and newspaper clippings through the decades. He was a mellow and generous man in his eighties then—far removed from the snarling sideline presence who brought his Bears to Met Stadium for the Vikings' first-ever game on September 17, 1961.

Halas had gone from a big promoter of Minnesota's NFL franchise to a condescending rival in the days leading to the opener. In late August, as the Bears prepared to play the Vikings in the exhibition game in Cedar Rapids, Halas accused the new team of not following NFL rules to promptly send films of the previous game to an opponent.

"It saddens me to see those nice Vikings people pitching us a curve ball," he said. "They told us we would have films of the Colts exhibition game in our hands by Friday. This is Monday. Still no films."

A concerned Van Brocklin watches the action during the Vikings' final exhibition game of 1961, a 21-17 loss to the Rams at Met Stadium.
John Croft/Star Tribune

MINNESOTA VIKINGS ORIGINAL STARTING LINEUP

The following list shows the first starting lineup fielded by the Vikings when they opened the 1961 season against the Chicago Bears on September 17 at Met Stadium. (Note the change in terminology from the NFL of 1961 compared to today's game. The offensive ends were just that, not a tight end or a wide receiver. There were the traditional two halfbacks and a fullback behind the quarterback. On defense, cornerbacks still were referred to as halfbacks, and safeties were left and right, not strong and free.)

Offense

Ends . . . . .Bob Schnelker,
                          Dave Middleton
Left Tackle. . . . . .Grady Alderman
Left Guard . . . . .Gerry Huth
Center . . . . .Bill Lapham
Right Guard . . . . . . .Mike Rabold
Right Tackle. . . . . . . .Frank Youso
Quarterback. . . . . . .George Shaw
Left Halfback . . . . . .Dick Haley
Right Halfback . . . . .Hugh McElhenny
Fullback. . . . . .Mel Triplett

Defense

Left End . . . . .Jim Marshall
Left Tackle. . . . . . . .Jim Prestel
Right Tackle. . . . . . .Bill Bishop
Right End . . . . .Don Joyce
Left Linebacker. . . . .Clancy Osborne
Middle Linebacker . .Rip Hawkins
Right Linebacker. . . .Karl Rubke
Left Halfback . . . . . .Jack Morris
Right Halfback . . . . .Dick Pesonen
Left Safety. . . . . . . .Rich Mostardi
Right Safety. . . . . . .Charlie Sumner

draft to Cleveland for what turned out to be seven players: defensive linemen Jim Marshall, Paul Dickson, and Jim Prestel; linebacker Dick Grecni; cornerback Billy Gault; running back Jamie Caleb; and guard Bob Denton.

All seven ex-Browns were on the season-opening roster in 1961, as were quarterback George Shaw, fullback Mel Triplett, and receivers Bob Schnelker and Jerry Reichow—acquired in trades with the Giants and the Eagles that cost the Vikings the first-, fifth-, and seventh-round selections in the 1962 draft. Those 11 players were all expendable veterans on established teams, while teams such as the Vikings didn't consider draft choices as valuable back then in the days of a 20-round draft.

The only rookie in Van Brocklin's opening-day starting lineup against the Bears was Rip Hawkins, the middle linebacker.

"Not many learn faster than Hawkins," Van Brocklin said. "He played a tough game for us in the Rams' exhibition last week—and that was his first as a pro. He's the man we want our defense to rally around."

The Vikings figured Shaw as the man for the offense to rally around. Van Brocklin was convinced that he needed a veteran, pocket-passing quarterback for the Vikings to compete at a professional level. As a result, they gave up a first-round pick in 1962 for Shaw, the backup with the New York Giants.

Shaw's standing as the Vikings' number-one quarterback did not last through the first quarter of the first game.

Van Brocklin had issued a challenge to his players through the Twin Cities media: "If we're not hungry for this one, we'll never be."

Halas' Bears came out turnover-prone and the Vikings had a chance to jump to a big lead. But the score was only 3-0 late in the first quarter, and Van Brocklin was upset at how his offense had bogged down on a couple of drives.

The coach brought in Tarkenton, the rookie from Georgia, and suddenly this undersized 21-year-old was dashing away from wheezing Bears pass rushers and finding open receivers. The "Scrambler" was born on that first afternoon at Met Stadium.

Tarkenton threw four touchdown passes and ran for another, igniting the Vikings to a 37-6 lead midway in the fourth quarter. The Bears managed to get a consolation touchdown, and the shocking final score was Dutchman's Expansion Team 37, Monsters of the Midway 13.

"How could anything top this?" Tarkenton said.

How, indeed. Tarkenton went 17-for-23 for 250 yards, with four touchdowns and no interceptions. The NFL had no such thing as a formula for a quarterback rating in 1961. But if you apply today's formula to those numbers, Tarkenton's rating in his first game was 148.6, on a scale where 158.3 is perfect.

Fresh-faced Jim Marshall came to the Vikings from Cleveland in exchange for draft choices before the 1961 season. The defensive end would go on to start 270 consecutive games for Minnesota in 19 seasons.
John Croft/Star Tribune

"We are dying to see what that rough-and-tough football team has been doing."

Later, Bill Bishop, a long-time Bears defensive tackle who was dispensed to the Vikings in the expansion draft, took some shots at Halas and how he treated his players. "I feel sorry for him," was Halas' response during the week before the game.

The Vikings still were trying to assemble a competitive roster in the days before the opener. They sent their second-, tenth-, and eleventh-round choices in the 1962

Coach Van Brocklin and General Manager Bert Rose celebrate with the players in the locker room after defeating the Chicago Bears in the franchise's debut regular-season game on September 17, 1961.
John Croft/Star Tribune

Among those impressed with the performance was Pete Rozelle, the new NFL commissioner. He was in attendance and visited the home locker room at Met Stadium after the game. He was overheard proclaiming to Van Brocklin: "It was fantastic! And Tarkenton—what a rookie!"

The first touchdown in Vikings' history was a 14-yard pass to Bob Schnelker early in the second quarter. "The one Francis threw to me, the ball just hooked in there to me, like a baseball," Schnelker said.

Jerry Reichow, the recipient of a 29-yard touchdown toss, was more succinct: "Francis throws a fine pass."

Van Brocklin made the rounds in the locker room to shake hands with his players. Then he gave the ultimate endorsement of the emotion of this victory: "It felt like the day in Philadelphia last year, when we beat the Packers for the NFL title. It's a wonderful moment."

Halas could not share in the joy. His quarterbacks threw four interceptions and the Bears lost one of their four fumbles; they also had a snap that sailed over the punter's head.

"I've never seen anything like it," Halas said. "Give the Vikings credit for capitalizing on our mistakes. But I've been with the Bears for 42 [seasons], and I've never seen so many things go wrong for a football team as they did for us today."

Halas was much more acerbic in private. There's a famous anecdote about Halas being the last man on the bus as the Bears were departing for the airport for the return flight to Chicago. He stepped on, stared at the players for a few seconds, and said, "You're all a bunch of ___."

It was a very impolite word that we wouldn't even want adults to read.

Coach Van Brocklin, General Manager Bert Rose, and the Vikings players whooped it up for a celebration photograph in the winning locker room.

That photo, taken by the *Tribune*'s John Croft, might have made the front page on Monday morning, September 18, but the Vikings' victory was overshadowed by a tragic event in Chicago. A Northwest Airlines Electra jet, with 32 passengers and an all-Twin Cities crew of five aboard, crashed seconds after takeoff at O'Hare International Airport.

The pilot radioed a frantic "no control," as the plane lost power from 250 feet in the air, went into a high-tension line, careened to the ground, and exploded. Everyone on the Florida-bound flight was killed.

REALITY FOLLOWS GLORY

The Vikings' opening-game victory caused euphoria to sweep across the Midwestern plains and led to giddy discussions of how the Vikings were going to be competitive in their very first season.

Tarkenton talked about the class with which Shaw handled being benched. "I'll never forget what a big man George was Sunday when I had a good day," the rookie quarterback said. "He was the first to congratulate me when I came off the field."

Shaw had a chance to continue his magnanimous ways a couple of days after the opener, when Van Brocklin announced that Tarkenton was his starting quarterback. Over the final three months of the season, Tarkenton started ten games and Shaw started three.

Reality kicked in at the season's second game during a visit to Dallas. The Vikings were punchless in a 21-7 loss to the second-year Cowboys. It was the start of a seven-game losing streak that included back-to-back losses to the Green Bay Packers.

The Vikings were the new hometown franchise for Minnesotans, but the Packers always had been the NFL team that was shown on television in the Twin Cities area. Green Bay also had emerged as a powerhouse,

Halfback Hugh McElhenny cuts back for some extra yardage against the Dallas Cowboys at Met Stadium on October 8, 1961. The Vikings were shutout, 28-0, by their expansion elders.
John Croft/Star Tribune

with Vince Lombardi replacing Halas as the league's most-commanding presence on the sidelines.

The first loss was a 33-7 trouncing at Met Stadium on October 22. The score was 28-10 one week later at Lambeau Field.

The Packers opened this now-longstanding rivalry with a 78-yard touchdown pass from Bart Starr to Boyd Dowler on their first play from scrimmage in Bloomington.

"Who would have thought they were going to pull that long pass to Dowler on the first play?" Vikings safety Rich Mostardi said. "I was looking for them to come out running. They worked a double cross-buck fake. I just spent too much time looking at it."

Van Brocklin took umbrage at Mostardi's confusion. The following week, two new safeties, Charlie Sumner and Dean Derby, were starting for Mostardi and Will Sherman at Lambeau Field.

The coach made other defensive changes as well, although it made no difference. Starr ripped up the Vikings by completing 18 of 24 passes for 311 yards and two touchdowns.

The highlight for the Vikings was a 39-yard run by Hurryin' Hugh McElhenny that set up the visitors' only touchdown. The veteran McElhenny played ahead of number-one draft choice Tommy Mason throughout the first season. McElhenny had 99 yards on 12 carries on that rainy day in Green Bay. He led the Vikings with 570 yards on 120 carries for the season.

The 28-10 loss at Lambeau Field also was the first of many times through the years that the folks back in Minnesota would hear complaints about the officiating.

The league was not yet into fining coaches and players large sums for ripping officials, so Van Brocklin had at 'em. "That's the worst officiated game I've seen in my 13 years in the National Football League," the Dutchman said. "And you can print that. I mean it."

The Vikings practice on the frozen gridiron of Met Stadium in late November 1961. The team headed to the relative warmth of San Francisco that Sunday but fell to the 49ers 38-28.
John Croft/Star Tribune

Fran Tarkenton scrambles free of the Detroit pass rush on November 19, 1961. It was the first of two Vikings losses to the Lions in 1961—a team against which they would later post 13 consecutive wins from 1968 to 1974.
John Croft/Star Tribune

The Vikings won two more home games—28-20 over Baltimore on November 12 and 42-21 over the Los Angeles Rams on December 3—to finish the first season with a record of 3 wins and 13 losses.

The Bears exacted some revenge in the final game of the season by putting up 52 points (to 35 for the Vikings) in Chicago.

The Bears also got the better of the Vikings in the Rookie of the Year voting. Chicago receiver Mike Ditka beat out runner-up Tarkenton by a wide margin for the Associated Press award. He finished with 27 first-place votes compared to Tarkenton's 4.

During the season, Ditka caught 56 passes for 1,076 yards and 12 touchdowns. He joined Baltimore's John Mackey as the prototype for what was starting to be called the tight end position in the NFL.

Tarkenton was a pioneer in his own right; he introduced scrambling as an art form to NFL quarterbacking. He finished with 157 completions in 280 attempts for 1,997 yards, 18 touchdowns, and 17 interceptions. He rushed 56 times—a huge total for a quarterback of that era—for 308 yards and 5 more touchdowns.

The young quarterback also took 44 sacks for a loss of 414 yards, or an average loss of more than nine yards per sack. Whenever Tarkenton was trapped on one of his scrambles, he put the Vikings offense in a considerable hole.

Asked at a fan club meeting in St. Paul about his quarterback's running, Van Brocklin said, "If they have to run, they do, but they ought to be running for that sideline.

At Met Stadium on December 3, 1961, Coach Van Brocklin has some choice words for official Red Pace after Pace nullified a Minnesota touchdown because of a penalty. The Vikings didn't need the points, however, as they trounced Los Angeles 42-21 for their third and final win of the season.
John Croft/Star Tribune

We play a quarterback system, not a four halfback system with one of them over the center."

This may have been the first real hint of the troubles to come between Van Brocklin, a former championship NFL quarterback as a pocket passer, and a young dynamo from Georgia whose crazy runs still can be found playing to cartoon music on NFL Films.

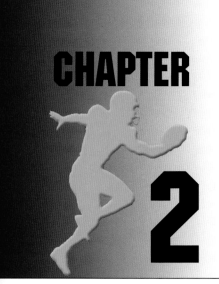
FUN WITH DUTCH AND FRAN
1962–1966

The best thing that happened to the Vikings in 1962 did not take place on the field, but rather on the business front. When Pete Rozelle was named commissioner two years earlier, he brought with him a vision of a national television contract and the league's teams sharing revenues equally.

Previously, there were regional television deals and the individual teams kept the revenues from those. Rozelle's first national contract with CBS was turned down in 1961 when the courts ruled it a violation of antitrust laws.

Congress intervened and granted sports leagues an antitrust exemption to execute such television contracts. This revenue sharing of national TV money would lead to astounding riches and allow a small-market franchise such as the Green Bay Packers to remain profitable and competitive.

In January 1962, a two-year, $9 million television contract was approved with equal shares for the 14 teams. "This deal would be a big break for us," said Bert Rose, the Vikings general manager.

The NFL also was in a battle for the top college seniors with the rival American Football League. The impact on the Vikings in the draft for the 1962 season was not as significant as it was for other NFL teams, since Minnesota had given up six of its top 11 choices (numbers 1, 2, 5, 7, 10, and 11) in order to obtain veteran reinforcements for the inaugural season.

If a team were to make such deals in this modern sports era, the media, bloggers, and the public would be screaming about a franchise "mortgaging its future." Back then, draft choices were not held in the same reverence, and the media was much less likely to lead a chorus of criticism about a home team.

The Vikings' first pick in the draft for the 1962 season was Bill Miller, a wide receiver from the University of Miami. He was a third-rounder, selected thirtieth overall. He signed with the Dallas Texans of the AFL.

Minnesota columnists saw this as revenge by Lamar Hunt, the Texans owner, who allegedly was still upset by the decision of Max Winter and his partners to drop out as an original AFL member in order to acquire an NFL expansion team.

Quarterback Fran Tarkenton confers with Coach Van Brocklin during an exhibition game in September 1962. The duo would spend an at-times tumultuous six years together in Minnesota before both men departed after the 1966 season.
Donald Black/Star Tribune

The only players from the 1962 draft who would have an impact on the Vikings were Roy Winston, a linebacker and fourth-round pick from LSU, and Larry Bowie, a guard and sixth-rounder from Purdue. Winston was a Vikings starter for 13 seasons and Bowie for 5.

The lack of assistance from the draft did not deter Van Brocklin. "We should have had six wins last year," he said. "What's more, we are going to do better this year."

To improve on the three-victory total, Van Brocklin decided that what was needed was a more hard-nosed approach at Vikings' training camp in Bemidji.

"We're going to do a lot more hitting in camp this year," he said. "We have a week less time than last year to get ready for our first [exhibition] game, so we'll hold more live drills."

As the opener approached, Van Brocklin declared that Tarkenton, his starting quarterback, was "the most-important man in our organization, bar none."

The public had been reading anecdotal evidence of a tight bond between the coach and the quarterback for over a year in the Twin Cities newspapers.

A scene relayed by Jim Klobuchar of the *Minneapolis Tribune* had Van Brocklin, Tarkenton, and a receiver going through a long drill on a hot day in training camp:

Sweat flowed down the young man's face. He bowed his head and, for a moment, he stood hunched over in the steaming sun, breathing heavily.

"Tired, Francis?" asked Norm Van Brocklin.

There was no cut in his voice, but Van Brocklin and Tarkenton both understood what the question really meant: "Do you want to play quarterback in the NFL?"

They worked until Tarkenton could scarcely hold up his arm. When it was over, the coach draped an arm around his 21-year-old quarterback and said, "Francis, you're getting the idea."

Tarkenton gave him a grimy smile and said, "Thank you, sir. It was a pleasure to work with you."

This took place in Bemidji, 1961. A year later, Tarkenton spent a week of August in a hospital with a severe virus that led to pneumonia. He missed two exhibitions, and there was no halcyon start to the Vikings' second season as there had been to the first.

Tarkenton had thrown four touchdown passes and ran for another in the 1961 opener against the Bears. One month into the 1962 season, the Vikings were 0-4 and had scored a total of three touchdowns. They lost 34-7 to Green Bay, 34-7 again to Baltimore, 21-7 to San Francisco, and 13-0 to the Bears.

The season's fifth game was at Met Stadium against Green Bay. The Packers rolled to 506 total yards and a 48-21 victory. Bart Starr went 20 for 28 for 297 yards

and three touchdowns. Fullback Jim Taylor barged for 164 yards on 17 carries, an average of 9.6 yards per rush. The Vikings generated some offense late in the drubbing, but it was a horrific mismatch.

The lousy start to the season had the Vikings badly trailing the University of Minnesota's Golden Gophers in attendance and in level of interest. Murray Warmath's Gophers had been to two straight Rose Bowls and were contenders for a third in the fall of 1962.

The Green Bay game attracted a crowd of 41,475 to Met Stadium. The other six home games peaked at 33,141 for a visit by the Bears in week four. The Vikings hit a low of 26,728 for a game against the L.A. Rams on November 25.

The Vikings did manage a two-game winning streak in the middle of the schedule—beating the Rams 38-14 in Los Angeles, and Philadelphia 31-21 at Met Stadium. A 24-24 tie with the Rams in week 11 left the team at 2-11-1 in its second season.

The Vikings took their only pride in providing Van Brocklin with a victory over the Eagles, the team that he had quarterbacked to a championship two years earlier.

"He's done a lot of things for young guys on this club," Tarkenton said after the victory. "This was the game we knew he wanted. I never in my life wanted to win a game more, for this guy's sake."

Van Brocklin wasn't willing to go along with the theory, at least publicly. "Just another ball game," he said. "You try to win them all."

"Scramblin' Fran" races for extra yardage against the Baltimore Colts during the 1962 home opener on September 23. Tarkenton ran for 361 yards that season, second only to halfback Tommy Mason on the team. *John Croft/Star Tribune*

Mick Tingelhoff earned the starting job at center in 1962—and he didn't give it up until 1979, for a stretch of 240 consecutive games. *Star Tribune*

Tommy Mason, the franchise's first-ever draft choice, did emerge as an outstanding two-way back in 1962. He rushed for 740 yards, caught 36 passes for a team-leading 603 yards, and made his first of three consecutive Pro Bowl appearances.

Another emerging star on the 1962 Vikings team was Mick Tingelhoff, an undrafted free agent from Nebraska who won the job as the starting center. Tingelhoff remained in the middle for 17 seasons, and his 240 games (and starts) are second on the all-time franchise list to Jim Marshall, the defensive end acquired from the Cleveland Browns before the start of the 1961 season.

ALL-OUT WAR WITH THE AFL

The draft for the 1963 season was held on December 3, 1962, with two games still remaining on the schedule. The NFL went with this early distribution of college seniors in an attempt to keep the AFL from getting to them first.

The Vikings' first two selections were Jim Dunaway, a defensive tackle from Mississippi State, and Bobby Lee Bell from the University of Minnesota. Bell had played defensive tackle for the Gophers at 220 pounds (or less). He won the Outland Trophy in 1962 as the nation's best lineman and is looked at by many of Minnesota's post-

World War II sports fans as the greatest player they ever saw with the Gophers.

Bell was projected as a linebacker in the pros because of his modest weight, his ranginess, and his outstanding speed. He would go on to have a Hall of Fame career at that position.

As suggested by the attendance figures in 1962, the Vikings were in need of the public relations boost that would come with signing a Gophers superstar. Bill Boyer, the Vikings president, said before the draft, "We have to sign our first five draft choices. If money is the difference, we'll get them, because we won't let it stand in our way."

In the end, the Vikings were unable to sign either Dunaway or Bell. Dunaway received a lucrative contract from the AFL's Buffalo Bills, and Bell signed with the Dallas Texans (soon to become the Kansas City Chiefs).

Not surprisingly, the local sportswriters rallied to the Vikings' defense, again blaming Lamar Hunt's disdain for the Vikings' owners and their alleged betrayal of the AFL. The local press also adopted the team's contention that Bell had reneged on a deal to sign with the Vikings.

Bell agreed to a guaranteed five-year contract worth $150,000 with Hunt's AFL team on December 13, 1962.

The Vikings-Lions game at Met Stadium attracted a sparse crowd on November 24, 1963—two days after the assassination of President John F. Kennedy.
John Croft/Star Tribune

This dwarfed the Vikings' offer of three years for a total of $62,000, not fully guaranteed.

Sid Hartman offered this version of events in the next morning's *Tribune*:

> Lamar Hunt, president of the Dallas Texans, is angry at Bill Boyer, H. P. Skoglund, and Max Winter, three owners of the Minnesota Vikings.
>
> He is still unhappy because the Vikings trio walked out on the American Football League. To gain revenge, Hunt signed Bill Miller of Miami, the Vikings' top draft choice last year. Thursday, he struck another blow at the Vikings when he signed Minnesota's Bobby Bell, the Vikings' second draft choice.
>
> When Bell told the Dallas team early this week that it looked like he was going to sign with the Vikings, the Texans sent their head talent scout, Don Klosterman, to Minneapolis with instructions to sign Bell regardless of the cost.

None of the Minneapolis newspapers mentioned that Boyer had pledged a month earlier to sign the top five draft choices and not let money stand in the way.

Different times, obviously. Today, when the Vikings or another pro sports team dawdles in negotiations, they have a tendency to get beat up in print, on talk radio, and in other media outlets.

Back in 1962, the Vikings lost a Hall of Fame linebacker from the local university to a rival and then were presented as the aggrieved party by Twin Cities sportswriters.

ROZELLE'S BLUNDER

The NFL's major story during the 1963 offseason was the suspension of Green Bay's Paul Hornung and Detroit's Alex Karras, two of the league's prominent stars, for gambling on games and "associating with undesirables."

In mid-April, Commissioner Pete Rozelle announced the suspensions for the 1963 season. He received praise for the decisive action from around the league, including from Vikings president Bill Boyer.

"I think we can be thankful this has come to a head and that Rozelle acted with that kind of forcefulness," Boyer said.

Rozelle was not so universally praised several months later, when he chose to have the NFL games played as scheduled on Sunday, November 24, two days after the assassination of President John F. Kennedy in Dallas.

Rozelle's explanation was that it was traditional for sports teams to play in times of "great tragedy." Many years later, Rozelle admitted that going ahead with the games in the wake of the president's murder was a decision that he came to regret.

There was immediate backlash toward the NFL. Many colleges had chosen to postpone their games. The Minnesota Gophers moved back their traditional

Fullback Bill "Boom Boom" Brown emerged as a dangerous weapon for the Vikings when he assumed a regular role in 1963. He led the team in rushing in four of the next five seasons while also serving as an effective pass receiver.
John Croft/Star Tribune

season-closer with Wisconsin to the following week, on Thanksgiving morning.

Francis E. Phelan, a Twin Cities resident, wrote a letter to Bert Rose at the Vikings' offices.

"In this day of materialism," Phelan wrote, "I suppose that making a dollar has to be first and foremost even when our beloved President is dead. I am a very rabid football fan, but playing a game during a national tragedy such as this is unbelievable.

"The Big Ten finally suspended all games. The American Football League grasped the international significance of the assassination of our great leader. The 'National' League (what nation, I wonder?) decided in the words of Pete Rozelle that it is tradition for athletes to perform in times of great personal tragedy. It sounds like some halfback's nephew scratched his knee."

The Vikings defeated Detroit 34-31 on that Sunday afternoon, for their fourth victory of the 1963 season.

Minnesota had the youngest roster in the NFL in 1963, averaging 25 and a fraction in years. The youth movement was led in part by two new offensive weapons: Bill Brown, previously a backup fullback, and rookie receiver Paul Flatley. Brown rushed for 445 yards and also hinted at a talent for catching the ball with 17 receptions. The Vikings would exploit that facet of Brown's game much more fully in the seasons to follow.

A leaping Paul Flatley is about to haul in one of his team-high 51 receptions in 1963. The 22-year-old receiver earned numerous honors for his outstanding rookie campaign.
John Croft/Star Tribune

Flatley, a fourth-round draft choice out of Northwestern, ran precise routes and also figured out how to his work his way open for Tarkenton as the quarterback took off on a scramble.

Flatley set team records with 51 catches and 867 yards in 1963. He was named the NFL's Rookie of the Year by the Associated Press, United Press International, and two other organizations.

"He's an amazing kid," Van Brocklin said of Flatley. "Paul Flatley has got everything a great end needs, except blazing speed. And I'm not sure how important that is. He's got the moves, hands, and stomach, and he's thinking all the time."

Tommy Mason also had a big season, with 763 yards rushing, 40 catches for 365 yards, and a combined nine touchdowns. He became the first Vikings player to be voted onto the Associated Press' All-Pro team.

The 1963 Vikings opened the season with a 24-20 victory over San Francisco and closed with a 34-13 win against Philadelphia to finish with a record of 5-8-1. The team scored more points (309) and allowed fewer (390) than it had in either of the previous two seasons.

The first signs of tangible progress toward a competitive team were in place.

Amidst all this improvement, it also was a season during which the first signs of discord involving Coach Van Brocklin became public in the Twin Cities newspapers.

Veteran tackle Frank Youso, who initially had refused to sign a contract in the hopes of getting more money out of the Vikings, was cut by Van Brocklin at the end of August.

"Norm is bullheaded and stubborn," he said. "I think my not signing had a lot to do with [getting cut]."

The Vikings went 4-1 in the 1963 exhibition season, as compared to a combined 2-8 in the first two years. After the last of those exhibition victories (a 34-24 win over Baltimore), Van Brocklin said of Tarkenton: "He ran the ballclub as never before. And he made it a great game with his headwork. It's like baseball. You have to be strong in the middle, between your ears. And that's where Tarkenton had it."

By season's end, the mutual admiration had waned. Van Brocklin started Ron VanderKelen, the rookie free agent signed out of Wisconsin after the 1963 Rose

Halfback Tommy Mason plows through the Detroit defense in a game at Met Stadium. Named an All-Pro in 1963, Mason led the Vikings with a career-high 763 rushing yards that year.
John Croft/Star Tribune

Two-hundred-fifty-pound lineman Paul Dickson works out in the August heat during training camp. Dickson was a cornerstone of Minnesota's defensive line from 1962 to 1967, until he took a reserve role behind Alan Page.
John Croft/Star Tribune

Bowl, as the quarterback in the season's final game at Philadelphia.

Publicly, Tarkenton offered his support, saying, "I wish Vandy the best. We've always gotten along well." Privately, the quarterback was very unhappy, as the *Tribune*'s Jim Klobuchar hinted in his advance story on that Eagles' finale.

It's a reasonable observation that some of the vitality and mutual regard have gone out of the Van Brocklin-Tarkenton association.

Van Brocklin is plainly offended to see his game plan transformed into what occasionally looks like an intramural offense. Tarkenton has had VanderKelen's presence flung at him frequently. Occasionally, he has been made to appear [by Van Brocklin] the chief instrument of a Vikings defeat.

Both are proud men with contrasting temperaments. Three years of odds-bucking, for both of them, have wrought some changes.

Klobuchar was referring to changes in the relationship between the coach and the quarterback, and in time, the discontent would lead both of them to leave Minnesota.

SUCCESS WITHIN REACH

Before the 1963 season, the Vikings signed Van Brocklin to a three-year contract extension that would carry him through the 1966 season. Bert Rose, Van Brocklin's titular boss as the general manager, received only a one-year extension that would expire in May 1964.

The Vikings were much more aggressive in signing draft choices in December 1963. Now wary of the AFL competition, they drafted and signed their top two picks—Minnesota tackle Carl Eller and Southern Cal tight end Hal Bedsole—on the same day.

The final selection in that draft was Milt Sunde, a Gophers guard. A 20th-round selection, Sunde would be the Vikings' starting guard for nine seasons (1965–1973).

"We couldn't have expected to do any better in the draft," Van Brocklin said. "We signed the two big ones. All of a sudden the world looks a little better."

Carl Eller (left) admires the hardware awarded to Paul Flatley (Vikings Outstanding Rookie) and Jim Marshall (Outstanding Defensive Player) after the 1963 season. *John Croft/Star Tribune*

That view of the world took a huge hit during the 1964 offseason.

Terry Dillon, an undrafted safety from Hopkins, Minnesota, and then Montana State, had been a tremendous surprise for the Vikings as a rookie in 1963. He was extra-impressive in training camp in Bemidji and was targeted to make the season-opening roster. Then, he suffered a severe ankle sprain and was placed on the taxi squad (now the practice squad) as he recuperated.

The 1963 Vikings were vulnerable in the secondary. Halfway through the schedule, Dillon showed in practice that he was healthy. He was taken off the taxi squad and replaced veteran Tom Franckhauser as a starting safety.

When informed by Van Brocklin that he was starting, Dillon remarked, "It's quite a shock, and quite a thrill. I suppose every kid who plays high school football dreams of playing in the pros, but I don't think I was ever really serious about it."

In late May of 1964, Dillon was back in Missoula, Montana, to finish his degree and to earn some extra money working for the construction crew that was building a bridge over the Clark Fork River. The river was swollen and running rapidly because of the spring snow melt.

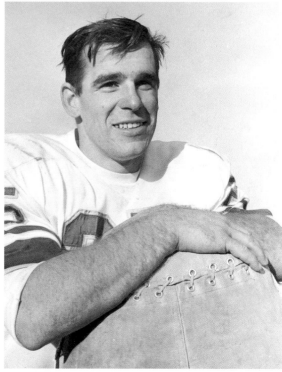

Terry Dillon's promising NFL career came to a sudden and tragic end when he drowned in a river while working construction in the 1964 offseason. The defensive back appeared in seven games for the Vikings in 1963. *John Croft/Star Tribune*

On May 28, Dillon was operating a cement bucket. It plunged through the bridge deck, carrying Dillon into the river. He was able to ride debris for a while, but he eventually was carried away by the current and drowned. He was 23 years old.

"He had the perfect temperament to play safety in the NFL," Van Brocklin said. "He wanted to learn, and he learned quickly. In our postseason grading, he was near the top."

The death of this young man was followed a few days later by a different type of Vikings headline: Rose resigned as general manager on June 1. In a fine use of semantics, Vikings President Bill Boyer denied that Rose was fired, saying, "That just isn't true. We have had problems. We got together and resolved them."

The immediate rumors were that Rose was forced out in order to give manpower decisions fully to Van Brocklin. "With Rose leaving, the assumption is that general managership will become almost exclusively an administrative post—while Van Brocklin handles all squad personnel matters," read a paragraph in the *Tribune* the day after Rose resigned.

This wasn't remotely the case. It took more than three months, but when the Vikings did get around to announcing a general manager, it was a true football man:

Jim Finks, the general manager of the Calgary Stampeders of the Canadian Football League.

The 37-year-old Finks had spent seven seasons as a quarterback in the NFL. The legend was that the Pittsburgh Steelers cut Johnny Unitas in order to retain Finks, which was one of the many blunders that kept the Steelers as also-rans until the 1970s.

Finks was announced as the Vikings' second GM on September 11, two days before the 1964 season opener.

When hired, Van Brocklin had talked about turning his expansion team into a championship contender by its fifth year. This was the season when it appeared the Dutchman was on track to make good on that boast.

This was also the season in which Van Brocklin earned his first victory over Vince Lombardi and the Green Bay Packers, 24-23 on October 4 at Lambeau Field.

Tom Hall, a former Gophers star, had been acquired from Detroit before the 1964 season in exchange for a fifth-round draft choice. He caught seven passes for 103 yards and a touchdown on that Sunday in Green Bay. He received a game ball in the winning locker room, tossed to him by quarterback Tarkenton, not Van Brocklin.

The Vikings won on a late field goal by Fred Cox. In order to set up Freddie the Foot's 27-yarder, they had

Newly named General Manager Jim Finks (right) with Coach Van Brocklin in September 1964. Finks would remain with the team through the 1973 season and help to build the Vikings into championship contenders.
John Croft/Star Tribune

During the 1964 election season, thousands showed up at Met Stadium donning helmets in support of the referendum for the Taconite Amendment. On the field, the Vikings trounced the Pittsburgh Steelers, 30-10, on October 18.
John Croft/Star Tribune

to convert on fourth-and-22. Tight end Gordie Smith made a 43-yard run-and-catch to convert that first down. Tarkenton eluded a Packers' rush with a scramble, saw a receiver near the right sideline, and unloaded. The intended receiver was Hall. Smith didn't know this, and he went lunging upward for the football.

"It was right on the money to Tom Hall," Tarkenton said later. "Then, I saw Gordie Smith going after it and said, 'Oh, no, Gordie, let it go.' And then Gordie went up and got it and was running down the sideline. I could hardly believe it."

The victory gave the Vikings a 2-2 record and a temporary reprieve in the Van Brocklin-Tarkenton tensions. "Francis was the greatest today when we needed him the most," the coach said.

The Vikings split the next two games and headed to San Francisco's Kezar Stadium on October 25, 1964, with a 3-3 record. A 27-22 victory over the 49ers brought them to the season's halfway mark with a better than .500 record. They accomplished this despite defensive end Jim Marshall recovering a San Francisco fumble and running 60 yards to the wrong end zone for a 49ers safety.

The Vikings escaped the snow in late November 1964 and found a more comfortable practice facility at the Hippodrome on the State Fair Grounds. That Sunday, they hosted the Los Angeles Rams in the cold, open air of Met Stadium and won handily, 34-13.
John Croft/Star Tribune

"WRONG WAY" MARSHALL

All but 12 of Jim Marshall's 282 consecutive games played (a record for non-punters) were as a member of the Minnesota Vikings, from 1961 to 1979. The left end led or tied for the team lead in sacks in each of the franchise's first six seasons. Later, he was a cornerstone of the famed Purple People Eaters that helped make the Vikings a dominating defensive force for so many years. In 1999, Marshall was inducted into the team's ring of honor.

Even with all these accomplishments, there is one slip-up that Marshall never will be able to escape: His 66-yard wrong-way run that resulted in a safety for the San Francisco 49ers on October 25, 1964. NFL Films listed Marshall's run as the number-one miscue in its *NFL's 100 Greatest Follies* video (released in 1994).

The infamous play proved to be relatively harmless in Minnesota's 27-22 victory at Kezar Stadium, and it occurred during a game in which Marshall and the defense otherwise played well.

In the second quarter, Marshall had recovered a fumble by 49ers quarterback John Brodie. In the fourth quarter, just a few minutes before his notorious return, Marshall forced a fumble by Brodie's replacement, George Mira. Fellow defensive end Carl Eller recovered the ball and took it 45 yards for a touchdown to give the Vikings a 27-17 lead.

That was of little consolation later in the fourth quarter. Mira completed a pass to receiver Bill Kilmer, who proceeded to fumble the ball at about the San Francisco 35-yard line. Marshall jumped over a fallen player to grab the ball and took off running—only he headed the wrong way! According to one account, quarterback Fran Tarkenton raced down the sideline stride-for-stride with Marshall trying to get his attention. Coach Norm Van Brocklin couldn't believe what he was seeing.

"At first I thought Marshall was kidding," Van Brocklin remarked later. "He does some of that in practice. He's kind of a cutup. But when I saw him pouring on the coal, I just put my hands over my eyes."

Marshall's teammates had no hope of catching him, and the 49ers certainly weren't about to stop him. Once he reached the end zone, Marshall threw the ball out of play in celebration.

The first indication for Marshall that something was wrong was when Niners guard Bruce Bosley embraced Marshall and said, "Thanks for the favor." Moments later, a distraught and embarrassed Marshall doubled over with his head in his hands.

"I couldn't hear our guys yelling that I was going the wrong way," he said. "I had to jump over a guy to get the ball after Kilmer fumbled, and just before that I was going the other way on the pass rush. I just got mixed up. I can't remember even picking up the ball, the thing was that confused.

"I saw my teammates running down the sidelines. I thought they were cheering for me. I think it dawned on me as I was crossing the goal line. Maybe I flipped the ball over my head to get it out of bounds. I don't know."

Afterwards, Marshall received an outpouring of support from Van Brocklin and his teammates. "He played a hell of a football game," Van Brocklin said. "He always does."

Jim Marshall pounces on a fumble by San Francisco receiver Bill Kilmer and takes off running. Unfortunately for Marshall and the Vikings, their end zone is in the opposite direction.
AP/Wide World Photos

The Vikings were whipped by Green Bay 42-13 at Met Stadium the following week, then they closed the season with a flurry. They went 4-1-1 down the stretch to finish at 8-5-1.

The NFL had something called the Playoff Bowl for the 10 seasons from 1960 through 1969. This game pitted the runners-up of the Western and Eastern Conferences for "third place" in the NFL. Green Bay's Lombardi hated the game, calling it the "Losers Bowl," and more profane terms.

Van Brocklin and the Vikings didn't feel that way. They were a young team on the rise. An appearance in the Playoff Bowl would have served to validate their improvement.

Baltimore had locked up the Western Conference entering the final week. The Packers were second at 8-5, and the Vikings were 7-5-1. The Vikings clobbered the Bears 41-14 in Chicago. The Packers were closing the schedule in Los Angeles against the Rams.

Van Brocklin, Tarkenton, and Bill Brown (who scored three touchdowns in the final game) were on a postgame television show celebrating the Purple's first winning season. When asked about the possibility of advancing to the Playoff Bowl, the Dutchman grinned into the TV camera and said the Vikings would be there if they could get some help from "those oversexed beach boys from Los Angeles."

The Packers rallied for a 24-24 tie with the Rams, putting both Green Bay and the Vikings at 8-5-1. The Packers had the tie-breaker on the basis of outscoring the Vikings in the head-to-head games, and Lombardi had to take his team to the "Losers Bowl."

Tarkenton didn't need the Playoff Bowl to feel giddy after a season-ending three-game winning streak over the Rams, Giants, and Bears. "If we continue to progress the way we have this year, we should be as good as any team in the NFL next season," the quarterback said.

THE VOLATILE DUTCHMAN

During the 1960s, regulars played in exhibition games more often than they do today, and there was more PR value in exhibition results. The Vikings went 5-0 in the 1965 exhibition schedule, including a 57-17 thrashing of Dallas, their former expansion rivals, in Birmingham, Alabama.

The optimism was high for the season opener in Baltimore against the defending Western Conference champion Colts. The game was being billed by Van Brocklin as the biggest game in franchise history.

The 35-16 loss at the hands of the Colts in the opener was a disappointment, but the optimism carried over to the ticket window when the Vikings opened at home against Detroit. The Vikings attracted their largest home crowd to date, 46,826.

The result was a bitter 31-29 loss to the Lions. The season of great expectations was looking as if it might be

headed off the rails, but the Vikings rallied to win five of the next six games.

The Tarkenton-led offense was lighting up the scoreboard with point totals of 38, 40, and 42 in victories over the Rams, Giants, and 49ers, and 37 in a loss to Chicago. Four consecutive crowds reached the Met's new sellout capacity of 47,426.

In the November 7 game against the Rams, Tommy Mason suffered an injury to his right knee, which knocked him out for three games and eventually short-circuited the chance of a Hall of Fame career. He had made

Van Brocklin enjoys a lighter moment as he looks ahead to the 1966 season. The "Big Board" for that season's draft is sketched out on the blackboard behind him. The team's top pick for 1966, tackle Jerry Shay, played just 15 games in a Vikings uniform. *John Croft/Star Tribune*

41

three consecutive Pro Bowls (1962–1964) and earned the nickname "Touchdown Tommy" for his ability to get to the end zone either as a runner or receiver. He was also a unique character. He had a pet monkey named Dutch, in honor of his coach. He played a guitar, sang country music, drove a silver Cadillac, and was a notorious ladies man.

Roy Winston, a fellow Louisianan, recalled in 2007, "I don't remember the monkey, but I remember the Cadillac and the guitar, and I remember that Tommy was never short of dates with good-lookin' women."

Mason was a favorite of the Twin Cities reporters, and a feature story made mention of those trappings. Shortly after the article came out, Mason missed a block during a game and caused Tarkenton to take a vicious hit.

Van Brocklin was running film in an otherwise darkened room. He came to Mason's missed block, ran the play back and forth several times, then turned off the projector and from the darkness said, "Mason, take that guitar, that monkey, that Cadillac, stick 'em you know where, and play some football!"

Mason's injury in the Rams game allowed Dave Osborn, a rookie 13th-round draft choice from North Dakota, to get his first significant action. Osborn carried the ball nine times for 48 yards and a touchdown. He played extensively in place of Mason over the final weeks of 1965 and emerged as backfield partner to fullback Bill Brown during the course of the 1966 season.

The Vikings, standing with a 5-3 record after the victory over the Rams, had a rematch with the Colts at Met Stadium on November 14. Van Brocklin, his players, and the team's newly enthused public saw this as the ultimate test: Were the Vikings contending or pretending?

The final score was Baltimore 41, Vikings 21.

An emotionally defeated Van Brocklin said, "The Vikings learned today what it means to be outplayed, outhit, and outscored by a team which wanted to win a little more badly.

"Baltimore did that, and that's why they're contending for the Western Division championship, and we're just where we are."

A day later, the extent of Van Brocklin's melancholy became clearer when he called reporters into his office on Monday morning and announced he was quitting.

Immediately.

"I've taken the team as far as I can," he said. "I can't get the team over the hump. It's been going this way for five years. We come to the big game and we blow it. I've gone as far as I can go. Maybe another guy can do it.

"I want to get out of football. I have no intention of reconsidering."

A copy boy working in the sports department at the *Minneapolis Tribune* overheard an interesting exchange that afternoon: Charley Johnson, the executive sports editor for the Minneapolis newspapers and a *Star* columnist, and Sid Hartman, the *Tribune*'s sports editor, were discussing Van Brocklin's decision.

These two gentlemen had many bad things to say about Van Brocklin. The theme of the conversation was "good riddance." Yet, they were also suspicious that Van Brocklin might change his mind, so Sid's next-day column carried the headline, "Van Can Name Terms If He Comes Back."

By the time Johnson's column appeared in the Tuesday afternoon newspaper, Van Brocklin indeed had changed his mind and was back as the Vikings' coach. The first paragraph of Charley's column read: "Norm Van Brocklin's decision this noon to reconsider his resignation as football coach of the Vikings was the best news that has come out of 24 hours of surprise, disappointment, and concern."

Over in St. Paul, Bill Boni, the executive sports editor and columnist for the afternoon *Dispatch*, ordered his column ripping Van Brocklin pulled from publication when it was announced that the Dutchman was returning.

Years later, I asked Hartman and Boni about the decisions to pull their punches on Van Brocklin, and they both said roughly the same thing, "Nobody wanted to deal with the guy even when he wasn't mad at you."

Van Brocklin's public comment after his 26-hour resignation was that he was "ashamed and embarrassed."

"I realized that by walking out at this time I would be a quitter," said Van Brocklin, who still was only 39 and in his fifth season as an NFL head coach.

Jim Klobuchar, at this time a general columnist for the afternoon *Star* as well as a Vikings' writer, wrote that he was surprised Van Brocklin's resignation lasted more than eight hours. He also was the only reporter to hint that the Dutchman's decision to quit might have been fueled by several Sunday night cocktails.

"After five years of sharing each other's triumphs and travails, a man concludes he understands the other guy's rhythm and blues," Klobuchar wrote. "I knew, for example, that Van Brocklin begins drifting wide after the third ginger ale."

He didn't mean ginger ale, literally.

Predictably, the players were publicly supportive of Van Brocklin's rapid return. The results on the field said otherwise. The Vikings lost the next three games, twice to Green Bay and at San Francisco.

They closed the 1965 season with victories over Detroit and Chicago, but the season of high expectations ended at 7-7. There were also considerable doubts about the future of a coach who had publicly demanded toughness from his players for five years, and then chose to quit (however briefly) on his team in midseason after a tough loss.

GOING DOWN IN FLAMES

The fire was gone from the 1966 Vikings from the get-go. Tommy Mason, the team's first All-Pro, was limited to 58 carries with his bad knee. Dave Osborn was the new running back.

The Vikings opened the season with a tie at San Francisco, then followed it with three straight losses. They were 3-6-1 in mid-November when Van Brocklin gave the start to Ron VanderKelen, over Tarkenton, in Los Angeles. He was pulled after three quarters. Tarkenton played the fourth in a 21-6 loss to the Rams.

On December 4, Atlanta came to Met Stadium. Tarkenton had played at Georgia, lived in Atlanta, and had several business interests there. This was the first chance for his Atlanta friends to see him play on television against the Falcons.

Van Brocklin knew that—and that's why he gave Bob Berry his first NFL start. The actual crowd on the snowy afternoon was 21,000, with 16,000 no-shows among the ticketholders. Berry had an unproductive day in a 20-13 loss.

Atlanta reporter Jim Minter asked Tarkenton why he didn't play. Tarkenton pointed across the locker room toward Van Brocklin's office and said, "You will have to ask the man in there."

The season closed two weeks later with a 41-21 loss in Chicago. The Vikings had gone from 8-5-1 in 1964 to 7-7 in 1965, and their downhill slide was official with a 4-9-1 finish in Van Brocklin's sixth season.

The animus between the coach and the quarterback was clear, yet there was little public speculation in Twin Cities newspapers on their Vikings' futures in the weeks following the season.

Then, all Hades broke loose in a period of 48 hours. On Friday, February 10, it was revealed that Tarkenton had sent a letter of resignation directed to General Manager Jim Finks, with copies to Van Brocklin and all five of the team's board members.

"It is impossible for me to return to the Vikings with a clear and open mind," Tarkenton said in his letter. "Feeling as I do, I am sure that this decision is the best for the Vikings, you, and myself. I hope you and the organization understand that nothing can be done which would change my decision."

One day later, Van Brocklin resigned for the second time. There was no attempt to get him to return this time. Indeed, everyone connected with the Vikings seemed to be relieved that the unpredictable coach was moving on.

Receiver Paul Flatley, who played for Van Brocklin in Minnesota for four seasons, reflected on the coach's relationship with the team. "He could dissect a defense in one glance, but his volatile personality got in the way of that brilliant mind," Flatley said. "I always felt that the best thing that happened to the Vikings was going from pro-

peller-driven aircraft to jets, so it didn't take so long to get home after a loss. That meant Norm didn't have as much time to go down the aisle chewing on everybody."

As he was headed out the door, Van Brocklin took the opportunity to take another shot at Tarkenton. He said that Tarkenton had started to "pull away" from him a couple of years earlier, harming his development as a quarterback. He also said Tarkenton "split the squad" by talking to teammates about the decision to start Berry against the Falcons.

Tarkenton responded by saying he wasn't going to "give a rebuttal or get into a debate with Van Brocklin" on his ability as a quarterback or his relationship with teammates.

Finks made a blockbuster trade on March 6, sending Tarkenton to the New York Giants for elite draft choices that the GM would turn into running back Clinton Jones and receiver Bobby Grim in 1967, and Ron Yary, a Hall of Fame offensive tackle, in 1968.

Tarkenton would play five seasons in New York before returning to the Vikings in a 1972 trade. Van Brocklin resurfaced as a coach in the NFL with the Falcons (the team against which he did not play Tarkenton) two weeks into the 1968 season.

Shown here in 1961, the volatile "Dutchman" butted heads with his quarterback numerous times in their six season together. The 1966 campaign was Van Brocklin's last in Minnesota.
John Croft/Star Tribune

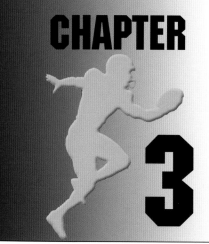
BUILDUP TO A SUPER BOWL
1967–1969

During his first three seasons as general manager of the Minnesota Vikings, Jim Finks was a secondary presence in the football operation behind Coach Norm Van Brocklin.

Finks was given much credit for calming down Van Brocklin and getting him to return quickly after the coach's one-day resignation in November 1965. On the flip side, Finks' first two drafts, for the 1965 and 1966 seasons, were less than sterling.

Jack Snow was the first-rounder in 1965. He was a receiver from Notre Dame but a Californian at heart. He refused to play for the cold-weather Vikings. Finks made the best of that and traded Snow to the Los Angeles Rams for receiver Jim (Red) Phillips and Gary Larsen, a defensive tackle from Concordia College in Moorhead, Minnesota.

Larsen would become one-fourth of the Vikings' vaunted Purple People Eaters, with Jim Marshall, Carl Eller, and Alan Page.

General Manager Jim Finks gained greater leeway in shaping the team after the departure of Coach Van Brocklin in February 1967. Finks quickly went to work to bring in new talent.
AP/Wide World Photos

Minnesota's four top rookies arrive at Minneapolis-St. Paul International Airport in August 1967, ready for training camp. They are (left to right) defensive back Bob Grim, receiver Gene Washington, defensive end Alan Page, and halfback Clint Jones.
Donald Black/Star Tribune

A pair of second-rounders in 1965—tackle Archie Sutton from Illinois and receiver Lance Rentzel from Oklahoma—had spotty careers with the Vikings. The only player to amount to anything in that draft was running back Dave Osborn, a 13th rounder from North Dakota.

The 1966 draft was another bust. Only running back Jim Lindsey from Arkansas and offensive tackle Doug Davis from Kentucky played much for the Vikings.

In February 1967, within 24 hours of one another, Fran Tarkenton demanded a trade and Van Brocklin resigned. That's when Vikings fans discovered that they had a pretty crafty football man in charge.

Finks had gained influence by increments over the previous seasons, but once Van Brocklin's mighty presence was out of the picture, Finks started to put his stamp on the organization.

His first bold moves came in a period of one week from March 7 to 13. On the 7th, he traded Tarkenton to the New York Giants for three top draft choices. On the 10th, Finks announced that Bud Grant, the former Gopher and highly successful young coach of the Winnipeg Blue Bombers, would be the Vikings' second head coach.

The draft was held on the March 13, and Finks did more than bring in running back Clinton Jones (second overall) and receiver Bobby Grim (28th overall) from the Tarkenton trade. He also drafted receiver Gene Washington (eighth overall) with the Vikings' regular pick. Then he pulled off the coup that made him famous: Finks traded Tommy Mason, the once-great running back now plagued by bad knees; tight end Hal Bedsole; and a second-round choice to the Rams for the 15th selection in the first round and tight end Marlin McKeever. The Vikings used the 15th pick to take Alan Page, the Notre Dame lineman who would become perhaps the most-dominant Vikings player of all-time and one of the NFL's greatest-ever defensive tackles.

A year later, Finks made the most of the Giants' bonus pick that he had also acquired in the Tarkenton trade. (The Giants received a special first overall pick in the draft as compensation for allowing the Jets into their market in the merger with the American Football League.) Finks used that choice in 1968 to take Southern Cal's Ron Yary, who would go on to be a Hall of Fame offensive tackle.

Defensive end Jim Marshall and running back Bill Brown check out the highlight film from the 1966 season in February 1967. The two returned as vital pieces under the new coach, Bud Grant. *John Croft/Star Tribune*

The arrival in Minnesota of those five outstanding collegians—Page, Yary, Jones, Washington, and Grim—completely changed the Vikings' talent level and launched the team's transformation into a contender.

For a new head coach, Finks had narrowed his choices to Grant, Cleveland assistant Nick Skorich, and San Francisco assistant Bill "Tiger" Johnson. Skorich had coached the Eagles from 1961 to 1963 and posted a 15-24-3 record. Johnson later coached the Cincinnati Bengals for three seasons in the 1970s and went 18-15.

A famous anecdote tells how Bill McGrane, a former *Minneapolis Tribune* sportswriter who had been hired as the Vikings' public relations director, was told by Finks to go to the Twin Cities airport to pick up Bud Grant.

"I don't know Grant; I don't know what he looks like," McGrane said.

Finks' reply was, "He'll be the fellow who looks like the town marshal."

McGrane met the airplane from Winnipeg and there he was: a younger version of Gary Cooper in *High Noon;* he was tall, slender, and had piercing eyes.

Finks' maneuvering to trade Tarkenton and other veterans and hire Grant as coach gained him praise in the Twin Cities media. Charley Johnson, the voice of the *Star,* wrote in late March: "We hope the five owners will realize what a sound leader they have in their general manager. Up to now, these magnates haven't done too good of a job of supervising their overall operations."

By the standards of that time, this was harsh criticism aimed at Max Winter, Bill Boyer, H. P. Skoglund, Bernie Ridder, and Ole Haugsrud—although mostly at Boyer (the team's first president) and Winter (the second).

THE ICEMAN COMETH

Grant was 10 days shy of his 40th birthday when he was hired by the Vikings. He came from Superior, Wisconsin, and was a talented and versatile athlete. He had been a three-sport star at Superior Central High and played fullback for the football team.

When he graduated in 1945, he enlisted in the Navy. The famous Grant practicality was on display way back then. "There still was a war on," he said. "It was either enlist or get drafted."

He was sent to the Great Lakes Naval Training Center and was told to go out for the football team. Billy Bye, later a teammate of his with the Gophers, told a Grant story to the *Tribune's* Merrill Swanson many years later.

"The first day they called the fullbacks," Bye said. "Marion Motley, who at the time weighed 235 pounds and was already a famous power runner, was lined up at fullback. Grant kept right on walking over to the ends."

Grant went on to become a top-flight end for the Gophers and also played basketball for the University in the late 1940s. He earned his summer money by

New coach Bud Grant confers with new quarterback Joe Kapp during training camp prior to the 1967 season. Despite a 3-8-3 finish that season, Grant and Kapp were Super-Bowl bound by the end of the decade.
Charles Bjorgen/Star Tribune

pitching town-team baseball in Minnesota and western Wisconsin.

Sid Hartman and Grant became friends when Grant was at the university. Hartman was involved in running the Minneapolis Lakers, a dynastic team for a time in the NBA with George Mikan. The Lakers had a habit of giving the eighth, ninth, and tenth spots on the roster to locals, and Grant landed one of those jobs after he was done playing football for the Gophers.

In 1950, Grant was Philadelphia's choice as the 12th overall selection in the NFL Draft. He declined an invitation to play in the College All-Star Game, because that was the day that he and Pat were married.

Then he turned down the Eagles because the Lakers offered him a raise for the 1950–1951 season, and he could stay in the Twin Cities. He didn't sign with the Eagles until the summer of 1951, then he played one season on defense and the next on offense.

Grant did not have a contract for 1953 and the Eagles had no hold on his services. So, he called the Winnipeg Blue Bombers and signed to play there. Legend says that this made Grant the NFL's first free agent, although it was more a case of him being unsigned and taking what he considered a better offer to play in Canada.

Grant played three seasons for Winnipeg, and then the Blue Bombers hired him as coach. He was 29 years old when he started his coaching career in 1956. During Grant's decade of coaching in the CFL, the Blue Bombers won four Grey Cups and posted a record of 105-53-2.

Finks' Calgary teams had competed against Grant's Blue Bombers without much success.

"We never beat him in a playoff game," Finks said. "There were a number of coaches available who probably could have adjusted quicker to the Vikings personnel and the NFL, but the deciding factor was Grant's record as a winner at Winnipeg."

The Twin Cities sportswriters knew Grant well from his Gophers days and wrote about his arrival with the Vikings in 1967 in a familiar style.

Dick Cullum had been writing columns in Minneapolis for decades; he demonstrated a combination of subtle humor and analytical opinion. He was a boxing, football, and baseball man; he made no secret of his disdain for basketball. That's why the locals certainly chuckled at "Cullum's Column" a couple of weeks after the hiring:

"Coach Bud Grant of the Minnesota Vikings is remembered as a university and professional basketball player. This may no longer be held against him. The statute of limitation has run in his favor.

"His overt presence at every session of [this week's] high school basketball tournament may be a violation of his parole and an indication that he is incorrigible. However, there is the extenuating fact that his mind can be diverted from the whistle symphony by a few questions about hunting and fishing."

Cullum followed with Grant's comments on the outdoors activities he engaged in while in Canada.

"After a football season, the coaching staffs of the league gathered for a game dinner," Grant told Cullum. "My assignment was to bring the moose."

Lo and behold, Grant discovered a two-legged "Moose"—Carl Eller—when he arrived at Mankato for training camp.

The training camp location was another sign of Grant's practicality. He saw no sense in conducting training camp in the woods of Bemidji, which was located four hours away from the Twin Cities. The camp was moved to Mankato, which could be reached in 70 minutes.

Training camp is still held there, making it more than 40 years for the Vikings at Mankato State (now Minnesota State University, Mankato). It has been an annual destination for thousands of Purple fans over the decades,

although that certainly wasn't the case when Grant assembled his Vikings for the first time on July 18, 1967.

An estimated 100 spectators were on hand to watch the team workout. The early workouts were mostly for rookies, which accounted for 24 of the 37 players at camp. There were four assistant coaches: Bob Hollway, defensive line; Jimmy Carr, linebackers and defensive backs; Bus Mertes, offensive backs; and John Michels, offensive line. Jerry Reichow, Finks' chief scout, helped with receivers in training camp. (By comparison, 40 years later, Coach Brad Childress has 16 assistants, a personal assistant, two quality coordinators, and three strength coaches on his staff.)

Grant arrived for that first afternoon workout without ceremony. He wore a blue short-sleeve shirt with a Vikings logo, gold Bermuda shorts, calf-high white socks, and a baseball cap.

He forgot one thing: a whistle. None of his assistants had a whistle, either. After 50 minutes, he looked at his watch and five minutes later used his hand to signal the end of his first Vikings' practice.

There were no mini-camps, optional team workouts, or formal offseason workout programs. The players were on their own until the morning they showed up in Mankato.

If there was a home exhibition game, the players drove themselves from Mankato to Met Stadium, since they wouldn't have to be back in camp until late the next afternoon.

"Bud wouldn't let 'em leave until exactly 4:30 p.m.," trainer Fred Zamberletti recalled. "Anyone caught leaving early would be fined. They would all have the cars lined up three abreast on the road in front of the dormitory. Jim Marshall would stand there looking at his watch and fire a pistol in the air when the second hand hit 4:30.

"It wasn't a starter's pistol. It was a real pistol."

Grant also did not want his athletes driving 90 miles per hour to the Twin Cities to meet someone for a brief interlude of companionship.

"Bud was known to call the Highway Patrol and say, 'They are on the way,'" Zamberletti said. "And if he saw someone pulled over on the highway, he would get a devilish smile on his face."

INAUSPICIOUS BEGINNING

Grant's arrival did little to inspire the Minnesota sporting public. Tarkenton had been the most popular Viking from game one, when he led the astonishing upset of the Bears in September 1961, and his departure made tickets more difficult to sell.

Ron VanderKelen, now in his fifth season, was being advertised as Tarkenton's replacement, although Finks and Grant had other ideas. Joe Kapp, the quarterback who took California to the 1959 Rose Bowl, was hav-

ing contract problems in Vancouver with the British Columbia Lions.

Kapp had played eight seasons in Canada and was number two on the CFL's all-time passing list for yards and touchdowns. Obviously, he was familiar to Finks and Grant as competitors in the Canadian league.

Kapp had refused to report to his Vancouver team. There were reports throughout August 1967 that the Vikings were trying to purchase his rights. Simultaneously, Minnesota's offense was struggling in exhibitions with VanderKelen, Bob Berry, and former Gophers star John Hankinson as the quarterback options.

The Vikings completed the acquisition of Kapp on September 3, costing Hankinson his spot as a third quarterback.

Grant offered the following description of Kapp: "He's about 6-3 and can buggy-whip the ball. He's not graceful, but he's tough. You never could discourage him, knock him out of there. He also was his team's leader."

Grant said this on Kapp's first day as a Viking, and it remained an immaculate scouting report on the quarterback until the end of his time in Minnesota.

The Vikings were unwilling to pull the plug on VanderKelen immediately. He was the starter in the

On November 5, 1967, eight months after being traded to the Giants, Fran Tarkenton made his first visit to Minnesota in an enemy uniform. The quarterback and his new team lost to his old team, but there were no hard feelings when Tarkenton greeted former teammate Dale Hackbart after the game. *Star Tribune*

season opener against San Francisco. The Met Stadium crowd was 8,000 below capacity.

VanderKelen was booed lustily during a futile first half. The Vikings were down 27-0 heading into the fourth quarter. The quarterback from Wisconsin triggered a three-touchdown comeback but came up short, with a final score of 27-21.

"I made the right decision staying with VanderKelen," Grant said after the game. "Yes, he'll start next week."

The Vikings were at Los Angeles to play the Rams in a Friday night game. It was a 39-3 slaughter. The Vikings were trailing 32-0 early in the fourth quarter when Grant called on kicker Fred Cox to attempt a field goal.

The Rams fans in the L.A. Coliseum booed lustily. Grant was nonplussed—and candid. He had Cox kick the field goal so that his team could avoid a shutout.

Kapp had replaced VanderKelen at quarterback in the second quarter of the Rams game. Kapp went on to start the final 12 games of the season, and VanderKelen was gone after the 1967 season.

The Vikings were 0-4 when they headed to Milwaukee to play the Packers on October 15. In six seasons, Van Brocklin had been 2-10 against Vince Lombardi's powerhouse teams.

In 1967, the Vikings were facing a Green Bay team that was headed for its second consecutive Super Bowl victory. But on that October day in Milwaukee's County Stadium, the Vikings showed the makings of what soon would become a ferocious defense. They won the game 10-7 on Cox's field goal from the 12-yard line with 13 seconds remaining.

The Vikings had three-fourths of the notorious Purple People Eaters in place on that afternoon: Jim Marshall and Carl Eller at the ends and Alan Page at tackle. Veteran Paul Dickson, an original Viking, still was starting at the other tackle. He would be supplanted by Gary Larsen, the tackle obtained in the Mason-Bedsole deal, a season later.

"We got a heck of a rush from the line," said cornerback Earsell Mackbee, who had two interceptions of Green Bay's legendary Bart Starr. "That gives the defensive backs a chance to react."

That victory was the highlight of Grant's first season, which ended with three wins, eight losses, and three ties. There were a lot of jokes about Bud kicking the field goal in Los Angeles and about his alleged contentment with ties.

That same autumn the Gophers tied for the Big Ten title with Indiana and Purdue. The crowds at Memorial Stadium were far from what they used to be, but in 1967, the Gophers remained at least equals to the Vikings when it came to the public's interest.

That lack of public interest changed dramatically in 1968, when Grant took the Vikings to the playoffs for the first time and the Gophers started a slide from contention that lasted for the next four decades.

KAPP TAKES CHARGE

Joe Kapp was far from the answer at quarterback for the Vikings in 1967. He completed only 47.7 percent of his passes. He threw 17 interceptions compared to eight touchdowns. His quarterback rating of 48.2 would get someone benched after a first half in today's game.

The Vikings were unsure enough about Kapp that they traded a first-round draft choice to New Orleans for Gary Cuozzo. He had been the understudy to Johnny Unitas in Baltimore for four seasons before going to New Orleans in the 1967 expansion draft. Cuozzo was not happy about being forced to split time with Bill Kilmer with the Saints.

The Vikings basically declared an open competition for the quarterback job for 1968. "I love competition," Kapp said. "It makes for better athletes."

A year earlier, the Vikings offense had been punchless in exhibition play. In the 1968 preseason, they put up 39 and 52 points in back-to-back victories against Denver and Philadelphia.

Kapp won the preseason quarterback competition. The regular-season opener was against Atlanta, a team against which Kapp had started and played pitifully in 1967. In that game, he lasted five series, the offense totaled 23 yards, and he got the hook from Grant.

The results were a tad different in the 1968 opener, which was played on a Saturday night.

When Kapp was introduced as the starter, there were some boos from the Met Stadium crowd. By halftime, the Vikings were leading 31-0. Kapp and his teammates were saluted with a triumphant roar from the crowd as the team headed for the locker room. Kapp finished the game 16-for-20 for 191 yards, with three touchdowns and no interceptions. When all the damage was done, the final score read Vikings 47, Falcons 7.

A week later, the Vikings went to Milwaukee to play the Packers. Lombardi had quit as coach to become general manager before the season, and Phil Bengtson was his replacement. The balance of power between these rivals was about to shift.

The Vikings won the game, 26-13. Kapp was outstanding again, and Grant—after getting criticized in 1967 for his conservative approach to offense—showed a side that Minnesotans hadn't seen.

The Packers had cut the lead to 16-6 with a touchdown drive after the second-half kickoff. On the Vikings' next possession, they faced fourth down and a few inches at their 26 yard line.

Rather than punt, Grant sent in an extra tight end and had Kapp run a sneak. When the chains came out, the Vikings had the first down by a fraction of an inch.

After the game, Kapp was asked if it ever occurred to him that he might not make the first down.

"Not until just now, when you mentioned it," Kapp replied.

The Vikings made it a sweep of Green Bay in 1968 with a 14-10 victory on October 10 at Met Stadium. It was the first time in eight seasons that the Vikings had won both games against the Packers. It also was the first time a team had beaten Green Bay twice in a season since Baltimore did it in 1964.

The Vikings held the 14-10 lead halfway through the third quarter and made it stand with some astounding defense. The most memorable play came when Carl Eller charged through Forrest Gregg, a fabled offensive tackle, ripped off his helmet as he went past, and then "crashed into Bart Starr like a runaway rhino," as Merrill Swanson wrote in the next day's *Tribune*.

Starr was knocked woozy and had to leave the game.

He came back briefly before being replaced by Zeke Bratkowski.

Larry Bowie, who had been the Vikings' starting right guard, was in a St. Paul hospital after having surgery to remove a blood clot from the base of his brain. Offensive linemen Grady Alderman and Milt Sunde, along with defensive tackle Gary Larsen, went to Miller Hospital to present Bowie with a game ball.

"He listened on the radio," Alderman said. "He said it had to be the greatest game played in the NFL this year."

The Vikings were 5-4 after the Green Bay win. They slipped to 6-6, then won the season's last two games on the road—in San Francisco and in Philadelphia—to finish at 8-6. When Green Bay defeated Chicago on the final

Joe Kapp, who took the starting quarterback job early in 1967, hands off to halfback Dave Osborn during a snowy game against Detroit.
Martin Mills/Getty Images

Bill Brown remained an integral part of the offense in 1968, leading the Vikings with 805 yards rushing and chipping in an additional 329 receiving yards. Here he plows through the Cowboys defense during a losing effort on October 20.
Kent Kobersteen/Star Tribune

weekend, it gave the Vikings the NFL Central Division title and their first playoff berth.

The NFL was in the midst of a three-year period (1967–1969) as a 16-team league with four divisions. The Vikings' 8-6 record put them in the Western Conference final against the 13-1 Baltimore Colts, who were champions of what was called the Coastal Division.

"Baltimore is superior to every team in the league," Grant said on the eve of his team's game at Baltimore's Memorial Stadium. "They are superior to us in all departments. The only place we could challenge them in personnel would be running back, with Bill Brown.

"If we play our best game and they play their best game, our chances of winning are slight."

But? "We can't afford the luxury of mistakes, and we have to cause them to make some mistakes," the coach said.

Grant's original thesis proved correct. The Colts played their best and the Vikings didn't have much of a chance. They were down 14-0 in the third quarter when defeat became inevitable.

Bubba Smith, the Colts' storied defensive end, crashed into Kapp. The ball popped to Mike Curtis and the linebacker ran 60 yards for a touchdown, to make it 21-0. The final was 24-14 in favor of the Colts.

"I don't know how we could've played any better than we did," Grant said. "We went bang-bang back and forth with them until the break came, and they got it."

The Colts embarrassed the Browns 34-0 in Cleveland in the NFL title game on December 29. Two weeks later, the team gained infamy with a 16-7 loss to the AFL's underdog New York Jets in the third Super Bowl.

The Vikings played Dallas in the NFL Playoff Bowl. The Cowboys won, 17-13. It was such a meaningless game that the statistics for those Playoff Bowls do not count in the career playoff numbers for teams or individuals.

DEFENSE FOR THE AGES

The Purple People Eaters—Carl Eller, Alan Page, Jim Marshall, Gary Larsen—were in their first full season together as starters in 1968. They started every game together and would duplicate that feat for the five seasons that followed.

The linebackers—Roy Winston, Lonnie Warwick, and Wally Hilgenberg—also had become a familiar unit. Two talented cover men—Bobby Bryant, a draftee in 1967, and Earsell Mackbee—were the corners. Karl Kassulke and Paul Krause were in their second year together as the safeties. Kassulke was the hitter and Krause was the finesse player. Krause earned nine All-Pro selections in his career and is enshrined in the Football Hall of Fame. He still holds the all-time NFL record for career interceptions.

The 1969 season opened with a 24-23 loss to the New York Giants and Fran Tarkenton at Yankee Stadium. It ended with a 10-3 loss to the Atlanta Falcons and Norm Van Brocklin at Atlanta Stadium.

In between, the Vikings won 12 straight games in dominating fashion. Included in this destruction were six victories against division rivals Green Bay, Detroit, and Chicago by a combined 141-38 score. The last of those wins was a 27-0 shutout in the Vikings' first-ever visit to Detroit for the Lions' traditional Thanksgiving Day game.

The opening-game loss to the Giants came after Gene Washington, Minnesota's big-play receiver, fumbled on the 36-yard line with less than three minutes left in the game. Tarkenton followed with his second touchdown pass of the fourth quarter to receiver Don Herrmann, a 15th-round draft choice from Waynesburg (Pa.) State.

"Herrmann made the touchdown passes work, not me," said Tarkenton, trying to display humility.

The opening defeat did not cool the enthusiasm back in Minnesota. The first playoff appearance in 1968 finally had assured that sellouts (now 47,900 capacity) would be routine at Met Stadium.

In the late 1960s, opposing quarterbacks had to face a fearsome Vikings defense, including the intimidating Lonnie Warwick at middle linebacker. He started every game from 1966 to 1970.
Kent Kobersteen/Star Tribune

Kapp celebrates with some young fans after the Vikings defeated the rival Packers 19-7 in week three of the 1969 season.
John Croft/Star Tribune

THE PURPLE PEOPLE EATERS

The *Star Tribune* had a series with monthly installments in 1999 on Minnesota's "Century of Sports." This is Patrick Reusse's article from January 1999 on Alan Page, Carl Eller, and Jim Marshall, the staples of the Purple People Eaters, the Vikings famed defensive line.

There was a long, curved wall of dark wood behind the desk of Doreen Garrett, a judicial secretary for the Minnesota Supreme Court. Garrett was chatting with two visitors when a door was revealed in that wall and Justice Alan Page stepped into the opening. As always, Page's gray beard was neatly trimmed, his suit draped exquisitely and the bow tie was in place—the picture of judicial dignity.

"How you doing, A. P.?" said Jim Marshall, as Page smiled and reached out for a handshake. Carl Eller, also smiling, stepped around Garrett's desk, and another handshake was exchanged.

Normally, a handshake with any of these men would cause a hand to be engulfed, but when Page and Marshall and Eller do so among themselves, there are matched mitts. The greeting is powerful and sincere, and the grip lasts for several seconds.

Minnesota's period of glory in professional football in this century came from 1968 through 1977, a decade in which the Vikings played in five NFL/NFC championship games and won

Left tackle Gary Larsen and right tackle Alan Page catch their breath on the sidelines in 1970. The two started side by side in every game from 1968 through 1973. *John Croft/Star Tribune*

four. This success was driven by a defense called the "Purple Gang," and it was powered by a front-loaded engine—Marshall at right end, Page at right tackle, and Eller at left end.

When Page, Marshall, and Eller assembled for a photograph last week, they made several mentions of the absence of Gary Larsen, the left tackle generally associated with the Vikings' famed front four.

Marshall came to the Vikings from the Cleveland Browns in the expansion draft of 1961. Eller arrived in 1964 as the No. 1 draft choice—sixth overall—from the University of Minnesota. Page came from Notre Dame and was the Vikings' third first-round choice in the 1967 draft.

The 1967 season started with Larsen and Paul Dickson at the tackles and Page in a backup role. Page moved into the lineup in the season's fifth game, starting alongside Dickson in nine games and Larsen in one.

Larsen was the left tackle from the first game of the 1968 season through the seventh game of the 1974 season, when Doug Sutherland replaced him in the starting lineup. Sutherland was

Gary Larsen, Alan Page, Jim Marshall, and Carl Eller formed a fearsome foursome during Minnesota's glory years of the late 1960s and early 1970s.

teamed with Page, Marshall, and Eller for the next three and a half seasons.

Left tackle was a position of flux for Bud Grant's NFC dynasty, in comparison to the astounding stability that the Vikings had in Page, Marshall, and Eller.

From Page's arrival in the lineup in the fifth game of 1967 through the 1977 season, the Vikings played a combined 169 games in the regular season and postseason. Page and Marshall started all 169. Eller missed a start in the 1976 season opener because of a broken thumb.

"I played in the game," Eller said. "I probably could have started. I guess as players and coaches we weren't as aware of streaks and history back then."

That broken thumb ended a streak in which Page, Marshall, and Eller had started 136 consecutive games together. They started another 32 consecutive games through a 23-6 loss in Dallas in the 1977 NFC Championship Game—this group's last of five NFC title games and its only defeat.

Page and Coach Bud Grant feuded over Page's weight loss and other matters during the 1978 season. Page was waived in October and claimed by the Chicago Bears, for whom he played into the 1981 season.

Eller was traded to Seattle for a draft choice in 1979 and played a final season for the Seahawks. Marshall, then 41, retired at the end of the 1979 season with an NFL's ironman record of 282 consecutive games that stands today.

"We played together for such a long time that we had an opportunity to really know each other," Marshall said. "One of the unique things for the four of us—Gary Larsen included—was that most of our communication during a game was not verbalized. We had a sense for each other that was almost telepathic.

"Alan, Carl, and I see each other only from time to time now. There's a purity to the relationship because we don't make demands on one another. It's a relationship that doesn't require maintenance."

Eller said, "You care about how their lives are going. You celebrate Alan's great accomplishments after football. You congratulate Jim for the outstanding program that he has put together for young people."

Page was asked if it was a situation where Marshall, Eller, and he could look into one another's eyes and tell that a quarterback was in trouble.

Jim Marshall celebrates a sack by fellow defensive end Carl Eller against Los Angeles quarterback John Hadl in October 1973.
John Croft/Star Tribune

"I don't know if you had to look at the other person's eyes," Page said. "We made the assumption that the quarterback was in trouble anyway."

The Vikings' record book remains a testament to that theory. They played in an era when the run was more popular than the pass, yet they stand 1-2-3 in sacks [in franchise history]—130 for Eller, 127 for Marshall, and 108 for Page. They played in the era of 14-game schedules, not 16, yet they stand 1-2-3 in fumbles recovered—29 for Marshall, 24 for Eller, and 18 for Page (tied with Matt Blair).

Page was inducted into the Pro Football Hall of Fame in his hometown of Canton, Ohio, in 1988. The new group of inductees will be announced next Saturday at the Super Bowl site of Miami and, once again, Eller is among the 15 finalists.

Eller has handled the past rejections with calmness and hope for the future. Now, he's not so sure. "It would be a verification of a career and a period of time when we had a great football team," he said.

"I don't think I could shrug it off again, not at this point. It is now about being unfair and unjust. When there is an injustice, that is something that has to be taken as directly aimed at a person."

[Eller would have to wait another five years, but he finally was voted into the Pro Football Hall of Fame in 2004.]

There are a number of symbols in Justice Page's office at the Judicial Center that serve as a reminder of injustices that black citizens have faced. Behind Page's desk, there is a sign that used to be located somewhere in North Carolina that reads, "Colored Waiting Room."

Asked if this was a daily reminder of the way things used to be in this country, Page said: "Used to be . . . and still is on occasion."

Page decided long ago that the best route to equality was education. He used the attention surrounding his Hall of Fame induction to start the Alan Page Education Foundation. For 10 years, the Page Foundation has evaluated applications and awarded grants to minority students to help pay for a college education. This year there are 390 Minnesota kids going to Minnesota schools as Page Scholars.

Page's relationship with Grant went from strained to mutual dislike when Page started to miss the early period of training camps while attending law school. Long-term, you would have to say that Page's defiance was a stroke of genius.

Page's first law work was with Ed Garvey and the NFL Players Association in the early '80s. He worked as an assistant attorney general in Skip Humphrey's office and served on the University of Minnesota's Board in Regents.

Page ran for and was elected to the Minnesota Supreme Court in 1992. He was challenged for re-election in 1998. "We took it seriously, and the campaign worked hard," Page said.

Page won last November with more votes—1.3 million—than any candidate on the state-wide ballot. "I can tell you that is a humbling experience to have 1.3 million citizens of your state take the time to vote for you," he said. [Page was re-elected to the state Supreme Court again in 2004.]

Marshall and Eller have had more difficult moments of humility. Marshall's life reached its low point in 1990, when he was arrested at gunpoint by Duluth police. He pleaded guilty to cocaine possession and was sentenced to 90 days of electronic monitoring and 3,000 hours of community service.

In the eight years since, Marshall's service has gone well beyond 3,000 hours. In 1991, Marshall started a non-profit organization with former Viking Oscar Reed called Professional

Sports Linkage. The Minneapolis-based organization is now called Life's Missing Link.

A major emphasis is a juvenile justice program. Marshall, Reed, and their staff work with Hennepin County males (ages 15 to 18) who are serving the final weeks of a sentence at the Red Wing Correctional Facility.

"Our mission is to help these young men develop the skills to get away from the things that have led them to their past problems," Marshall said.

Eller went through treatment for chemical abuse at St. Mary's Rehabilitation Center in March 1981. He entered the treatment field. He ran the Triumph Life Centers from 1986 through 1994. Eller's program treated more than 1,000 chemical-dependency patients during those eight years.

This month, Eller started a job with the state's Human Services Department. The enemy again will be chemical dependency and the main beneficiaries will be high-risk young people.

They were the pillars on which the Vikings' period of glory was built.

The three pillars of the Purple People Eaters are reunited in 1999: Jim Marshall, Alan Page, and Carl Eller. *Jeff Wheeler/Star Tribune*

The Colts came to Bloomington for the 1969 home opener on September 28. They were the defending NFL champions. They also held a dominating 12-2-1 lifetime record against the Vikings, including the victory nine months earlier in the Western Conference title game.

Johnny Unitas had missed most of the 1968 season with an injury, but he was back as the Colts' quarterback. Before the game, he was asked about the Vikings defensive line and made a favorable comparison with the Rams' famed Fearsome Foursome.

"From what I've seen in films, they're devastating," Unitas said. "They're as potent, or more potent, than the Rams."

The devastation in week two of the 1969 season came from the other side of the ball. Vikings defensive end Carl Eller commented, "You know who played the best defense? Our offense."

The final score was 52-14 in favor of the Vikings. Kapp threw for seven touchdown passes to tie an NFL record. He was 28-for-43 with 449 yards passing, despite hurting his left wrist early in the fourth quarter and sitting for a time.

Backups Gary Cuozzo and Bobby Lee stepped in and continued to throw, adding eight completions and pushing the passing yardage to 530. Overall, the Vikings totaled 622 yards and 34 first downs.

Grant had no qualms about rubbing it in to the Colts. When he learned that Kapp was five yards short of Tarkenton's club record of 407 yards passing, he put Kapp back in the game. Kapp led the Vikings on another drive and connected with running back Jim Lindsey for the seventh touchdown pass.

Two game balls were presented after the game: one to Kapp and one to Doug Davis, the right offensive tackle who had handled Colts defensive end Bubba Smith throughout the afternoon.

"Personally, I've been waiting all year for this to get back at the Colts after that playoff loss last year," Kapp said. "It's a big win, but I think we're looking forward to some bigger wins in terms of winning championships."

Baltimore coach Don Shula was fuming about his team's play, not the Vikings' quest to surpass 50 points.

"We stunk the joint out," he said. "I've never been ashamed of a football team before. I'm ashamed not only of the team, but of my coaching performance."

It was such a stirring performance that even Van Brocklin, now coaching in Atlanta, checked in with praise. "The Vikings did everything so easy," he said. "They looked like a bunch of guys out in the backyard playing catch."

The following week, the Vikings hosted Green Bay at Memorial Stadium—the Gophers' historic Brickhouse—because the Twins were scheduled to play Baltimore at Met Stadium the next day in the first-ever American League Championship Series.

They didn't come much tougher than number 81, Carl Eller. The 250-pound end enjoyed his third straight All-Pro season in 1969 and would go on to earn six more All-Pro selections in the next six seasons.

Kapp followed all the praise from the Colts' carnage with a horrendous game against the Packers. He completed six passes (in 20 attempts) for 87 yards. But it made no difference, because the Vikings were overwhelming Green Bay with the other half of their arsenal: defense.

The Vikings crunched the Packers 19-7 before a crowd of 60,740 in Memorial Stadium.

"Our defense was fantastic," Jim Marshall said. "Before looking at films, I would say this is the best our front four has ever played."

The Vikings kept winning in solid fashion. Cleveland came to Met Stadium for the eighth game of the season. Jim Brown was long gone. Cleveland couldn't move the ball and couldn't stop the Vikings.

Final: Vikings 51, Browns 3.

Kapp threw three touchdown passes to Gene Washington. The Vikings had 31 first downs and 454 yards, compared to Cleveland's eight first downs and 151 total yards.

Following the thrashing of the Browns, the Vikings added five more games to the winning streak, including another 50-point performance in a 52-14 victory over Pittsburgh two weeks later.

The Vikings had the NFL's best record locked up when they went to Atlanta for the final regular-season

The recipients of the Vikings team awards for 1969 included Joe Kapp, top offensive player; Jim Marshall, top defensive player; and Bobby Lee, top rookie. Kapp's statement that the team's most valuable player trophy should not go to him but rather to all 40 Vikings brought renewed admiration from teammates and fans alike. *Pete Hohn/Star Tribune*

contest. The 10-3 loss was significant only in the satisfaction it brought Van Brocklin.

Bob Berry was the Falcons' starting quarterback that day. He was the same Bob Berry who used to be the Vikings' backup and that Van Brocklin had started against the Falcons late in the 1965 season, which inflamed the feud that ultimately led to his and Tarkenton's departure from Minnesota.

THE MVP DECLINES

Four days before the Atlanta game, the Vikings' annual awards banquet was held at the Prom Center in St. Paul.

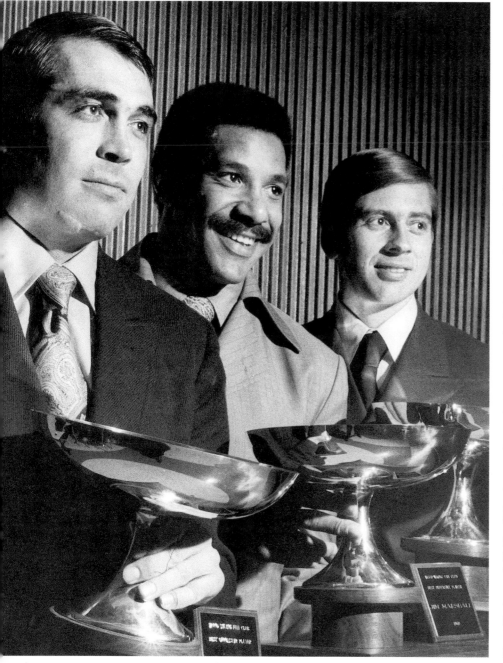

The event came on the same day that the Associated Press announced Grant as its NFL Coach of the Year.

This was the only time that Grant was the recipient of that award during an 18-season NFL career that would land him in the Hall of Fame.

On that Wednesday night in St. Paul, the recipients of the Vikings team awards were announced. Joe Kapp was named the top offensive player. Jim Marshall was named the top defensive player. Bobby Lee, the third-team quarterback and punter, was named the top rookie.

Then it came time for the big award: Most Valuable Player.

The winner was Kapp. He walked to the podium and said, "I know for a fact there is no Most Valuable Viking. There are 40 of them. This should go to 40 for 60."

This was a reference to Kapp's battle cry that was adopted as the slogan of the 1969 Vikings: 40 players for 60 minutes.

"I can't accept this," Kapp said, then he put the trophy on the table next to the podium and walked away.

The ovation from the 1,000 people inside the banquet room was deafening. Joe Kapp, the quarterback who was booed when introduced to fans before the home opener two years earlier, became a hero to fans with that gesture. He was able to win over the fans as few athletes had in the first decade since the Twin Cities became a bona fide major-league area.

Minnesota loved everything about Joe Kapp, even the tales of his fight with middle linebacker Lonnie Warwick late in the 1967 season after a 30-27 loss to Green Bay at Met Stadium. Legend has it that there was much tequila consumed before the argument started. Everyone drank tequila when Kapp—once called by *Sports Illustrated* football's "toughest Chicano," and golfer Lee Trevino's rival as the "Merry Mex"—was around.

What made this fight unique was that Kapp was blaming his offense for the defeat and Warwick was blaming his defense. The debate turned to shoves and the shoves turned to punches.

"And we left the party with our arms around one another," Kapp would say later.

PLAYOFFS IN BLOOMINGTON

The first-ever NFL playoff game at Met Stadium was played on December 27, 1969. The opponents for the Western Conference title game were the Los Angeles Rams, champions of the Coastal Division. The two teams had played on the same field 20 days earlier and the Vikings had won 20-13.

Observers commented that this game matched two of the most famous front fours in NFL history: Minnesota's Purple People Eaters and the Rams' Fearsome Foursome.

This wasn't exactly true. The Vikings quartet of Eller, Page, Marshall, and Larsen was entering its prime as a group, while the Rams were down to just two of the original Fearsome Foursome: Merlin Olsen and Deacon Jones. Rosey Grier had retired after the 1966 season. Lamar Lundy played in only four games in 1969. Roger Brown, Grier's replacement, was now a backup. The starters alongside Olsen and Jones for that playoff game at Met Stadium were Coy Bacon at tackle and Diron Talbert at end.

Los Angeles coach George Allen was wired very tight. He was paranoid about secrecy, and he worked for every advantage. He decided to bring his southern California team to Minnesota four days early in an attempt to acclimate his players to the cold.

Merrill Swanson's story in the *Tribune* on the Rams' arrival suggested that they had brought hand warmers, foot warmers, heat blowers, a variety of gloves, and arm bands to regulate circulation and further warm hands.

Allen rented Macalester Stadium for his team. He had tarps placed over the fences surrounding the field, and security was on hand to make sure that people weren't peeking through the tarps.

Ralph Reeve was the Vikings' beat reporter for the St. Paul newspapers. He had access to a house across the street from Macalester. An upper-level window gave him a clear view of the field with binoculars. He watched the Rams' practice for a time and included enough details in his article to cause considerable trauma for Allen.

Bud Grant loved to chide people such as Allen. He said of the Rams' stock of gear to fight the cold, "We will not wear gloves. Some teams do, which is fine. But what we've been learning to do is to play in the cold."

The cold weather never showed up (at least not by Minnesota standards). It was 21 degrees with calm winds. Rams quarterback Roman Gabriel led three scoring drives, and the visitors led 17-7 at halftime.

"The feeling at halftime was that we had to pull ourselves together and hold them," Alan Page said. "Our offense had started out moving the ball, and we knew they could do that in the second half. But the defense had to hold the Rams for the offense to do its work."

The Vikings cut the score to 17-14 on a six-play, 72-yard drive on their first possession of the second half. Dave Osborn dived over from the one yard line for the touchdown.

Richie Petitbon's interception of a Kapp pass set up a Bruce Gossett field goal to make it 20-14 early in the fourth quarter. Now, it was clutch time for Kapp, and he met the challenge with a 10-play, 65-yard drive.

Those crazy legs of his did much of the damage. First, he rumbled and stumbled 12 yards to the Rams' 4-yard line. Then he kept the ball and went around the left end from two yards out for the touchdown and a 21-20 Vikings lead.

The Vikings went into an emotional frenzy. First, Dale Hackbart covered the kickoff and brought the Rams' Ron Smith to a crushing halt.

Joe Kapp threw and ran the ball to help lead the Vikings to their first playoff win, a 23-20 triumph over the Rams on December 27, 1969.
James Flores/NFL/Getty Images

Receiver Gene Washington sprints to the end zone to complete a 75-yard touchdown pass against Cleveland in the NFC championship game on January 4, 1970. It was the second scoring play in two possessions for Minnesota and contributed to Washington's 120 receiving yards on the day. *AP/Wide World Photos*

The Vikings drove the Rams farther back. Then Eller came plowing through Bob Brown, Los Angeles' vaunted offensive tackle, and sacked Gabriel in the end zone for a safety.

It was 23-20 Vikings and the Rams had one more shot. They moved into Vikings territory, but Page intercepted a Gabriel pass and rumbled 29 yards to the Rams' 26 yard line. Victory was clinched.

"I had a bad first half," Page said after the game. "I was so tense I didn't know what was going on. I had to do something to make up for that poor play."

Cleveland defeated Dallas 38-14 in the Eastern Conference title game and earned the right to come to Met Stadium on January 4, 1970, for the NFL championship game, returning to the site of the Browns' 51-3 loss in early November.

"From everything I've heard, we shouldn't even have bothered to come up here," Cleveland receiver Gary Collins said before the game. "The way I hear it, we already have lost 30-0."

This was the day the cold weather showed up—it was 15 degrees below zero with the windchill.

The Vikings came out hot and scored on their first two possessions. The second TD was a 75-yard pass from Kapp to Gene Washington.

Swanson's game story in the *Tribune* offered this candid assessment: "After the first few minutes of play, it appeared the Browns already knew what the outcome was going to be and played like that—like losers."

Kapp didn't have to throw much after that. The Vikings rushed 45 times for 222 yards, with 108 coming from Dave Osborn and 57 from Kapp on eight carries. On

one of his carries, Kapp knocked out Cleveland's Jim Houston when he kicked Houston in the head while trying to hurdle the 240-pound linebacker.

"I guess I hit him with my purse," said Kapp, joking about how quarterbacks are supposed to take punishment and not dish it out.

Asked further about his unique style, Kapp said: "Am I a classic quarterback? Classics are for Greeks. I can pass the ball when necessary. I can do a little more."

Kapp had given bottles of champagne to his offensive linemen at practice on the Saturday before the game. The bottles were broken open in the winning locker room, which was contrary to NFL rules. Kapp was slurping champagne as Grady Alderman, his left tackle, was answering questions.

"I asked 'Joe Saturday' if the champagne was for services rendered or expected," Alderman said. "He gave that big grin of his and said, 'You figure it out.'"

The 27-7 victory over Cleveland put the Vikings in the fourth and last NFL-AFL Super Bowl against the Kansas City Chiefs. (Beginning with the 1970 season, the leagues fully merged under the NFL umbrella.)

"We still have the biggest one of all left," Bud Grant said in his post-game interview after the victory. "We won't be the national champions until we beat the American Football League winner and take the Super Bowl.

"This was Kapp's best game in the NFL, but I think he feels like I do: The most important game is yet to come."

As usual, Bud was right.

Kapp enjoys some bubbly in the locker room after the Vikings secured a trip to their first Super Bowl.
Kent Kobersteen/Star Tribune

61

SUPER BOWL IV

MINNESOTA VIKINGS VS. KANSAS CITY CHIEFS, JANUARY 11, 1970

The Minnesota Vikings had good reason to be full of confidence as they arrived in New Orleans in January 1970 for their first Super Bowl appearance, in the fourth edition of the game.

The Vikings had captured the NFL championship with a dominating 27-7 victory over the Cleveland Browns on January 4 at Metropolitan Stadium to improve to 14-2 for the season. This record included a 12-game winning streak during the regular season that was sandwiched between an opening-day loss to the New York Giants and a season-ending defeat at Atlanta.

Minnesota had a swagger not only on defense, but also with their offense led by quarterback Joe Kapp. Kapp's seldom-pretty, rough-and-tumble approach epitomized the Vikings' style of play. Unlike the quarterbacks of today, Kapp had no interest in sliding to avoid getting hit when he took off running with the ball.

Cleveland linebacker Jim Houston found this out the hard way in the NFL title game when he collided with Kapp as the quarterback scrambled for a first down. Kapp got up; Houston did not. "My head is still ringing after getting kicked," Houston said. "I just woke up to a bad dream. I hit John Unitas once like that and he didn't get up. Kapp? He's too tough."

The popular assumption was that the Vikings also would be too tough for the Kansas City Chiefs, whom many considered to be an inferior club in part because they were from the AFL. The Chiefs had gone 11-3 in the regular season and captured a playoff spot by finishing second in the Western Division. The Chiefs beat the New York Jets, 13-6, in their opening playoff game and then defeated the host Oakland Raiders, 17-7, in the AFL title game.

Third-year coach Bud Grant's team was a 13-point favorite for the January 11 match-up at Tulane Stadium. The national press jumped on the Vikings' bandwagon in the days after the victory over Cleveland.

Jack Griffith of the *Chicago Sun-Times* wrote: "The Minnesota Vikings, newly crowned lords of the National Football League, play this game about as gracefully as a three-ton truck, and they're about as deadly.

"Even in Green Bay's clover days, the Packers might have had trouble matching muscle with this gang of ice-age ruffians. And the Kansas City Chiefs, who have resumed ownership of the American Football League, are going to find out on Super Bowl Sunday."

At Tulane Stadium on January 11, 1970, quarterback Joe Kapp completed 16 of 25 passes in Super Bowl IV, but two interceptions and an inability to put the ball in the end zone left the Vikings on the outside looking in. *Focus on Sport/Getty Images*

Griffith wasn't the only Illinois resident who liked the Vikings' chances against the Chiefs.

"The Vikings are the best team we played this season," said star running back Gale Sayers, whose Bears had been outscored 62-14 in two losses to the Vikings. "I don't know how good Kansas City is. But I think Kansas City will have trouble moving on Minnesota. There can't be a better defense in football."

How much simpler was the Super Bowl back then? Tickets cost $15 and kickoff took place at 2:35 p.m., about three hours earlier than the game begins today. New Orleans residents were excited to be hosting the title game for the first time.

Bob Lundegaard of the *Minneapolis Tribune* reported that "residents of New Orleans were offering Super Bowl tickets for color television sets, Yorkshire terriers, and even—in an undoubted burst of whimsy—a Rolls Royce last week.

"But on the eve of the Vikings-Chiefs game, many of them are happy to get merely their $15 (the legal price) back. A combination of police surveillance and an earlier threat of rain probably accounted for the falloff in the ticket market."

It was Chiefs coach Hank Stram and his team's play that would account for a falloff in the Vikings' performance in front of 80,562 fans.

Kansas City put up points four of the first five times the team touched the ball, including three field goals by Jan Stenerud, en route to a 23-7 victory. It didn't help that in their first five possessions, the Vikings committed two fumbles and a dropped pass that cost a first down.

The key miscue came when Minnesota was trailing 9-0 in the second quarter. The Vikings' Charlie West fumbled a kickoff, and the Chiefs recovered on the Minnesota 19-yard line. Kansas City went on to score on Mike Garrett's 5-yard touchdown run to give them a 16-0 advantage at halftime.

Minnesota was able to pull within 16-7 following a 4-yard touchdown run by Osborn in the third quarter, but any hopes of a comeback vanished with one play. Chiefs quarterback Len Dawson completed a pass to Otis Taylor that should have gone for a short gain, but Taylor pulled away from cornerback Earsell Mackbee and went 46 yards for a touchdown.

Kansas City used a variety of formations in an attempt to confuse the Vikings on both offense and defense, but the Minnesota players claimed they were not fooled. "There weren't really any surprises," defensive end Carl Eller said. "They didn't fool us. They beat us with execution."

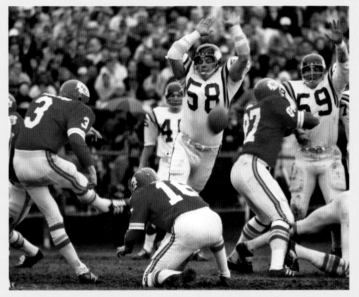

Kansas City's Jan Stenerud kicked three field goals in the first half to put the Chiefs up 9-0 early. They added two touchdowns for an easy 23-7 win over the favored Vikings. *Focus on Sport/Getty Images*

The Kansas City defense was able to drive Kapp from the game with an injury to his left shoulder. Kapp and backup Gary Cuozzo combined to throw three second-half interceptions. Dawson earned Most Valuable Player honors by completing 12 of 17 passes for 142 yards with a touchdown and an interception.

"They played a better basic game than we did," said Grant, whose team generated only 67 yards rushing.

The New Orleans Super Bowl was likely the most memorable of the Vikings' four Super Bowl losses, thanks to NFL Films. Stram wore a microphone during the game, and there have been countless replays of his commentary. The famed replays featured phrases such as, "Keep matriculating the ball down the field, boys," and, "You can't do that in our league," in reference to the Vikings' struggles. The most famous words to come from Stram's lips that day might have been the call for "65 Toss Power Trap," the play that led to Garrett's 5-yard TD run.

Among the Minnesota residents lamenting the loss in the postgame locker room was former Vice President Hubert Humphrey. "I've lost some big Super Bowls myself in the past," he told a group of players. "I know how you must feel."

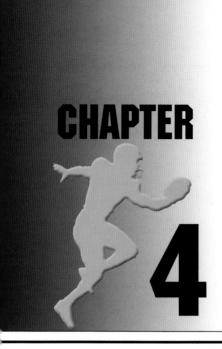

BACK-TO-BACK BOWLS
1970–1974

KAPP TAKES A HIKE

When the decade of the 1970s opened, the Vikings had a reasonably young nucleus, football's best defense, and a Joe Kapp-led offense that was explosive enough to score 50 points three times in 1969. They finished that 12-2 regular season scoring 379 points and allowing a meager 133.

The NFL-AFL merger was coming into full effect in 1970. The two leagues had made peace in 1966 and agreed to hold a common draft and to play a championship game between the champions of each league, with the first one played after the 1966 season. The AFL officially came under the NFL umbrella in 1970. Three of the 16 existing NFL teams would have to join the 10 former AFL teams to create two balanced conferences, the NFC and the AFC.

William Clay Ford, the new owner of the Detroit Lions, and Russ Thomas, his general manager, had an idea: They wanted the Vikings to be one of those three teams. For sure, the Lions wanted the Vikings to be moved from the four-team Central Division (Minnesota, Detroit, Chicago, Green Bay) that had existed for the three previous seasons.

The publicly stated reason for this was to get a team from a southern climate in the division, so some warm-weather games could be played in December. Another reason was that Grant's Vikings had gone 4-0 against the Lions in 1968 and 1969, and it did not look as if that domination would end any time soon.

Eventually, Pittsburgh, Baltimore, and Cleveland agreed to move to the AFC; the Vikings stayed put in a four-team NFC Central; Grant's winning streak against Detroit eventually reached 13, lasting until the teams' second meeting of 1974; and the division did not get a warm-weather team until the Tampa Bay Buccaneers became the fifth Central Division member in 1977.

Meantime, back in Minnesota, the shock of the Super Bowl loss to Kansas City had worn off with the populace. There was a wide fascination with all things Vikings. The most popular figure of the bunch was Joe Kapp, called "Zorba" or "Mr. 40 for 60" or "There Ain't No MVP" or "Hennepin Avenue Joe" (in contrast to New York's "Broadway Joe" Namath)—take your pick.

In early May 1970, a 31-mile hike was being held to raise money for hungry kids in the Twin Cities. Kapp had signed up as the grand marshal, which meant he was supposed to walk at the front of the nearly 20,000 school children who had hit up the neighborhood and family adults for financial pledges based on the distance they covered.

Kapp showed up in one of those hats usually associated with Mexican musicians. He was accompanied by Dale Hackbart, the Vikings' veteran defensive back.

Jim Klobuchar, writing in the Minneapolis Star, described the scene:

"Here was a 12-year-old girl trying to walk the last five miles on the soles of her feet, and the football player leaned down to comfort her."

Kapp lifted the girl and carried her for those final miles, so she could collect her full pledges.

"We finished and so did better than half of the 20,000. They raised more than $160,000. [Kapp] was the guy who had grappled and cursed and slugged encroaching linemen to bring his football team a title. But he nearly wept now at the sight of a 15-year-old boy, nearly blind, finishing the walk with his cane."

You could not give Minnesotans their fill of yarns such as this about Kapp, who grew up hungry in California, became a winning quarterback at Cal-Berkeley and in Canada, and then became the symbol of the Vikings' first real success.

Kapp started only 43 games, including playoffs, for the Vikings in his career, yet he was Minnesota's Brett Favre in popularity, and the events surrounding his departure were a bitter pill for the Minnesota masses.

John Elliott Cook, Joe Kapp's 71-year-old agent from the Bay Area, announced in July that the quarterback would not be present in Mankato when the 1970 training camp opened.

Cook, a law professor from the University of California, had gained some notoriety among players a couple of years earlier when he was able to get San Francisco quarterback John Brodie a contract totaling nearly $1 million from the 49ers.

Cook's real goal was to beat the so-called Rozelle Rule, which was the rule instituted by Commissioner Pete Rozelle that served to keep players under the thumb of their teams, whether or not they had signed a contract.

According to the Rozelle Rule, any team signing a free agent had to give heavy compensation, in players and draft choices, to the team that the player was leaving. If the teams could not agree, Rozelle set the compensation. This effectively discouraged teams from signing free agents away from other teams.

"Hennepin Avenue Joe" was a popular and charismatic figure on the Minnesota sports scene for three seasons, but his career came to a premature end following deadlocked contract negotiations prior to the 1970 season.
Larry Schreiber/Star Tribune

"Kapp is 1,000 percent a free agent," Cook said. "He's going to wind up where the opportunity is the best. Kapp will go to training camp of whatever, if any, football team he signs a contract with. And he won't go to training camp until he does sign."

According to the Vikings, Kapp was seeking a five-year, $1.25 million deal. In a *Minneapolis Tribune* story in early August, Jim Finks said, "I don't know whether Joe will play or not this year. I doubt any team in pro football could meet Joe's salary demands."

The contract problem with Kapp—the man behind the "40 for 60" spirit that inspired the 1969 Vikings—was so traumatic that Klobuchar started a mid-July column in the *Minneapolis Star* thusly:

I have been receiving telephone calls from my 10-year-old daughter Amy about the horrifying reports involving Joe Kapp. The girl has been visiting relatives out of town and clearly is hungering for news that will let the sunbeams back into her life and change her latest plans to join a hooded order.

You are aware that Joe Kapp has not signed his contract with the Vikings. At the moment, he is independent and incommunicado. His attorney has despaired of all hope that Joe will be in Vikings training camps. The disputants plainly are at an impasse, Joe in California and the Vikings in their bullion vaults.

Kapp never again played for the Vikings. Young Amy Klobuchar did overcome this trauma of her childhood and eventually became the first woman elected from Minnesota to the U.S. Senate.

As the impasse dragged into training camp, Cook continued with his eloquent rhetoric. He suggested that the Vikings and the rest of the NFL were blackballing Kapp. On August 17, he told Merrill Swanson: "[The Vikings] know what forces come into play. They know what will happen. And a good old American jury of 12 people will decide."

It took until October for the Vikings to make a move with Kapp. He was traded to the Boston Patriots, and under the Rozelle Rule, the Vikings received safety John Charles and Boston's number one selection in the 1972 draft in return.

Kapp played the remainder of that 1970 season with the lowly Patriots. He refused to sign a standard players' contract in 1971 and walked out of training camp. This was part of Cook's legal strategy to defeat the Rozelle Rule in court and win large damages.

They wound up with a bittersweet verdict: The Rozelle Rule was found to be a restraint of trade, but a jury awarded Kapp no compensation for what remained on his Patriots' contract. Kapp never played another game in the NFL.

The Rozelle Rule remained in effect from 1963 to 1976. It survived a 44-day strike by the veteran players in 1974 and several court verdicts. It was finally struck down in December 1975 by the verdict in John Mackey's federal lawsuit against the league.

A labor agreement was negotiated between the union and the players association. The Rozelle Rule was replaced by the "right of first refusal," which allowed the team that previously held a player's right to match any offer made by another club to a free agent. There was also a settlement of unannounced millions from the NFL to players who had been hurt financially by the Rozelle Rule.

The news of the 1970 Vikings offseason was not restricted to the Kapp drama. The veterans didn't report to camp on time, as a symbolic protest against the Rozelle Rule. Carl Eller held out for much of August, subjecting himself to fines because he was under contract.

It also was an eventful May for Bud Grant. It was announced on May 19 that he had signed a five-year contract extension through the 1974 season. A couple of days later, it was revealed that Grant had been cited in Canada for shooting wolves out of a bush plane.

This caused great outrage among conservationists and many sportsmen.

Jim Finks had referred to Grant as "Mark Trail," the outdoorsman from a newspaper comic strip, from their earliest days together in Minnesota. Finks had a fondness for needling people. After the wolf-shooting incident, a reporter called Finks and in the conversation asked if he knew of Grant's whereabouts.

"I don't know where Mark Trail is," Finks said. "Maybe he's out dynamiting walleye."

Grant later apologized for the event and admitted his mistake—something that never came easily for the steely-eyed coach.

Kapp's departure created a quarterback turmoil that lasted until Tarkenton was reacquired after the 1971 season. Still, with the exception of a 7-7 blip in 1972, Minnesota remained a powerhouse team during the first eight years of the NFC's existence.

Once Kapp was gone, the Vikings were left with Gary Cuozzo, the career backup who had been brought in to challenge Kapp for the job in 1968, and Bobby Lee, a 17th-round draft choice from that same season, as the main quarterback options. The Vikings also used a second-round choice on Florida State's Bill Cappleman in the 1970 draft.

Cuozzo had kicked up a fuss about wanting to be traded after the 1968 season, when it became obvious that Kapp was the team's quarterback. Now, with Kapp's contract impasse, the Vikings were fortunate that they had held on to Cuozzo.

"I didn't play much last year, but I still had the opportunity to work with these receivers every day in prac-

tice," Cuozzo said during training camp in 1970. "When we call a play, I have a feel for it, because we've done it so many times before."

The Vikings' season opener was against Kansas City at Met Stadium. These were the same Chiefs that had astounded the Vikings 23-7 in the fourth Super Bowl, and the same coach, Hank Stram, who had embarrassed them with his giddy sideline banter captured by NFL Films.

Stram had agreed to be miked while Grant had declined. Four decades later, Stram's ridicule still is a staple on NFL Films highlight shows. The comment that hurt the most concerned safety Karl Kassulke: "Kassulke is running around like a Chinese fire drill."

Stram also observed on that day that his team's exotic offense of the 1970s—with multiple formations and late shifts—was too much for the Vikings defense of the 1960s.

Grant showed no outward emotions before the opening game of 1970. His intensity was obvious to reporters such as Dick Gordon from the *Minneapolis Star*.

"Personally the Viking coach appears as self-controlled and emotionless as ever," Gordon wrote. "Deep inside

he wants a Chiefs-[beating] so bad he can taste it."

The game's big play came early in the second quarter when Carl Eller smashed Mike Garrett, the Kansas City running back, and caused Garrett to fumble. Jim Marshall picked up the ball at the Chiefs' 38-yard line and headed toward the (proper) end zone.

When he reached the 14-yard line, Marshall was about to be tackled and lateraled to linebacker Roy Winston, who ran the rest of the way for a touchdown to make it 10-0 in the Vikings' favor. The final score was Vikings 27, Super Bowl champs 10.

Following the game, Grant let out his resentments from the previous January.

"They've been shoving it down our throats for eight months," Grant said. "What can you say when you get beat. It's sour grapes then. But today we proved that the defense of the 1960s can beat the offense of the 1970s. We proved that we can play with the best of teams, including the Super Bowl champions."

The Vikings had not watched en masse the Super Bowl film featuring Stram's cackling until the Sunday morning pre-game meeting.

Bud "Mark Trail" Grant enjoyed hunting and fishing almost as much as football, although his hobby got him into some hot water during the 1970 offseason.
Star Tribune

Hub Meeds first donned a Vikings costume as a lark when he and his brother went to New Orleans for Super Bowl IV, where they cheered on the Purple from the sidelines. Beginning the following season and for many years thereafter, Meeds was a fixture at all Vikings home games. *Star Tribune*

Stram offered no excuses for the 17-point loss. "This is a game of now," he said. "On January 11, 1970, we were the better team. Today, we weren't."

The victory gained enough national publicity that even Kapp's agent, John Elliott Cook, checked in with a reaction.

"I watched the Vikings on television and so did Joe," Cook said. "He concurred with me that the Vikings looked good with Gary Cuozzo at quarterback.

"Joe was happy with the Vikings. Kapp is still pulling for those players, always has. We hope the Vikings keep going."

The Vikings defense was as ferocious as it had been in 1969. The Purple People Eaters and pals had two shutouts in the season's first four games: 26-0 against New Orleans at the Met and 24-0 in Chicago.

They equaled the 12-2 record of 1969, with Cuozzo starting 12 games and Lee starting 2. The only losses came in the third week, 13-10 against the Packers in Milwaukee, and in the 11th week, 20-10 against the Jets in New York.

The final season numbers were close to those of 1969: They outscored opponents 335-143 in 1970, compared to 379-133 the previous year. They had 49 sacks for 356 yards in losses, compared to 49 sacks for 404 yards in 1969. They allowed 200.5 yards per game, compared to 194.3 yards a year earlier.

The ferocity of this defense was perhaps best displayed in the shutout victory in Chicago. At one point, Bears quarterback Jack Concannon was hit by Gary Larsen, hit again by Carl Eller, and the football popped free. Alan Page plucked it out of the air and ran 65 yards for a touchdown. While in pursuit of Page, Chicago's great running back, Gale Sayers, suffered a leg injury that sent him to the hospital.

"I didn't think I'd ever make it to the end zone," Page said. "It seemed like it was taking forever."

There was also a 54-13 crunching of Dallas in mid-October. The point total was impressive enough, but two touchdowns came courtesy of veteran cornerback Ed Sharockman. One of the scores was on an interception return and another resulted when he picked up a blocked punt.

The Vikings totaled four interceptions, seven sacks of quarterbacks Roger Staubach and Craig Morton, and held the Cowboys wide receivers to three receptions.

"The Viking defense was tremendous," Dallas coach Tom Landry said. "When we got behind as easy as we did, the race was on. They can just come at you with everything. They hit us harder than we hit them."

The results of the 1970 postseason don't often get proper attention when long-time Vikings fans discuss their greatest heartbreaks. But consider this: The same Cowboys team that the Vikings bullied on October 11 ended up being the NFC's first Super Bowl representatives when that season's title game was held on January 17, 1971. Their opponents were the Baltimore Colts, one of the freshly minted AFC teams.

This was the first close Super Bowl—16-13, Colts—but also the most unimpressive winner. The Vikings of the 1970s would make three trips to the Super Bowl, but they never had a chance to play an AFC team that was as low-octane offensively as the Colts.

The path to the Super Bowl seemed clear for the Vikings on the opening playoff weekend of December 26–27. On Saturday, the Cowboys defeated Detroit

5-0 in Dallas. A Vikings' victory over San Francisco on Sunday would mean the Cowboys would be heading to Bloomington for the conference title game, with the memory of the 54-13 trouncing still in their helmets.

One problem: The 49ers came in from California and upset the Vikings 17-14 on a day when the high temperature was 9 degrees.

Merrill Swanson, writing in the next day's *Minneapolis Tribune*, made the following observation:

The 49ers were the underdogs and very tired of hearing about how easily the Vikings were going to win and march to the Super Bowl for a second straight season.

They reacted by playing like champions. The 49ers were good, very good. The Vikings were good only on defense.

The only meaningful touchdown the Vikings scored yesterday was by the defense—a 22-yard run by Paul Krause with a fumble recovery. The only touchdown scored by the offense came with one second to play—a gift really from the 49ers, who were willing to give ground in order to run out the clock.

Cuozzo threw the ball poorly and also was done in by drops. Jim Lindsey, a fullback with a reputation for good hands, had three drops.

"There's no excuse, no reason, no explanation," Lindsey said. "When you do something like that, you're not prepared mentally for the game."

Grant stood steely-eyed in front of 30 reporters after the game. No one wanted to ask the first question, so Grant finally said: "What do you say?"

He refused to blame the cold or the field conditions. After those comments, and another in response to a question about whether he had considered a quarterback change from Cuozzo to Lee ("Only in the final minutes"), Grant said, "You don't mind so much going down in flaming battle. But to be a victim of your own mistakes…."

Cuozzo threw a 46-yard pass to John Henderson early in the game. That was the highlight of an otherwise miserable day. He finished 9-for-27 for 146 yards, with two interceptions.

There was nothing said that afternoon, but it was obvious that the Vikings again would be looking for a quarterback during the offseason.

Gene Washington's touchdown catch in the waning seconds of the first-round playoff game against San Francisco on December 27, 1970, was a little too little, a little too late. The Vikings lost in the sloppily played contest by a score of 17-14.
AP/Wide World Photos

QUARTERBACK CAROUSEL

Before the 1971 draft, the Vikings sent three draft picks and defensive tackle Steve Smith to the Philadelphia Eagles for quarterback Norm Snead. Snead had been in the league for a decade since being the number-two overall selection (behind Vikings' running back Tommy Mason) in the draft for the 1961 season.

Snead had started as a rookie for Washington in 1961 and was the starter for all 42 games during his three seasons with the Redskins. He was sent to Philadelphia for Sonny Jurgensen prior to the 1964 season, and Snead went on to start 80 games for the Eagles in seven seasons.

He had been a Pro Bowl quarterback, and the Vikings assumed they were getting a new starter for 1971. Minnesota played six exhibitions prior to the season, and Snead didn't look that good. Neither did Cuozzo. Bobby Lee was the best of the three, but was also the least experienced.

Grant was the master of looking at a situation and making it appear as though it fit perfectly with his coaching theories. Here was a team with three flawed quarterbacks, but Grant tried to make it sound as though his decision came down to choosing from among three number-one-caliber quarterbacks.

"What's the use of having three quarterbacks if you're not going to use them?" he said before the season opener against Detroit.

Over the course of the season, Grant started Cuozzo in eight games, Lee in four, and Snead in two. They combined to throw 18 interceptions, compared to only nine touchdowns.

Jim Vellone spent five seasons on the Vikings offensive line before he was diagnosed with Hodgkin's disease during the 1971 offseason.
Skip Heine/Star Tribune

Yet, the Vikings managed to finish with a record of 11-3, thanks to their mighty defense. The Vikings again held the opposition to a meager point total—139, or less than 10 points per game. They scored only 245 points on the season, a 90-point decline from 1970 when Cuozzo threw 70 percent of the passes, and a 134-point decline from 1969 when Kapp was in charge.

Three of the victories came by shutout, including a 3-0 win over the Packers on November 14 at Met Stadium. This victory came despite club records for fewest total yards gained (87), fewest yards passing (21), and fewest first downs (5). Cuozzo was the quarterback for that offensive abomination.

Green Bay's John Brockington rushed for 142 yards. The Packers offense was able to move the ball to the Vikings' 16-, 1-, 20-, 10-, and 8-yard lines—and the Vikings defense stopped them each time thanks to a tipped field goal, two interceptions, a recovered fumble, and holding them on downs inside the 1.

"We are a defensive football team," safety Paul Krause said. "It's up to the defense to make big plays."

The Vikings opened the playoffs at home against Dallas. The game was played on a Saturday, which happened to be Christmas Day. The opinion pages of the local newspapers were dotted with letters complaining of the sacrilege of this scheduling. Commissioner Pete Rozelle was the target.

Grant started Bobby Lee against Dallas. The Vikings were now big enough news that a story on Lee was splayed across the front page of the *Minneapolis Tribune* on December 25.

Below it was the headline: "NWA jet hijacker seized in Chicago after takeoff here." The hijacker, Everett Holt of Indianapolis, had taken over the plane after it left Minneapolis-St. Paul. He surrendered five and a half hours later on the tarmac at O'Hare International Airport.

Above this story, Lee, 26 years old and making his first playoff start, was telling the *Tribune*'s Merrill Swanson: "If I play up to my ability, if we play as well as we're capable of playing, we'll come out as winners."

Lee threw two interceptions that set up 10 Cowboys' points. He was pulled in favor of Cuozzo, who threw two more of his own. The Vikings totaled five turnovers for the game and lost 20-12—the second consecutive first-round loss at Met Stadium.

The Vikings defense was so much responsible for the team's 11-3 record (equaling Dallas for the league's best record) that Page became the first defensive player ever to be named the NFL's Most Valuable Player.

Jim Marshall, the ironman defensive end, said of Page's honor, "I'd say he probably is the best football player I've seen since I've been in the league, and in 12 years I've seen a lot of good ones."

Page's award was a highlight in what was largely a chaotic season for the Vikings. It started when starting guard Jim Vellone, who had been getting ready for his sixth Vikings' training camp, was diagnosed with Hodgkin's disease right before the start of camp. He was unable to return to the Vikings and would die from complications of the disease on August 21, 1977, one day after his 33rd birthday.

It was also a year in which the Vikings dispatched defensive tackle Paul Dickson and hard-nosed safety Dale Hackbart, two of the team's popular veterans. Middle linebacker Lonnie Warwick had to give up his spot between Wally Hilgenberg and Roy Winston because of knee surgery.

Second-year player Carl Gersbach took Warwick's place as the starter in the middle in 1971, then Stanford's Jeff Siemon was taken as the 10th overall selection in the 1972 draft, with the pick that the Vikings had received when Joe Kapp signed with New England under the Rozelle Rule stipulations.

That was a big change for 1972—putting a rookie in the middle of the Vikings' veteran defense—but it didn't compare with the dramatic move General Manager Jim Finks was willing to make to fix the nagging quarterback problem.

THE RETURN OF TARKENTON

Fran Tarkenton's time with the New York Giants saw its share of turmoil. The veteran quarterback threatened to retire during a cantankerous contract dispute in the summer of 1971. He ultimately agreed to come back for the Giants' original offer of $125,000, although he wasn't happy about it.

The Giants posted a 33-37 record and didn't reach the playoffs during Tarkenton's five-year tenure with the team. Their best finish was a 9-5 record in 1970, but they fell to 4-10 in 1971.

On January 27, 1972, the Vikings announced a blockbuster trade: Tarkenton was returning to Minnesota in exchange for quarterback Norm Snead, receiver Bob Grim, running back Vince Clements, a first-round draft choice in 1972, and a second-rounder in 1973.

Finks, the same general manager who had sent Tarkenton to New York in 1967, said, "This one was a totally different kind of deal. In 1967, we gave up a proven quarterback for four intangibles, for four draft choices. We were at a disadvantage because Tarkenton had said he wanted to leave our club.

"This time, New York was doing the selling. They called us. This was the type of deal we couldn't afford to make two or three years ago. It's the type of deal only a contender can make."

Tarkenton was greeted at Minneapolis-St. Paul International Airport by former teammates Grady Alderman and Mick Tingelhoff on the day the trade was

announced. Another man that greeted him was Robert Evans, the director of marketing for Twin City Federal Savings and Loan (TCF).

Ray Foley from Colle & McVoy, TCF's advertising agency, soon joined the group. TCF wanted to sign Tarkenton for some instant radio and television commercials. The negotiations took place at the airport gate. Tarkenton got his price within 10 minutes and headed down the corridor and on his way to the press conference.

A month earlier, Alan Page had been named the NFL's Most Valuable Player, and he didn't get an ad deal. Tarkenton was on the air in Minnesota making a sales pitch within hours of his arrival.

Shown here recovering a fumble during a game against San Francisco on November 7, 1971, Alan Page had a dominating season that earned him NFL Most Valuable Player honors.
Kent Kobersteen/Star Tribune

Page had not played with Tarkenton. On the day of the announcement, he didn't express much enthusiasm.

"It's my personal opinion, and it may get me in trouble," he said. "But I don't think our offensive problems are one of personnel. We had three good quarterbacks in Bob Lee, Norm Snead, and Gary Cuozzo.

"It is the Viking [coaches'] theory not to make mistakes, to play conservatively, and rely on the defense to hold the other team. I don't think it makes that much difference who plays quarterback.

"Tarkenton's a good quarterback, but I don't think anybody is that good to give up this much. It reminds me of a song I heard on the radio last night: 'One monkey doesn't stop a show.'

"Nor does he start it. The quarterback is just one of eleven."

Page had given some indications of his status as an independent thinker during his earlier years, but this was the strongest evidence yet that he was not going to be one to join most of his teammates in toeing the Grant/Vikings party line.

Page's skepticism proved accurate in the first season of Tarkenton's return. The Vikings had gone 35-7 in the three previous regular seasons. They finished 7-7 in 1972.

Beano Cook, then a behind-the-scenes character on New York television, noted that in Tarkenton's first two seasons as the Giants' savior, the team also finished 7-7. Cook commented: "That's what they are going to put on Tarkenton's headstone: '7-7'."

Tarkenton would get the last laugh during the next few seasons.

With his new coach at his side, Fran Tarkenton addresses the media after the Vikings reacquired the veteran quarterback in January 1972. Although Minnesota missed the playoffs the following season, Tarkenton would help lead the team to three of the next four Super Bowls.
Don Black/Star Tribune

BACK TO THE BIG GAME

Before the start of the 1968 season, Jim Finks made one of his greatest deals when he acquired safety Paul Krause from Washington for tight end Marlin McKeever and a seventh-round draft choice. This trade rated along with the two Tarkenton trades and the deal that sent Tommy Mason and Hal Bedsole to the Los Angeles Rams for the draft choice that netted Alan Page.

Krause was the Vikings' starter at free safety for a decade. He had 53 interceptions with Minnesota and an

Tarkenton signals for the touchdown as Bill Brown tumbles into the end zone during a 23-20 Vikings win over the Broncos on October 15, 1972. Brown had a reserve role that season behind Oscar Reed and Ed Marinaro, but he contributed a team-high eight touchdowns (four rushing and four receiving). *Star Tribune*

Four months after being paralyzed in a motorcycle accident, former defensive back Karl Kassulke was greeted enthusiastically by the Met Stadium crowd on November 25, 1973. He is being wheeled onto the field by teammates Jim Marshall (70), Bill Brown (30), and Grady Alderman (67). *Kent Kobersteen/Star Tribune*

all-time NFL record 81 for his career. He was inducted into the Pro Football Hall of Fame in 1998, after much campaigning by Bud Grant, his Vikings coach.

Karl Kassulke, a free agent from Drake University, took over as the Vikings' strong safety as a rookie in 1963 and held on to the spot for the better part of ten seasons. He played five seasons (1968–72) alongside Krause.

Kassulke was one of the most popular players among the early generation of Vikings fans. He had a reckless, hard-tackling style and a mischievous edge to him that came across both on and off the field.

On July 24, 1973, Kassulke was a passenger on a motorcycle being driven by Monty Krizan on Highway

494 near Minnetonka Boulevard. The motorcycle collided with the rear of a car in front of it. Kassulke was wearing a helmet, but he was thrown 60 feet and wound up paralyzed from his midsection.

The Vikings were set to open training camp the next day in Mankato. The devastating injury to the effervescent Kassulke was a horrid beginning for a team trying to come back from the flop of 1972.

Jeff Wright, a late-round choice out of the University of Minnesota in 1971, replaced Kassulke in the lineup. That was one of three changes that had occurred from the defensive squad of the 1969 Super Bowl team: Jeff Siemon was now the middle linebacker, replacing Lonnie

Warwick, and Nate Wright had replaced Earsell Mackbee as a cornerback.

The turnover in four seasons was much greater on the offensive side. Ed White was the left guard, not Jim Vellone. Ron Yary was the right tackle, not Doug Davis. John Gilliam and Carroll Dale were the wide receivers, not Gene Washington and John Henderson. Stu Voigt was playing ahead of John Beasley at tight end.

The starting running backs were Chuck Foreman and Oscar Reed; Ed Marinaro was the number three back. Bill "Boom Boom" Brown, the Vikings' greatest-ever fullback, and Dave Osborn, the starting halfback in 1969, were now down the depth chart.

The Vikings had decided after two first-round playoff departures following the 1970 and 1971 seasons that they had to fix the quarterback situation, and they brought in Tarkenton. They decided after missing the playoffs again in 1972 that what the offense was missing was a dynamic running back.

The Vikings had tried to add such a running back in 1971, when they drafted Ohio State's Leo Hayden with the 24th overall pick. He was a historic bust—never had a carry or caught a pass for the Vikings.

Minnesota tried again with the 12th overall pick in 1973. They selected Foreman, a combination runner and receiver out of the University of Miami (Florida), and wound up with the greatest running back in franchise history.

Grant and his offensive boss, Jerry Burns, had found success throwing the ball out of the backfield to Brown and Osborn, and later to Reed and Marinaro. Now with Foreman, throwing to the backs became the trademark of the Vikings attack. They did it so often that Grant, Burns, and the Vikings can legitimately claim that the West Coast offense actually started on the Bloomington prairie, not with Bill Walsh in San Francisco. (See sidebar in Chapter 7.)

The Vikings would make an opposing defense paranoid about the short throws to Foreman, Marinaro, Reed, and tight end Voigt, then Tarkenton would go over the top to Gilliam when the safeties started creeping forward. Gilliam caught 42 passes in 1973, for an average of 21.7 yards and eight touchdowns.

Shown here in action against New Orleans in November 1972, Jeff Wright became the regular strong safety in 1973 after Kassulke's career-ending injury. Wright nabbed three interceptions as a backup in 1972 and added seven more over the next two seasons as a starter.
Star Tribune

The Vikings opened the season with nine straight victories. In week 10, they went to Atlanta for a Monday night game on November 19. Norm Van Brocklin was still the coach of the Falcons. The Atlanta quarterback was Bobby Lee.

The Vikings had acceded to Lee's wishes to get a chance to be a starter, trading him, along with Warwick, to the Falcons for backup quarterback Bob Berry and a 1974 first-round draft choice (which they used to take UCLA linebacker Fred McNeill).

Berry had been Van Brocklin's starter in Atlanta in the last game of 1969 when the Falcons broke Minnesota's 12-game winning streak. This time, Lee and the Falcons handed the Vikings a 20-14 loss.

Lee made a Tarkenton-like scramble to elude the Vikings' rush and hit Eddie Ray for a 39-yard touchdown pass. Those proved to be the winning points.

Van Brocklin, ecstatic in victory, said, "So, you want to be a coach? That was a sweat job all the way. When Lee

got away for that second touchdown [pass] it was like getting money from mother without writing home."

Van Brocklin made the following comment about Tarkenton, his old friend the scrambler: "Bud Grant has restricted him, gotten a little more control over him than I had."

The Vikings were beaten again two weeks later, 27-0 in Cincinnati. It was the first shutout against Grant in seven Minnesota seasons and the first for the Vikings since the fourth game of 1962.

No matter. The Vikings closed with back-to-back 31-7 victories over the Packers in Green Bay and the Giants in New York. They finished 12-2 for the third time in five seasons and were heading home for the playoffs.

The first opponent was Washington at Met Stadium. A victory would likely take them to Dallas to play the Cowboys, now their rivals as the NFC's "team of the 1970s."

The ecstasy during those two December weekends in 1973 was so great for the franchise that they receive

All-Pro receiver John Gilliam was a popular target for Tarkenton in 1973. Here he scores easily on a reverse against Philadelphia on October 21, while Tarkenton offers some company and blocking.
Charles Bjorgen/Star Tribune

special attention in the Introduction of this book. The victories over Washington and Dallas carried the 1973 Vikings to the franchise's second Super Bowl berth, where they faced the defending-champion Miami Dolphins in Houston, Texas. (See pages 78–79.)

WELCOME, MR. LYNN

In 1973, Fran Tarkenton had effectively buried the 7-7 jokes and led a team to the playoffs for the first time in his career. The selection of Chuck Foreman in the 1973 draft had brought an infusion of new energy to the offense. In the first two rounds of the 1974 draft, the Vikings picked up a pair of linebackers in Fred McNeill and Matt Blair, good-sized athletic players who were brought in as the eventual replacements for Wally Hilgenberg and Roy Winston.

Things were looking smooth in Vikingsland. Then a shocking story appeared in the Twin Cities' morning newspapers on May 20, 1974: Jim Finks had resigned as the team's general manager due to "fundamental differences" with Max Winter, the team president.

Finks had been carrying the ball for the Vikings in an effort to get a larger stadium, preferably one with a dome. A new stadium would substantially increase the value of the team and Finks wanted to be able to profit in some way. He asked the Board of Directors if he could purchase 100 shares (2 percent) of non-voting stock, but was turned down by the votes of Winter, H. P. Skoglund, and Jack Steele (representing the family of the late Bill Boyer).

Bernie Ridder, the St. Paul newspaper publisher, and his friend Ole Haugsrud had voted to sell the stock to

The 1974 Vikings team awards were handed out in the week prior to the season's final game. The honorees were (left to right): tackle Alan Page, best defensive player; halfback Chuck Foreman, best offensive player; tackle Doug Sutherland, most improved player; and linebacker Matt Blair, best rookie.
Powell Krueger/Star Tribune

SUPER BOWL VIII

MINNESOTA VIKINGS VS. MIAMI DOLPHINS, JANUARY 13, 1974

These days, any team heading for the Super Bowl can count on first-class treatment at every turn. But that wasn't the case for the Minnesota Vikings in January 1974 as they prepared for their second Super Bowl appearance in five years.

Coach Bud Grant was livid when he saw the facility at which the Vikings would be housed in the days leading up to their game against the Miami Dolphins in Houston. The Dolphins were headquartered at the Houston Oilers' facilities because both franchises were in the American Football Conference, which made Miami the home team.

The Vikings were left with the locker room at James M. Delmar Stadium, a high school facility without lockers and only nails in the wall for hanging clothes. The room, which according to the *Minneapolis Star* was 50 by 100 feet, had a concrete floor and walls and a basketball hoop at one end. There was barely any room for the coaches.

"This is the Super Bowl, not some pick-up game," Grant said. "The league had a year to find a place for the teams to work, and

they come up with the type of room your kids would play in on a Saturday afternoon. I call this shabby treatment. Our schedule is off. All the things we do to get here are changed."

The Vikings also didn't have blocking sleds or tackling dummies with which to work. Grant did not mince his words when asked whom he blamed for putting the Vikings in this situation. "The league," he said. "It's a league responsibility. It gets down to [Commissioner] Pete Rozelle, I imagine. He runs the league."

Grant presented the media with visual evidence by inviting them to look at the locker room and take pictures of it. An NFL official tried to stop Grant, but to no avail.

The situation got worse later in the week when Grant learned that Miami had been allowed to work out in Rice Stadium on the Wednesday before the game. Rice Stadium was where the big game would be played, and Grant had been told it would be available to the teams only for the Saturday practice sessions.

The coach's disgust, which surely also was an attempt to motivate his club, came after the Vikings had completed a 12-2 regular season and then beat visiting Washington and host Dallas in the playoffs.

Grant knew the Vikings would have their hands full against the Don Shula-coached Dolphins. Miami had looked so good in playoff victories over Cincinnati and Oakland that Grant decided not to show his team the film of those games.

Instead, he had his players watch film of two late-season Dolphins games from 1973. The first was the second half of Miami's 30-26 victory over Pittsburgh—a game in which the Steelers outscored the Dolphins 23-0 in the final 30 minutes—and the second was Miami's 16-3 loss at Baltimore.

"I didn't want our players to get the impression Miami was unbeatable," Grant said. "In the earlier films we saw, they looked indefensible and unstoppable. I just thought it would be a good idea to take a look at the Dolphins getting whipped."

Grant went so far as to have the Vikings watch the fourth quarter of their 20-17 preseason victory over the Dolphins the previous August. The win ended Miami's 20-game winning streak and was the Dolphins' first defeat following a perfect 1972 campaign.

Unfortunately for Grant and the Vikings, the Dolphins did prove to be unbeatable on January 13, 1974, in Super Bowl VIII. Miami, making its third consecutive appearance in the Super Bowl,

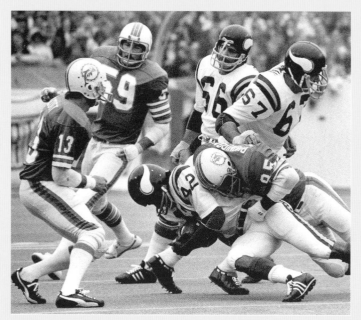

Receiver John Gilliam is stopped cold by Miami's defenders during Super Bowl VIII in Houston. While the Vikings gained 166 yards passing in the game, they were held to just 72 yards on the ground. *Star Tribune*

won its second title in a row with a 24-7 victory.

The Dolphins drove 62 and 56 yards on their first two possessions en route to a pair of first-quarter touchdowns.

Miami running back Larry Csonka set a Super Bowl record by rushing for 145 yards on 33 carries and had scoring runs of 5 yards and 2 yards. Miami led 24-0 after three quarters. The Vikings did not get on the board until Tarkenton scrambled on a keeper around right end for a 4-yard touchdown in the final 15 minutes.

"They took the ball and got 14 points up right away," Grant said. "That's tough to overcome against a good team. Csonka is at his best with a lead. They can work him 25 to 30 times a game, because they know he'll eat up the clock and give them good field position. But it mostly boiled down to the fact that Miami played very well and we didn't play well at all."

The Vikings also failed to get any breaks. John Gilliam's 65-yard kickoff return to open the second half was wiped off by a clipping penalty. Minnesota lost possession of an onside kick following its touchdown because of an offside ruling, and an apparent recovery of a fumbled punt was "foiled by an errant bounce," according to the *Minneapolis Tribune*'s game report.

"I've never seen a game any time in my career where we came up absolutely zero in the matter of breaks," veteran defensive end Carl Eller said. "We didn't play very well, but nothing was going our way, either."

Tarkenton, playing in his first championship game after 13 years in the league, completed 18 of 28 passes for 182 yards. "Went out there and gave it a whirl," Tarkenton said. "They were just a better football team today. I'm going to have a nice dinner and forget about this game."

It wasn't as easy for Grant to forget.

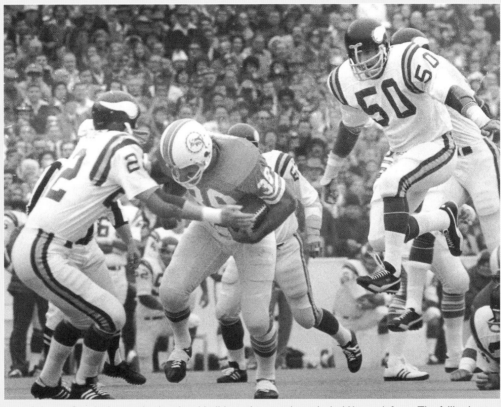

Miami's Larry Csonka lowers his head and bulldozes his way through the Vikings defense. The fullback ran for 145 yards on the day and scored two touchdowns. *John Croft/Star Tribune*

Rozelle had not taken kindly to Grant's remarks about the locker room situation and he fined the Vikings coach an undisclosed amount later in the month. All that the league would reveal was that the maximum allowable fine was $5,000.

Although Grant declined to comment after learning he had been fined, he had been well aware that the league might take action against him. "The commissioner took a dim view of my observations," Grant said a day after his initial comments in Houston. "In 17 years as a coach, I've never been fined. I still think there are better facilities available here, like at the University of Houston. Everything else is fine. I still believe when you are playing a game as important as the Super Bowl you should be able to find better dressing facilities when you have a year to do it in. In Minnesota we have the poorest stadium [the Met] in the National Football League. But our dressing room is 10 times as good as what we have here."

Finks. When the GM resigned, Ridder pulled no punches in blaming Winter for the departure.

"The heart of the matter is that Max Winter has been jealous of Jim Finks for years," Ridder told the *Minneapolis Star.* "Max was just bugging Jim too much."

Finks' on-the-record comments were politically prudent, that both he and the Vikings were better served by his moving on. Finks was soon hired as the executive vice president of the Chicago Bears. It was the first time that the day-to-day operations of the team left the hands of the Halas family.

This Winter-Ridder feud ended up being very profitable to the Winter-Skoglund-Steele voting bloc. Ridder wanted out and sold his shares, as did Haugsrud. The remaining three owners were able to ride the wave of huge increases in NFL franchise values in the years ahead.

As for Finks' replacement, speculation was that John Thompson or Bill McGrane, two of Finks' trusted front-office people, would get the job. Winter didn't want the Finks connection, however, and he passed on both. McGrane went to Chicago to work for Finks.

Grant received a five-year contract extension before the start of the 1974 season. His title remained head coach, but the new deal gave him power over trades and the draft, as well as roster cuts. Previously, Finks was the one who ran the draft and made the trades.

Later that year, a mysterious figure named Mike Lynn was seen with Winter. Lynn, who had no football background, had met Winter at league meetings while lobbying for an expansion franchise in his hometown of Memphis, Tennessee.

With Finks gone, Winter needed help to negotiate contracts with players, which was the original reason

Chuck Foreman goes over the top for one of his team-high nine rushing touchdowns in 1974. It wasn't enough on this October afternoon, however, as the Vikings fell to Detroit, 20-16.
John Croft/Star Tribune

behind hiring Lynn. A year later, on July 15, 1975, Lynn received the title of general manager.

The departure of Finks was not as big an issue at the start of training camp as the labor situation between league management and the NFL Players Association, which was run by Minneapolis lawyer Ed Garvey. There was talk of a strike or a camp boycott.

The season went on as scheduled. The Vikings opened 1974 with five straight victories, the fifth of which was a 51-10 rout of the Houston Oilers at Met Stadium.

The 1974 Vikings team featured two notable changes from previous years. Fullback Bill Brown was phased out of the offense in his 13th and final season in the league.

During his Vikings career, he amassed 5,757 rushing yards, 3,177 receiving yards, and 75 touchdowns. On the defensive side, Doug Sutherland moved ahead of Gary Larsen on the depth chart to become a starting tackle and the fourth member of the Purple People Eaters alongside Page, Eller, and Marshall.

The Vikings' first loss in 1974 was to Detroit, 20-16, at Met Stadium on October 20. This was significant because it ended the Lions' 13-game losing streak against Grant's Vikings.

The Vikings finished the season with a 10-4 record to claim their sixth Central Division title (two NFL, four NFC) in seven seasons. This time around, an unusual

Jim Marshall and the Vikings defense limited St. Louis All-Pro running back Terry Metcalf to just 55 yards rushing in the first-round playoff game on December 21, 1974, at Met Stadium. *John Croft/Star Tribune*

While Alan Page smothers Terry Metcalf, Nate Wright eyes the ball as it flies loose from Metcalf's grasp. Wright scooped up the fumble and ran 20 yards to the end zone to add to the Vikings' lead over St. Louis.
Earl Seubert/Star Tribune

playoff opponent was coming to Met Stadium: the St. Louis Cardinals.

The Vikings had defeated the Cardinals 28-24 in a midseason meeting at St. Louis. The Cardinals had played that game without their star runner/receiver Terry Metcalf, so there was some cause for concern.

Some concern, but not much.

The teams were tied 7-7 heading into halftime in the December 21 playoff game. Then, the Vikings defenders turned into their old ferocious selves in the second half, and Minnesota cruised to a 30-14 victory. The back-

breaker for St. Louis came when Alan Page knocked the ball loose from Metcalf and cornerback Nate Wright picked up the fumble and ran it 20 yards for a touchdown to make it 17-7.

The win meant that the Los Angeles Rams, after defeating the Redskins in their game on December 22, were returning to Minnesota for a playoff game for the first time since 1969. Chuck Knox was now the coach, James Harris was the quarterback, and young ends Fred Dryer and Jack Youngblood were the stars of the Rams' defensive front line.

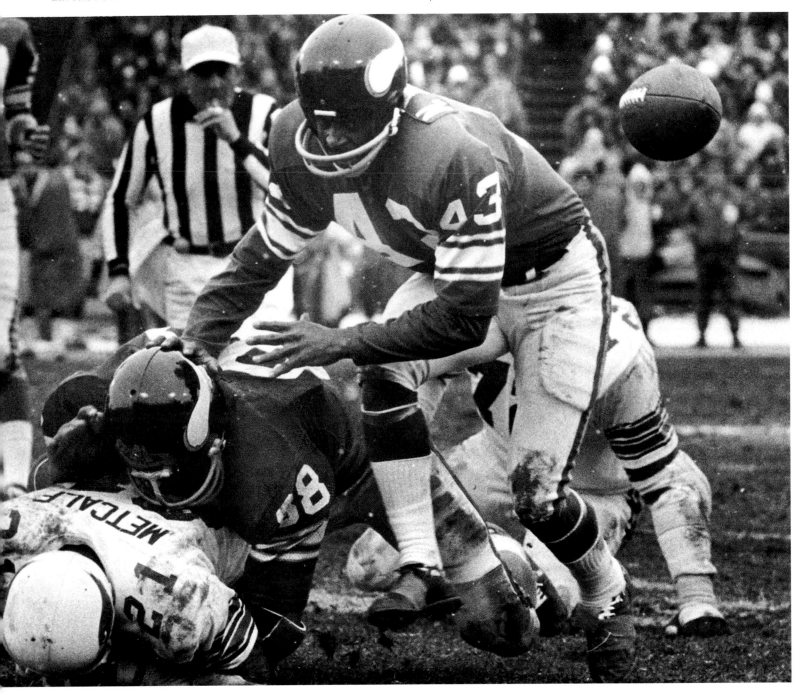

The Vikings survived with a 14-10 win on a frigid December day. It was a day on which an off-sides call against Dryer kept the Vikings alive on a fourth-quarter drive that led to the game-winning touchdown. It was a day on which the Rams drove 98 yards from their 1 to the Vikings' 1, only to have cornerback Jackie Wallace tip a Harris pass, which Hilgenberg intercepted in the end zone for a touchback. And it was a day on which the Vikings—trying to run out the game's final five minutes—saw a Foreman fumble scoot 21 yards forward before being recovered by a teammate, tackle Charles Goodrum.

"The big guy upstairs just didn't want us to win this one," Youngblood said in the losing locker room after the game.

He was referring, clearly, to Thor, the Norse God, who had helped get the Vikings to previous Super Bowls, only to disappear. This time, Minnesota's Super Bowl opponent was the Pittsburgh Steelers, a newcomer to the AFC's power elite. The location was Tulane Stadium in New Orleans, site of the Vikings' first Super Bowl disappointment five years earlier.

Linebacker Jeff Siemon subdues Rams fullback Jim Bertelsen during Minnesota's 14-10 win in the NFC title game on December 29, 1974.
John Croft/Star Tribune

As the Vikings sealed the victory over Los Angeles in the conference championship, at least one fan let it be known what his plans were for January 12, 1975. Thousands of Minnesota supporters had similar intentions as the team journeyed to another Super Bowl in the Big Easy.
Richard Olsenius/Star Tribune

SUPER BOWL IX

MINNESOTA VIKINGS VS. PITTSBURGH STEELERS, JANUARY 12, 1975

The Vikings didn't waste any time in returning to the Super Bowl after losing to the Miami Dolphins following the 1973 season.

The Vikings of 1974 did not have as much regular-season success as the previous year's team. They finished with two fewer victories and lost four in one six-game stretch for a 10-4 record. Minnesota got hot late in the season and won its final three regular-season games before beating St. Louis and the Los Angeles Rams in playoff games at Met Stadium.

"Our job this season really was to be as good as we were the year before with basically the same cast of characters," Grant said.

Heading to the Super Bowl for the second year in a row and the third time overall, Minnesota was set to face a first-time participant in the Pittsburgh Steelers.

The Vikings took a very businesslike approach to their arrival in New Orleans. As with their first Super Bowl appearance, the game was to be played at Tulane Stadium. Minnesota fans were anxious to get a victory in the big game after the previous losses to Kansas City and the Dolphins.

A week before the game, Twin Cities travel agents were telling the Vikings faithful that there was no possibility of staying in New Orleans for the game and that the closest accommodations would be in Baton Rouge, Louisiana (65 miles away), or Biloxi, Mississippi (90 miles away). "There is no way we can get anybody on a plane to New Orleans that weekend," one agent said. "There are no charters, there are no seats. No way."

And this didn't address the likelihood of landing a game ticket, even in a stadium that held more than 80,000 fans.

The Vikings arrived in New Orleans the Sunday before the game and quickly boarded a group of awaiting buses. Only Coach Grant and linebacker Wally Hilgenberg slowed down enough to talk to the assembled media members.

"We will do things as normal as possible," Grant said. "But this week is just not normal. Will things be different this time? Well, that's what we are here to find out."

Pittsburgh coach Chuck Noll seemed a bit more relaxed, saying, "We're here to have fun."

Back in the Super Bowl for the second year in a row, Minnesota's offense proved to be little match against Pittsburgh's "Steel Curtain" defense. The Vikings managed just 119 yards of total offense in Super Bowl IX, and their only points came on special teams, when Terry Brown recovered a blocked punt in the end zone. *Focus on Sport/Getty Images*

Grant's no-nonsense approach might have alienated some, but his dry sense of humor had to be appreciated by those who knew him. At the previous year's Super Bowl, Grant had got in trouble with Commissioner Pete Rozelle for criticizing the locker room facilities the Vikings had to use in the week leading up to the game.

The facilities were not a problem this time around because the Vikings were housed at the training site of the New Orleans Saints. Grant was well aware that he had given the media plenty to write about in Houston, and he knew his comments were appreciated.

"I am sympathetic with you people," he said at media day in Tulane Stadium. "I understand the fact that you always have to have a new angle. Last year we gave you the sparrows-in-the-shower story. We'll come up with one again this year. But you'll have to be patient. This is only Monday. We've got a whole week ahead of us."

Grant delivered on his promise when he divulged that quarterback Fran Tarkenton had a sore arm. "We consider it a good omen," Grant said. "Every time that happens, it starts the adrenalin flowing and he has a great game. The great athletes do that. They compensate for their nicks and troubles by digging for something extra."

There was debate as to whether Tarkenton really had a sore arm—essentially Grant was having fun with the injury report before it became fashionable—and Jim Klobuchar of the *Minneapolis Star* wrote that Grant was not "above a certain amount of cornfed dramatics in mid-week of the Super Bowl."

But Grant also was beginning to feel some heat after losing in his first two Super Bowl appearances. He was unwilling to take a life-or-death approach to the game, but he certainly didn't want to dismiss it.

"How could I say anything to minimize its importance when we spend so much effort getting here?" he explained. "But I just do not see any private glory in it for me. I've coached teams in four Canadian Grey Cups and three Super Bowls, and those things have been worth striving for. But life does go on, doesn't it."

Life would have to go on again for the Vikings after a 16-6 loss to the Steelers on January 12, 1975, in Super Bowl IX. Minnesota had only 119 yards of total offense, including 17 on the ground. Pro Bowl running back Chuck Foreman managed just 18 yards on 12 attempts. Terry Bradshaw, Pittsburgh's young quarterback who had started only half of the regular-season games, was far more poised than expected.

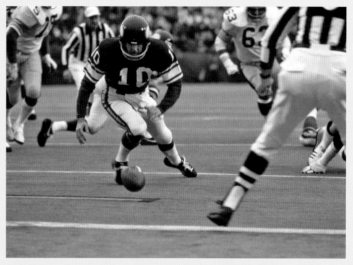

Fran Tarkenton scrambles after a fumble near the Vikings' own end zone. It was a tough day all around for Tarkenton, who completed only 11 of 26 pass attempts in the game. *Focus on Sport/Getty Images*

"They took away just about everything we do well," said Tarkenton, who completed 11 of 26 passes for 102 yards and three interceptions. "We were groping for something. It's obvious nothing much worked with consistency, and when we moved any place at all we hurt ourselves with fumbles or interceptions."

Pittsburgh scored the only two points of the first half when Dwight White tackled Tarkenton in the end zone for a safety in the second quarter. Tarkenton had pitched the ball to running back Dave Osborn, but the ball ended up on the ground.

The Vikings' Bill Brown fumbled the opening kickoff of the second half, and the Steelers recovered on the Minnesota 30-yard line. The turnover led to a 9-yard touchdown run by running back Franco Harris. The Vikings finally scored in the fourth quarter when Matt Blair blocked Bobby Walden's punt and Terry Brown recovered in the end zone to make it 9-6 (they missed the extra point), but the Steelers scored on their ensuing drive to seal the victory.

As the game neared its end, Vikings All-Pro defensive tackle Alan Page, who did not play in the last series on defense, threw his helmet on the ground and ran off the field. "I didn't think I'd need that helmet any more this afternoon," Page said, later adding, "It doesn't bother me all that much to lose. What does bother me more is that we had some players who didn't want the win when it was there."

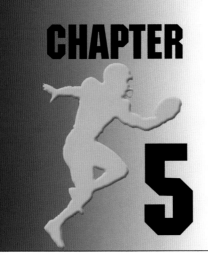
BLOOD, MUD, AND GOODBYE
1975–1978

TARK'S MVP SEASON

A touring group of student-actors from the University of Wisconsin-Superior made a stop in Mankato during the Vikings 1975 training camp. The name of the play was *Damn Vikings*, a regionalized version of the famed Broadway play, *Damn Yankees*.

In this adaptation, Joe Boyd is a middle-aged Green Bay fan who sells his soul to Applegate, the devil incarnate, in order to have his beloved Packers defeat the Vikings.

The play was a bow to the fact the Vikings had won 11 out of 14 games against the Packers since the start of the 1968 season. They also had won six division titles in seven seasons.

The Vikings earned two more victories over the Packers—by a combined score of 52-20—and another division title in 1975. Again, they won the division with a 12-2 record, the fourth such lofty mark in a stretch of seven years.

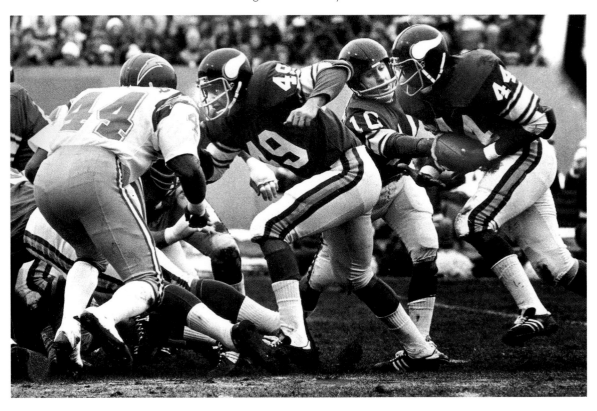

With an offense spearheaded by Fran Tarkenton (10) and Chuck Foreman (44), the Vikings charged out of the gate with 10 straight wins to open the 1975 season. Here Tarkenton hands off to his running back during a 28-13 victory over San Diego in week 10.
Charles Bjorgen/Star Tribune

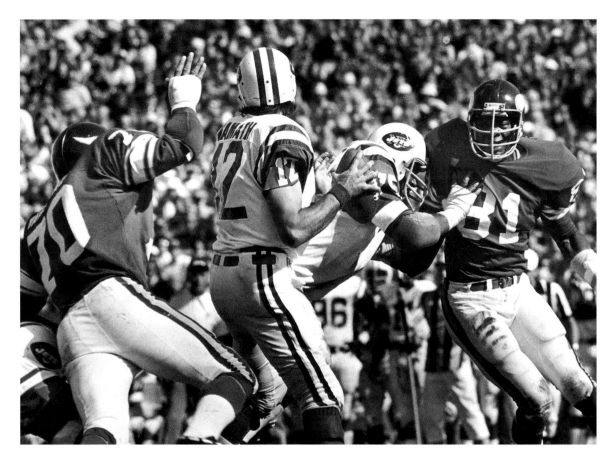

In a matchup of future Hall of Fame quarterbacks, New York's Joe Namath (12) faced intense pressure from Minnesota's Purple People Eater defense, while Tarkenton led the Vikings offense to a 29-21 win on October 12, 1975.

John Croft/Star Tribune

In 1973, Minnesota had opened the schedule with nine victories before losing at Atlanta. In 1975, they opened with 10 victories before losing 31-30 at Washington on November 30.

During the 1975 season, Chuck Foreman scored 22 touchdowns, 13 rushing and 9 receiving. Fran Tarkenton completed 64 percent of his passes for 25 touchdowns and was voted the NFL's Most Valuable Player by the Associated Press. Nine members of the 1975 Vikings were named to the Pro Bowl: Tarkenton, Foreman, John Gilliam, Ron Yary, and Ed White from the offense, and Alan Page, Jeff Siemon, Bobby Bryant, and Paul Krause from the defense.

Talk of strikes and boycotts again loomed over the start of training camp. The Vikings voted as a team to oust Ed Garvey as the head of the players association, even though Page was among Garvey's closest allies.

Grant allowed Page, Bobby Bryant, and Jim Marshall to boycott practice in support of the union without making a huge deal out of it.

"So three players missed some practice?" Grant said. "I still believe in all the rules we have, but I also think there can be exceptions to the rules as long as everyone involved realizes the rules still exist."

Again, the labor dispute did not impact the regular season. The big event on the Vikings' 1975 schedule was the first appearance by Joe Namath and the New York Jets at Met Stadium on October 12. Joe and his squad were far removed from the Jets team that had brought the AFL its first Super Bowl victory in January 1969, but the Vikings' ticket office said the demand was as great for this game as any in the team's history.

Tarkenton came away with a 29-21 victory over Namath, his former rival for the football headlines in New York.

There were some more raucous events that season. During a game against the Lions at Met Stadium on October 19, Alan Page and the Vikings were so upset by the holding by Detroit rookie Lynn Boden that a fight nearly started.

Yary, the Vikings' outstanding right tackle, said of Boden, "In all my career, I've never seen a guy grabbed like Page was grabbed by the Lions. It was more than bad; it was unreal."

Page said, "I threatened to start breaking arms. The problem was, I couldn't get an arm free to do it."

The Vikings won that game 25-19 for their fifth consecutive win of the season.

The loss to Washington in week 11 came when Fred Cox missed the extra point after the Vikings' third touchdown and then had a 45-yard field goal blocked by the Redskins' Ron McDole with five seconds left.

On a snowy December day in Buffalo, Chuck Foreman picks up a first-quarter first down by jumping over a mound of Bills and Vikings linemen. Toward the end of the game, the crowd bombarded the field with snowballs. Foreman was hit in the right eye and had blurred vision for several days.
Kent Kobersteen/Star Tribune

The Vikings shrugged off that loss, but Grant had a hard time shrugging off a 24-3 victory over Green Bay that followed on December 7. Two days later, the coach went on a rant at the Vikings' weekly media luncheon, ripping both NFL officials and the Vikings' stadium situation:

"With professional football, we've got a multimillion-dollar operation and every weekend is handled by amateurs. I've always maintained that they should be paid better and devote full-time to the business of officiating.

"If we're going to maintain our status in this area as being big league, a new stadium is mandatory."

Grant was fined $500 by Commissioner Pete Rozelle for his comments on the officiating. The Vikings would not get a new stadium until 1982.

The Vikings' second loss came in week 13—a 17-10 upset victory by the Lions in Detroit. Minnesota closed the season at Buffalo the following Saturday and won 35-13. Late in the game, the crowd started pelting the players with snowballs.

The snowballing turned into such a barrage late in the game that Grant sent his offensive players to the locker room with 45 seconds remaining. If the defense had taken the ball away from the Bills, Grant was going to have those players play offense.

"We had our offense already to go," reserve tackle Bob Lurtsema said. "I was going to play center, Paul Krause quarterback, Jim Marshall running back, Alan Page tight end. We wanted the ball."

No such luck. The game ended and the thrown object that surfaced when the Cowboys came to town for the playoffs became much more notorious in NFL history than those Buffalo snowballs.

FRAN'S SADDEST DAY

The Dallas Cowboys and the Minnesota Vikings came into the NFL as the league's 13th and 14th teams in 1960 and 1961. By the end of the decade, they were power teams.

The 1969 Vikings were the last team designated as NFL champions to appear in the Super Bowl, prior to the merger with the AFL. Dallas was there as the first NFC champions following the 1970 and 1971 seasons. Washington sneaked in after the 1972 season, then the 1973 and 1974 Vikings went to the Super Bowl as conference champions.

That made it five of the last six NFL/NFC titles for the Vikings or Cowboys, and the two teams were set to face each other in a first-round playoff game at Met Stadium on December 28, 1975. The teams had met twice previously in the playoffs, with the Cowboys winning 20-12 at Met Stadium on Christmas Day 1971 and the Vikings winning 27-10 in Dallas on December 30, 1973.

The 1975 contest became the game by which all others can be judged in this rivalry.

The Vikings were handed a 7-0 halftime lead when Dallas' Cliff Harris allowed a punt that was rolling on the Met's worn turf to hit his leg. The Vikings' Fred McNeill jumped on the ball at the Cowboys 4-yard line, and Chuck Foreman dove into the end zone from the 1-yard line on third down.

Dallas quarterback Roger Staubach led a 72-yard drive in the third quarter to tie the game at 7-7. Then the Cowboys went ahead 10-7 on a Toni Fritsch field goal early in the fourth.

Tarkenton mustered a 70-yard drive that was capped by Brent McClanahan's 1-yard dive to give the Vikings a

Vikings cornerback Nate Wright falls to the ground as Dallas receiver Drew Pearson hauls in Roger Staubach's "Hail Mary" pass in the final minute of the opening-round playoff game on December 28, 1975. *John F. Rhodes/Star Tribune*

As Pearson jogs untouched into the end zone with the game-winning touchdown, safeties Terry Brown (24) and Paul Krause (partially obscured by the official) plead for an offensive pass interference call—to no avail. *John F. Rhodes/Star Tribune*

14-10 lead with 5:56 remaining. Each team had a possession but failed to score. Then the Cowboys got the ball on their own 15-yard line with less than two minutes remaining.

The first crisis averted by the visitors came on fourth-and-16. From their own 25 yard line, Staubach threw a sideline pass that Drew Pearson caught at the 50. He landed out of bounds, but the officials ruled it a force-out by cornerback Nate Wright and gave Dallas the first down.

"Nate touched him and the official gave Pearson the benefit of the doubt," remarked Bud Grant.

Pearson said, "I would've been in if I hadn't been pushed. There's no question about it."

The push became a mild controversy compared to what transpired next. Staubach lofted a pass down the right sideline, where Pearson and Wright were running in unison inside the 10. Both players went up, Wright went to the ground, and Pearson secured the football and ran the last five yards into the end zone.

There were 24 seconds left on the game clock. Vikings defenders were racing after the officials to protest the absence of an offensive pass interference call against

An All-Pro in his first NFL season, rookie receiver Sammy White totaled 51 catches for 906 yards and 10 touchdowns in 1976. Here White pulls in a 37-yard reception against Detroit on November 7.
Richard Olsenius/Star Tribune

Pearson. Alan Page was so heated that Minnesota was assessed a 15-yard penalty on the kickoff.

Fran Tarkenton was dropped for a sack near his goal line. He raced over to scream again at the officials before heading for the line of scrimmage. This outrage inspired some fans to throw bottles from the right-field bleachers near the end zone where Pearson scored.

Armen Terzian, the field judge, reached over to pick up a bottle and was hit in the head with another flying bottle. It opened a cut and he started to bleed. Later, in the officials room, Terzian had a blood-stained cloth wrapped around his head.

The Vikings were unhappy with the bottle throwing and angry at the officials. "From our [opposite] side of the field, there is no question Nate was pushed," Grant said. "No question. Pearson had nothing to lose. If they called a penalty on him, what had they lost? They would just line up and try another long pass."

Tarkenton recalled, "I had a clear view. The man pushed his arm down and pushed Nate down."

Wright said he was ready to intercept the pass. "I had it, then suddenly I was on the ground."

Pearson said it was simply a case of two players going for the football. Staubach commented, "I just threw it and prayed. I couldn't see whether or not Drew had caught it. I didn't know we had the touchdown until I saw the official raise his arms.

"I'll admit we were very lucky on that play, but on the other hand, that touchdown we gave the Vikings in the second quarter was a fluke. I think we deserved to win."

Tarkenton left the stadium and was visiting friends when he received even worse news: His father, Dallas Tarkenton, had suffered a fatal heart attack while watching the game on television.

ONE MORE SHOT

Grant's ongoing problems with the officials surfaced before the end of the Vikings exhibition schedule in 1976. A headline in the *Minneapolis Star* on August 30 suggested the possibility of a vendetta against Grant.

Following a 20-16 victory over Philadelphia, Grant said, "My 'difficulties' with the league seem to be boomeranging on us."

He was referring to 15-yard penalties assessed against Carl Eller, Alan Page, and Ron Yary. Art McNally, the NFL's supervisor of officials, denied a vendetta and said Grant's official comments sent to the league after games "were calmer than most."

A more pressing issue for the Vikings was what to do at the wide receiver position.

John Gilliam, who was coming off a career-high 50 catches the previous season, was one of the players who became free agents after playing out their contract options in 1975, since the Rozelle Rule had been overturned in federal court that December. Gilliam had made $75,000 for with the Vikings. Atlanta signed him to a three-year, $275,000 contract.

That August, Tarkenton said, "Until we find somebody who is a super outside receiver, we are going to be at a disadvantage. If we don't come up with somebody to replace John Gilliam, we may have a hard time."

The Vikings replaced Gilliam and then some. With their second-round pick in the 1976 draft, the Vikings selected Sammy White from Grambling State. He became the third Viking to win the Rookie of the Year award (following Paul Flatley in 1963 and Chuck Foreman in 1973).

Then, right before the season, the Vikings acquired receiver Ahmad Rashad from the Seattle Seahawks for a fourth-round draft choice and defensive tackle Bob Lurtsema. It was another trade that rates among the Vikings' all-time best.

Tarkenton went from lamenting his wide-receiver situation to having the best receiving duo in his time in Minnesota.

Minnesota opened with a 40-9 thumping of the Saints in New Orleans and then came home to play the Los Angeles Rams. The NFL had adopted a 15-minute overtime period for regular-season games in 1974, and the Rams game was the first time the Vikings had gone to the extra period.

The score was still knotted 10-10 with 1:07 left in overtime. The Vikings had a first down at the Rams 11-yard line. They could have run down the clock and gone for a field goal. Instead, Tarkenton tried to hit White with a pass on the right sideline. It was intercepted a foot outside the goal line by linebacker Rick Kay. The game concluded as a 10-10 tie, one of only two tie games the Vikings have played since overtime was introduced to regular-season play. (The other was a 10-10 tie with Green Bay in 1978.)

A week later, things turned even more curious. The Vikings were on the road to play the Lions for only the second time since the Detroit franchise moved to the Pontiac Silverdome.

Grant was superstitious about getting to a stadium more than 70 minutes before a game. The Vikings' bus always left a hotel for road games later than any other team's bus. This time, the Vikings got stuck in traffic and the bus arrived at the stadium at 12:53 p.m., which was seven minutes before the scheduled kickoff. The kickoff was pushed back 30 minutes.

Despite the hectic pre-game activity, the Vikings edged the Lions, 10-9. Bobby Lee played the second half of the low-octane game after Tarkenton took a big hit.

General Manager Mike Lynn tried to head off a league fine for the team's late arrival by saying, "I'm sure the league will take into consideration that our showing up late at the stadium resulted primarily from an act of God. It was a rainy day, there was an enormous traffic jam, and there were some accidents."

Pete Rozelle wasn't amused. The Vikings were fined $5,000.

The Vikings continued to putter along, squeezing out a few narrow victories, and clinched another playoff berth with a 17-10 victory over Green Bay on November 21. There were still three games left on the schedule and already the Vikings were the Central Division champs for the eighth time in nine seasons.

The Vikings closed the season with a 29-7 whuppin' of the Dolphins in Miami. It was the 200th regular-season coaching victory of Grant's career—98 in the NFL and 102 in Canada.

Tarkenton repeatedly threw to White during the game in an effort to get the receiver the Rookie of the Year award. Sammy caught nine passes for 120 yards and three touchdowns. The first of those TDs concluded a drive that officially registered at 99 yards, although Tarkenton insisted it was longer.

"That's the longest drive I've ever been associated with," said the quarterback, then in his 16th NFL season. "The nose of the ball was an inch in front of the goal line."

Minnesota finished the season with an 11-2-1 record. Going back to 1969, the Vikings' regular-season record was 87-24-1.

"We weren't quite the team we had been," tight end Stu Voigt would say years later. "We had some wear-and-tear with key players."

"BENCHWARMER BOB"

Bob Lurtsema had spent two nondescript seasons as a defensive lineman with the Minnesota Vikings when he was summoned to the lobby of the team's training-camp headquarters in Mankato in the summer of 1973.

Jim Lovdahl, an executive at the Colle & McVoy advertising agency, was looking for a player to be a pitchman for Twin Cities Federal, and he came with specific requirements. According to Lurtsema, "Jim's criteria was, 'Let's get someone with a different name, a backup, of course, and a complete unknown.'"

The previous year, TCF's campaign had featured Vikings stars Fran Tarkenton and Carl Eller. The problem was that many viewers identified the spots with the team and not with the bank. Lovdahl's goal was to make people remember TCF, as well as find a player that the average person might believe would do his banking at the establishment.

TCF Marketing Director Bob Evans had the brainstorm that it might help to select someone with a funny name.

Center Godfrey Zaunbrecher and linebacker Carl Gersbach also were candidates. "They were OK," Lovdahl recalled in a 1998 interview. "I ran into Lurtsema in the hallway before his interview.

Defensive lineman Bob Lurtsema played in 55 games for Minnesota from 1971 to 1976, but "Benchwarmer Bob" is best remembered for his television adds for TCF bank after his playing days had passed. *Roy Swan/Star Tribune*

We talked for a couple of minutes and I could see he had humor. I knew this was a guy I could work with."

The humorous ads featuring "Benchwarmer Bob" Lurtsema began running shortly after that initial meeting in 1973 and proceeded through 1984. "A normal advertising campaign, if you do really well, lasts for two or three years," said Lurtsema, who still makes his home in the Twin Cities. "This one went for almost 12."

That's because research showed that Lurtsema was delivering exactly what TCF wanted. "They had a poll that showed 83 percent of the people in the state of Minnesota knew who I was through the television ads and 78 percent supposedly liked me," Lurtsema recalled. "Like Lovdahl said, 'Seventy-eight percent don't like Santa Claus.' Seventy-three percent knew the product. That's why it kept going."

The campaign lasted well after Lurtsema's tenure with the Vikings had finished. The day after the 1976 season opener, Lurtsema was informed that he was being sent to Seattle as the player-to-be-named in the deal for receiver Ahmad Rashad. The next morning, Lurtsema shot a TCF spot that featured him leaving for Seattle in a dented and rusted Falcon station wagon, which actually belonged to Lovdahl.

Lovdahl came up with the idea on short notice after being told that TCF wanted an ad to run the night after the trade. "I was sitting in the living room, feeling desperate," said Lovdahl, who died of lung cancer in 1999. "We were scheduled to do some filming at 7:30 the next morning. I knew I had to get the Benchwarmer to Seattle. I didn't know how.

"Then, I looked outside in the driveway and there it was—my Falcon station wagon. I said, 'That's how we're getting him to Seattle. He's driving there in my Falcon.'"

The next year, Lovdahl came up with a plan that had Lurtsema going to Seattle in a biplane.

In all, there were more than 150 ads featuring the "savings conscious" Lurtsema; at times during the hockey season he would be joined by former North Stars player and executive Lou Nanne. To this day, Lurtsema is still identified by many as "Benchwarmer Bob." It's a role he embraces.

"A lot of people said they were making fun of you," Lurtsema said. "Who cares? Were they laughing at me? No. I was laughing with them. . . . I came out being 6-6 and not the best looking guy in the world and I was a walking billboard [for TCF]. Something else that was important is what people saw in the commercial was me in real life. A fun-loving guy who loves kids and isn't intimidating. What they saw in their living rooms, that's what they got."

They still had enough to return to a fourth Super Bowl.

The NFC title push started with a visit from the Washington Redskins. George Allen was the Vikings' rival coach for a third time in the playoffs—first with the Rams in 1969, then with the Redskins in 1973 and 1976. Grant always enjoyed two things: beating George and agitating him.

Grant said before the 1976 playoff game that it appeared as though Mark Moseley, the Redskins' exceptional kicker, was wearing a "different-looking kind of shoe."

He said the Vikings had checked with the league and were told that any regularly manufactured show was okay—that the officials didn't check them anyway. Grant claimed that the Vikings had been experimenting with new shoes (maybe one with a steel shank in it) for Cox, and he was "kicking the ball way out of the end zone."

Grant's claim led Allen to say he planned to have Cox's shoes checked, but he never did.

The field-goal kickers had little import in this game, a 35-20 victory for the Vikings that put Allen at 0-3 in his December playoff trips to Minnesota. The lead was 35-6 before the Redskins scored twice in the fourth quarter.

That victory put the Vikings at home against the L.A. Rams in the NFC Championship game. The Rams had lost playoff games at the Met in 1969 and again in 1974.

Cornerback Bobby Bryant had missed most of the season because of a broken arm. He returned with three games left in the regular season. "Big Play" Bobby did it again against the Rams.

He opened the scoring in the first quarter by running the ball 90 yards after Nate Allen blocked a Tom Dempsey field goal. He also twice intercepted quarterback Pat Haden. In the second quarter, linebacker Matt Blair blocked a punt that ultimately set up a Minnesota field goal, and a 62-yard run by Chuck Foreman in the third quarter set up his own touchdown plunge two plays later.

The score was 17-0 early in the third quarter, but the Rams came back with two quick touchdowns to make a game of it.

In addition to leading the team with 55 pass receptions in 1976, Chuck Foreman ran for 1,155 yards—his career best and, at the time, a franchise record. Foreman contributed to the Vikings' 413 yards of total offense in a 20-9 win over the Packers in snowy Met Stadium on December 5.
John Croft/Star Tribune

93

SUPER BOWL XI

MINNESOTA VIKINGS VS. OAKLAND RAIDERS, JANUARY 9, 1977

Many longtime Vikings followers contend that the 1975 team was the most talented group assembled during Bud Grant's 18 seasons as head coach. But unlike Grant's previous two teams, the 1975 squad didn't make the Super Bowl.

Instead, the 1975 season came to a painful end in an NFC divisional playoff game when Roger Staubach's "Hail Mary" pass to receiver Drew Pearson gave the underdog Dallas Cowboys a 17-14 victory and infuriated fans at Met Stadium who thought Pearson should have been called for interference on Nate Wright.

The loss might have been tough to take in the short term, but the Vikings quickly recovered and the next year advanced to the Super Bowl for the third time in four seasons. Having lost in their previous three trips, Minnesota certainly felt the pressure as it prepared to face the Oakland Raiders at the Rose Bowl in Pasadena, California.

"I can't bear the idea of losing this game again, and nobody on the team can," Pro Bowl guard Ed White said. "Nobody thinks about that as a serious possibility. It's been a burden all these years, so much that all you want to do is stand there and tell the world, 'We've won it. We're a great football team and we've won it.'"

The Vikings players lined up on the Rose Bowl field prior to the start of Super Bowl XI, hoping to break their string of Super Bowl misfortunes. Once again, it was not to be. *Focus on Sport/Getty Images*

While many of the veterans who helped lead them to the NFC title in 1974 remained, the team's chemistry had changed. Receiver Ahmad Rashad, who arrived from Seattle early in the 1976 season, and another newcomer, defensive back Nate Allen, joined running back Chuck Foreman to bring some youthful enthusiasm to the team.

"It's real," veteran cornerback Bobby Bryant said. "It's cool. We used to have a pretty rigid attitude, a fixed idea of what constituted professionalism. I don't know if that kind of detached attitude won any football games or lost any. We won a lot and we had that attitude and we kept it. Maybe we didn't have enough fun. Who knows? All this stuff is theory anyhow. But we had enough people who were looking for a release, some way to let themselves express what they felt, so that we've really kind of transformed ourselves."

It didn't hurt that Foreman, Rashad, and Allen also backed-up their exuberance with big plays on the field. Foreman led the team in rushing (1,155 yards and 13 touchdowns) and receiving (55 catches). Rashad was second on the team with 53 receptions, and Allen had three interceptions. Receiver Sammy White, the second-round pick in 1976, provided a boost with his team-leading 10 touchdown receptions.

Quarterback Fran Tarkenton, playing in his 16th season, arrived in Los Angeles with a 0-2 record in Super Bowls. He also pointed to the positive chemistry.

"You come to a natural summing-up time in your personal and professional lives. I think the Super Bowl is one of those for the Minnesota Vikings," he said. "We have a new feeling that is superficially expressed in the go-crazy gimmicks. They're fine. But it goes deeper, the togetherness. It's a slap on the helmet on the practice field, a talk in the locker room, just a new appreciation of each other and what all of this means for us. It means so much, so much. . . . It has a good, strong, enduring feel. Yes, we could get beat. But if we did I would be very surprised."

Tarkenton spent the week of practice prior to the Super Bowl at far less than 100 percent. He had injured his right knee in the Vikings' victory over Washington in the first playoff game but played through the injury in the win against the Rams a week later.

Tarkenton attempted to downplay the problem, saying, "I'll be able to do anything I want to do." On the other side of the ball,

A battered Chuck Foreman is helped off the field by teammates after running into a tough Raiders defensive line. In three Super Bowl appearances, Foreman gained a combined total of 80 yards rushing on 36 carries. *Focus on Sport/Getty Images*

Pro Bowl defensive tackle Alan Page missed practice time that week because of hemorrhoids.

The Vikings' injuries didn't even address concerns about the hard-hitting Raiders, who presented plenty of problems with an offense led by quarterback Ken Stabler and a defense that featured, at the time, a rare three-man line.

Many were curious to see if the Vikings could finally win a Super Bowl. That curiosity combined with the frigid temperature reading of 17 degrees below zero meant that nearly everyone in the Twin Cities tuned into the game on January 9, 1977.

It proved to be a depressing experience for many. The Raiders humiliated the Vikings with a 32-14 victory in front of 103,438 fans at the Rose Bowl, plus 81 million television viewers. At the time, it was the largest television audience for a sporting event. The 18-point loss was a Super Bowl worst for Minnesota.

"I don't know how or why it happened, but for the first time in all the years I've been playing football, I was embarrassed," right tackle Ron Yary said.

With good reason.

The Raiders, who led 16-0 at halftime, gained a record-breaking 429 yards on offense. Running back Clarence Davis finished with 137 yards on the ground.

The Vikings appeared to catch a break late in the first quarter. They blocked a punt by Oakland's Ray Guy, and Fred McNeill recovered it at the Raiders' 3-yard line. On the second down in Minnesota's offensive series, fullback Brent McClanahan fumbled and Oakland recovered. The Raiders drove down the field, and Errol Mann hit a 24-yard field goal to give Oakland a 3-0 lead.

This game also featured a play that has been aired countless times in highlight reels. Sammy White, who had an 8-yard scoring grab in the third quarter, was running a crossing route on a third-down play. White caught Tarkenton's pass, and then Oakland's All-Pro safety, Jack Tatum, in combination with cornerback Skip Thomas, delivered a vicious hit that caused White's helmet to pop off. White did manage to hold onto the ball.

The catch did little to ease the Vikings' pain.

"I don't know how to handle this," Foreman said. "I mean, how I'm going to cope with another failure like this in the Super Bowl. Other guys, maybe they can shake it off. Me, it hurts. It grabs me and shakes me, and I just hate it. I wanted to be so proud of our team, and I guess I still am, but this was a terrible way to lose a championship football game. I'm just so damned depressed."

A dejected fan stands in disbelief after a fourth Super Bowl loss by her beloved Vikings. *Mike Zerby/Star Tribune*

The Vikings clinched the victory when backup running back Sammy Johnson barreled 12 yards for a touchdown with just minutes left in the game. Johnson's determined, tackle-breaking run remains a vivid memory for Vikings fans from the Super Bowl era.

The final was 24-13 Vikings, and it was on to Pasadena, California, to play the Oakland Raiders, the Vikings' fourth different Super Bowl opponent in an eight-year stretch.

YEAR OF TARKENTON

Sammy White received his Rookie of the Year Award in January 1977 and gave the credit to his quarterback, Fran Tarkenton.

"Francis started giving me special attention as soon as I got to camp," White said. "He helped me with the patterns, with the audibles. He told me to always catch the ball with my hands, not my body. He told me to watch the ball and not worry about defenders.

"He also told me he was going to make me a star, and he held to his word."

Tarkenton needed a few kind words, since he was bashed after losing his third Super Bowl to Oakland and then was ripped by other NFLers for bailing out on the Pro Bowl in San Diego.

"It's not the first time he's pulled this," said Jim Hart, the St. Louis quarterback who was added to the NFC

Nate Allen's block of a Tom Dempsey field goal in the first quarter set the stage for a Vikings victory in the 1976 NFC championship on December 26. Bobby Bryant picked up the ball and ran it 90 yards for the game's first points. *Earl Seubert/Star Tribune*

roster in Tarkenton's place. "Personally, I'm absolutely delighted to be here. But if a guy's chosen to play in this game, he should have the decency to be a part of it."

(Making up an excuse for missing the Pro Bowl in the 1970s was much less common than it is today, obviously.)

Some additional tension came to Tarkenton's offseason when the Vikings made Tommy Kramer, a quarterback from Rice University, the 27th selection in the first round of the 1977 draft.

Kramer's agent, Houston attorney Mike Thornell, said in May that he expected the rookie to be the Vikings' number one quarterback within a month of the start of the season.

At the same time, Tarkenton said he planned to offer no tutoring to Kramer. "That ain't my job," he said. "I don't train quarterbacks."

Minnesota's sporting public aimed considerable criticism at Tarkenton for taking that approach, just as Wisconsin fans would three decades later when Green Bay quarterback Brett Favre said he planned to do no tutoring of young quarterback Aaron Rodgers.

Tarkenton's offseason included a late-January appearance as the host of *Saturday Night Live*. John Belushi opened the show by saying to the audience: "Please help guide Fran Tarkenton in this show. Don't let him humiliate himself like he did in the Super Bowl."

Tarkenton's opening monologue included the line, "I guarantee we'll be in the Super Bowl, and I predict we'll lose again."

No doubt, this elicited many laughs throughout the country, with the exception of Minnesota.

The wear-and-tear on the Vikings' veteran team showed more clearly during the 1977 season. They were 5-3 in mid-November. In a game against Cincinnati at Met Stadium, the Vikings were on the way to 42-10 victory when the Bengals' Gary Burley sacked Tarkenton late in the third quarter.

Tarkenton suffered a broken right leg and missed the remainder of the season. Burley was shook up in the visiting locker room even before he heard the extent of the injury.

"I wouldn't be able to sleep thinking I hurt a player as great as Fran Tarkenton, a player who hadn't been injured in 17 years in this league," Burley said. "To me, he's the greatest quarterback in the history of football. He's just a wizard."

A week later, the Vikings defense surrendered an NFL-record 275 rushing yards to the Bears' Walter Payton in Chicago. Somehow, the Bears managed to turn Payton's sweetest day into just one touchdown and one field goal, squeezing out a 10-7 victory.

Kramer's first big moment as an NFL quarterback came against San Francisco on December 4 at Met Stadium.

Ahmad Rashad gives the OK sign during the Vikings' New Year's Eve practice session in 1976, eight days before their Super Bowl date with the Oakland Raiders.
William Seaman/Star Tribune

When the Vikings chose Tommy Kramer with the 27th pick in the 1977 draft, it was the first time the team took a quarterback with a first-round selection. (The only other time they've done so since was with Daunte Culpepper in 1999.)
Charles Bjorgen/Star Tribune

The Vikings were trailing 24-7 entering the fourth quarter. The rookie replaced Bobby Lee and proceeded to throw three touchdown passes to secure a 28-27 victory.

Immediately, Vikings fans insisted that Kramer should be the team's quarterback—over Lee and over Tarkenton, even if the NFL's all-time leading passer got healthy.

It didn't work out that way. Minnesota's 9-5 record was good for the ninth Central Division title in 10 years. The Vikings went to Los Angeles to face the Rams in the playoffs, with Lee as the starting quarterback.

The Rams had embarrassed the Vikings 35-3 in a late-October contest in Los Angeles. The Rams were 9-point favorites.

Jack Youngblood, the team's star defensive end, was one Ram who couldn't wait to play the Vikings in December in decent weather, instead of the frozen conditions of Minnesota.

Referring to the frigid weather of the previous year's playoff game, Youngblood said, "Games like that cheat the fans and threaten the players. I didn't have any feeling in my feet after the game. We've been trying to make it to the Super Bowl for years.

"Nobody has any complaints this year about the game conditions if we lose again."

Then it started raining in southern California and it didn't stop. The field at the Los Angeles Coliseum was soaked and water was standing. The game became known as the "Mud Bowl" in Vikings lore.

With Minnesota's Lee making more plays than Los Angeles' Pat Haden, the Vikings won 14-7. They scored on their first possession, thanks to a pair of spectacular catches by Ahmad Rashad.

That one touchdown held up until the fourth quarter, when the Vikings splashed to a 41-yard touchdown drive that was capped by Sammy Johnson's 1-yard run. Haden was not able to produce points until the game's final minute.

"I blame the entire game on myself," Haden said. "I didn't execute and, consequently, our offense didn't move."

Jeff Siemon intercepts a pass from San Francisco quarterback Jim Plunkett during the Vikings' dramatic 28-27 comeback win on December 4, 1977.
Duane Braley/Star Tribune

After the game, a television commentator asked Grant about an "unbelievable victory" for his team.

"It's only unbelievable if you're not a believer," Grant said. "I happen to be a believer. We all are.

"We liked the weather very much. When we saw what the weather would be like, we felt it was a good omen. We've been a bad-weather team for a long time, particularly late in the season."

The upset win sent the Vikings to Dallas, where they were 11-point underdogs in the NFC Championship Game. It was the Vikings' fifth title game in their nine-year run of excellence, and they were 4-0.

The Cowboys had been reinforced in their bid for a third Super Bowl: They had pulled off a trade with Seattle in order to get the right to draft Tony Dorsett, the great running back from Pittsburgh.

There was no mud to help Lee and the Vikings this time. The Cowboys cruised to a 23-6 victory on New Year's Day, 1978. The Vikings would not reach a conference title game for another decade.

GREATNESS DEPARTS

Fran Tarkenton was the most dynamic offensive player in Vikings history and the NFL's Most Valuable Player in 1975. Alan Page was the most dynamic defensive player in Vikings history and the NFL's MVP in 1971.

Tarkenton made it clear throughout the offseason that 1978 was to be his final year in the NFL. He was 38 years old, playing in his 18th season, and had started to be confronted by injuries.

The more surprising news was that Page's tenure with the Vikings would also come to an end during the 1978 season, and it would come three months before Tarkenton's retirement.

There had been coolness for several years in the relationship between the headstrong Page and the equally

In the fourth playoff meeting of the Rams and Vikings since 1969, Los Angeles played host for the first time in 1977—and the Los Angeles Memorial Coliseum resembled a giant mud pit on that December day. The Vikings prevailed 14-7 in the legendary "Mud Bowl."
George Long/NFL/Getty Images

headstrong Grant. Page had missed hunks of training camps in order to attend law school.

Grant tolerated it because Page remained the most important member of the defensive line, a group that had more to do with the Vikings' period of glory than any other element of the roster.

In 1978, Page had become a recreational runner and was trying to play at a substantially reduced weight. He had weighed 265 to 270 pounds at the peak of his efficiency and that year he showed up weighing less than 230 pounds.

Grant told him he couldn't be effective at that weight. Page told Grant that carrying all that weight was unhealthy and that he could play at the smaller size.

On September 25, the Vikings were in Chicago for the season's fourth game. James "Duck" White, the team's top draft choice from 1976, replaced Page for a series. When

told to return to the game, Page reportedly told the coaches, "What for?"

On October 10, two days after the Vikings had lost 29-28 in Seattle, Page was placed on waivers. The 33-year-old defensive tackle was available to any team for $100.

"Nobody has meant more to the Vikings, but he just can't make the plays anymore," Grant said.

The coach also said that the Vikings had too many defensive linemen (eight) and were short of offensive linemen.

"There were teams in the NFL interested in Mark Mullaney, Duck White, Randy Holloway, young players like that. They didn't want to make a deal for Alan," Grant said. "He's playing at 220 pounds now, and he doesn't have the strength or the stamina he used to. He was the most dispensable of our linemen in terms of future value to the team."

Fran Tarkenton acknowledges the cheers at a roast in his honor on June 29, 1978. Among the roasters was sports commentator Howard Cosell, seen here to Tarkenton's right.
Pete Hohn/Star Tribune

Many players saw it more as an indication of the friction between coach and player than of Page's effectiveness on the field.

Bobby Bryant, who had been a leader with Page in players' union matters, said that waiving the tackle showed "a lack of class by the Viking organization."

Page was picked up by Chicago. The Bears were now run by Jim Finks, the man who had maneuvered into position to draft Page in 1967 when Finks was the GM of the Vikings.

Page played for the Bears against Denver that weekend. When asked about being with a new club in the middle of his 12th season, Page was his usual imperial self.

"It's only a uniform," he said. "Nothing more."

To prove his contrary nature, Page responded to the Bears' failure to reach the playoffs that season by saying, "I don't miss the playoffs even a little bit. Money is important, but not as important as being able to spend the holidays with my family."

The Vikings faced Page and the Bears on November 12 at Met Stadium, and defeated Chicago 17-14.

Minnesota also squeezed into the playoffs for the 10th time in 11 seasons, although this was as much a tribute to the weakness of their NFC Central rivals—the Bears, Packers, Lions, and now the Tampa Bay Buccaneers—as it was to the strength of the 1978 Vikings.

Ahmad Rashad pulls in a Fran Tarkenton pass against the Packers in Met Stadium on October 22, 1978. Rashad led the Vikings with 66 receptions during his All-Pro season. *William Seaman/Star Tribune*

It was the first season of the 16-game schedule for NFL teams. The Vikings finished 8-7-1. They lost the last two games—45-17 at Detroit and 27-20 at Oakland—but made the playoffs when the Packers closed with a 31-14 loss to the Rams.

This playoff appearance was short-lived. A 34-10 loss to the Rams in Los Angeles sent the Vikings home early.

"I was rooting for this," Rams guard Tom Mack said. "I wanted the Vikings to come out here and play us. I never believed in that jinx business.

"We had found out every way to lose to them previously. And we finally ran out of ways to lose."

Bobby Bryant was nearing the end of his career in 1978, but the 34-year-old cornerback snared a team-best seven interceptions that season, adding to his eventual lifetime total of 51. Here he takes a pass away from San Diego's Charlie Joiner on November 20, 1978.
Steve Schluter/Star Tribune

TARK LEAVES SLINGING

Even if you prorate the numbers over a 16-game schedule, Tarkenton went out slinging the football as never before. He threw an astounding 572 passes in 1978 and completed 345 for 3,468 yards—tops in the league in all three categories. He threw 25 touchdown passes, but also an inflated 32 interceptions.

On September 17, the Vikings lost to Tampa Bay 16-10 to fall to a record of 1-2. The Met Stadium crowd of 46,152 booed Tarkenton and that stuck in his craw for the rest of the season. In late October, the quarterback said he had "played better than at any time in his life for the past five weeks," but still was simmering over the booing.

"I resent the hell out of it," Tarkenton said. "In other towns, to be a veteran player is to be revered. Look at Washington and the feeling they had for Sonny Jurgensen. Or Green Bay during Bart Starr's last years as a player. He didn't have it anymore, but the fans didn't get on his back.

"When you're an old guy in this town, it seems like they're trying to exterminate you. The real point is, in other cities, if a man plays well over the years, he's revered. But not in this place. Seems like all they want here is fresh blood, new people."

On November 5 against Detroit, Tarkenton showed some of the grit that carried this undersized quarterback to greatness. He was smashed in the mouth by Lions end Dave Pureifory and lost three teeth. He had a large cut in his mouth and was spitting blood. He stayed in the game and led Minnesota to a 17-7 victory.

"I've never seen a worse cut than that on a football field," center Mick Tingelhoff said. "It took a lot of guts to go back in the game after being all stitched up."

Tingelhoff, Minnesota's starting center for 17 years, joined Tarkenton in retirement after the 1978 season. It was a season of tremendous transition; the Vikings waved goodbye to greatness and, although they didn't know it, headed into a stretch of mediocrity.

In August 1986, Tarkenton became the first Vikings player inducted into the Pro Football Hall of Fame. When he retired, he was the NFL's all-time leader in passing attempts (6,467), completions (3,686), yards (47,003), and touchdowns (342). He also rushed for 32 touchdowns.

Two years later, Page became the second Vikings player elected to the Hall of Fame. He was enshrined on July 30, 1988, in his hometown of Canton, Ohio.

Hard-nosed to the end, a bloodied Tarkenton leaves the field to get his mouth stitched up after a vicious hit by Detroit's Dave Pureifory on November 5, 1978. Tark would return to the game and lead the Vikes to a 17-7 victory. *William Seaman/Star Tribune*

The 38-year-old Tarkenton wreaked havoc on the NFC in 1978. He posted league highs and career bests in pass attempts, pass completions, and passing yardage—as well as most interceptions. *Bruce Bisping/Star Tribune*

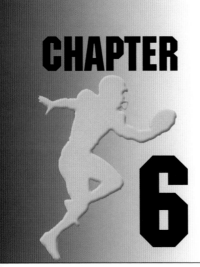

HOW THE OTHER HALF LIVES

6 1979–1985

When the Minnesota Vikings arrived at training camp prior to the 1979 season, many of the familiar faces were gone.

Fran Tarkenton and Alan Page had played their last games as Vikings in 1978. After 16 years with the Vikings, Carl Eller was traded to Seattle for defensive tackle Steve Niehaus prior to the 1979 season. Eller spent his final NFL season with the Seahawks in 1979; he would wait 25 years before being elected to the Pro Football Hall of Fame.

Mick Tingelhoff, the 17-year starter at center, was also missing when veteran Jim Marshall and the rest of

By 1979, veteran Jim Marshall was one of the few holdovers from the core of players that went to four Super Bowls between 1969 and 1977.
Donald Black/Star Tribune

the team arrived for the first day of training camp in Mankato.

Marshall told Bob Fowler of the *Minneapolis Star* that he walked into the dining room and thought, "Where is everybody?"

Marshall added, "Then I thought, 'They must be in their rooms.' It's too early for me to miss them. I haven't noticed their absence yet. But I know I will."

The 1979 season would be the last for Marshall, the NFL's all-time ironman (unless you want to count a punter, Jeff Feagles), with 282 consecutive games played, 270 of them (all starts) for Minnesota. Doug Sutherland

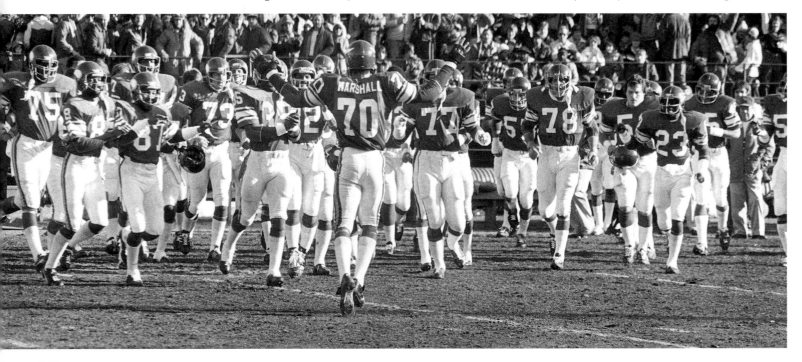

was the only other remaining representative of the Purple People Eaters, although he was not an original member but took Gary Larsen's spot in 1974.

Chuck Foreman was another Vikings star entering his final season with the team. He lost his starting position to Ted Brown, the rookie first-round draft choice from North Carolina State. Foreman's pass-catching total also fell from 61 receptions in 1978 to 19 in 1979, and Rickey Young became the first option as a backfield receiver. Foreman would finish his career as a New England Patriot in 1980.

At quarterback, the post-Tarkenton era started with Tommy Kramer, the third-year player from Rice, throwing every pass for the Vikings during the 16-game season. There were plenty of passes, too: 566 attempts, just six fewer than Tarkenton's club record from the previous season.

The first indication that the Vikings' decline was serious came with their winless record in four exhibition games. They opened the regular season with a 28-22 win over San Francisco and went to Chicago to face a Bears' team that featured Alan Page on the defensive line.

The Bears cruised to a 26-7 victory and a game ball went to Page. He sacked Kramer twice, which added to 27 yards lost. "I don't think there's any doubt in my mind that this meant a lot to Alan," said Bears coach Neil Armstrong, who had been an assistant for Grant with the Vikings.

Regarding his storied Vikings connection, Page said, "I was always an employee there. I was there to do a job. Now, I'm here—true, to do a job. But the feeling is different. It's a warmer organization."

The Bears organization was being run by Jim Finks, the man who had drafted Page in 1967 and was in charge of the Vikings during Page's first seven NFL seasons. His comment was an obvious shot at Grant, who bluntly had stated the previous fall that Page was being cut because he could no longer make plays.

When Page retired after the 1981 season, he did some work with the NFL Players Association. A union delegation that included Page visited the Vikings' training camp in 1982. Grant was walking out of the dormitory as Page was arriving. The eyes of these two proud, stubborn men met and you could see the icicles form between them—even on a hot August day in Mankato.

The Vikings captured a 30-27 win in a rematch against Page and the Bears in the teams' second meeting of the season, on October 21 at Met Stadium. The win put Minnesota's record at 4-4 and kept them in contention of the now-mediocre NFC Central. However, then the Vikings lost three straight to Tampa Bay, St. Louis, and Green Bay.

The season closed with a 27-23 loss at New England. Kramer went 35 for 61 for 308 yards in the game. The 61 attempts broke Tarkenton's team record by five. Rickey

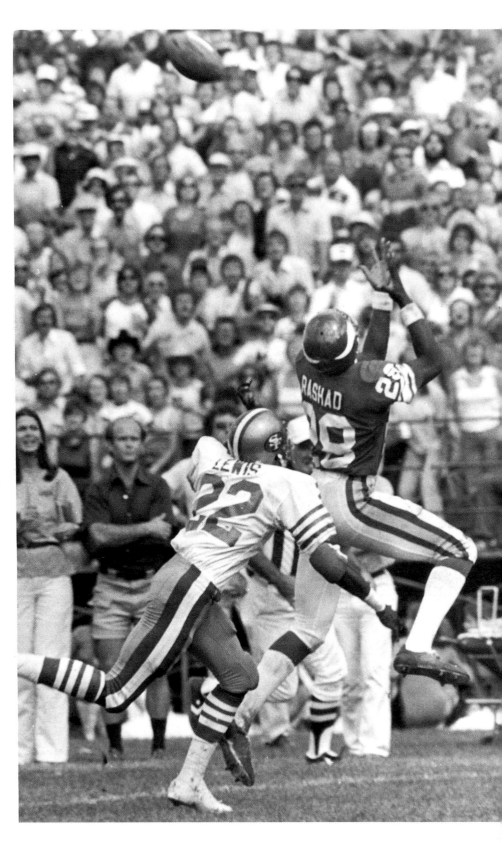

Ahmad Rashad's 1,156 receiving yards in 1979 set a team record that stood for nearly a decade. Here he outruns defensive back Eddie Lewis for one of his four touchdown catches on the day, a 28-22 win over San Francisco in the season opener. *Duane Braley/Star Tribune*

Young, slipping out of the backfield, caught 15 passes for 116 yards and broke his own team record for receptions by four.

The Vikings finished the year at 7-9—their first losing season since 1967, Bud Grant's first with the team. Although it also marked the end of a streak of six consecutive division titles, there was reason for optimism.

"I'm very encouraged," General Manager Mike Lynn said. "Against Los Angeles, the number-one defensive team in the NFC, we gained 409 yards [in week 14]. Against New England, we got 453."

Kramer summarized his first season as a starter by saying, "I think I have proved I can be one of the better quarterbacks in the league. I've gone through a learning process, and so has our entire team."

That was the theme—youth and a bright future—in the wake of missing the playoffs for the first time since 1972. "This entire team has made progress," Grant said. "The young players learned a lot that will help them next year."

BACK TO THE TOP

Lynn's good mood was not tied completely to the Vikings' display of high-powered offense during the final weeks of the season. In December 1979, ground was broken for the domed stadium that the Vikings had been trying to win from the state's politicians since early in the decade. It would be three more seasons before the Vikings moved into the Hubert H. Humphrey Metrodome on the eastern edge of downtown Minneapolis.

The optimism surrounding the Vikings' on-field fortunes at the end of 1979 was not misplaced. They regained the NFC Central Division title in 1980, even though it was earned with a modest 9-7 record.

The season opened with Tommy Kramer completing 30 of 42 passes for 395 yards and three touchdowns in a 24-23 win over the Atlanta Falcons at Met Stadium. Ahmad Rashad caught 11 passes for 160 yards.

"It wasn't just a bad day for the Atlanta secondary," Rashad said. "You have to realize that we have some of

Even at the age of 42, Jim Marshall was a threat to opposing quarterbacks, such as Buffalo's Joe Ferguson, in the lineman's farewell season of 1979.
Steve Schluter/Star Tribune

the best receivers in the league. It's not that we've got chopped meat out there.

"With Sammy White, Terry LeCount, and myself out there, who are you going to double-team? And that's what a receiver likes to see—man-to-man coverage."

The Vikings pulled out the victory when Kramer engineered a 69-yard touchdown drive that started with 3:06 remaining in the game. He had been involved in a couple of comebacks as Tarkenton's backup in 1977, and now the nickname was applied: Two-Minute Tommy.

"I feel we can move the ball against anybody, anytime, not just in the last two minutes," Kramer said.

At the midpoint of the schedule, the Vikings had a record of 3-5. After winning five of the next six games, they were 8-6 and in position to clinch the division, when the Cleveland Browns came to Met Stadium.

The Browns pummeled the Vikings throughout the sunny afternoon of December 14. They went ahead 23-7 after running back Cleo Miller crashed into the end zone with seven and a half minutes remaining.

Minnesota came back with two touchdowns, the second one set up by an interception by cornerback Bobby

Bryant, another veteran who was nearing the end of his Vikings career.

With 14 seconds remaining in the game and Minnesota trailing 23-21, the Vikings had the ball on their own 20-yard line. On the first play, Kramer threw a 10-yard pass to tight end Joe Senser, who then lateraled to Ted Brown—a "hook-and-ladder" play in football jargon. Brown ran 24 more yards before getting knocked out of bounds at Cleveland's 46. There were just a couple of seconds left on the clock. The only option now was for Kramer to heave a pass into a crowd near the end zone and hope for the best.

Rashad, White, and LeCount bunched to the right at the line of scrimmage and ran a sprint to the 5-yard line. From there, LeCount was supposed to leap and try to tip the ball with the hope it would ricochet to Rashad or White.

LeCount, who was held up briefly at the line, arrived late, and Cleveland defender Thom Darden leaped above the group to deflect the pass. Standing just beyond the defenders, Rashad reached out and grabbed the football, pulled it to his waist, and backed the final three yards into the end zone to secure the 28-23 victory.

In the fifteenth game of the 1980 season, two Cleveland defenders leap to deflect Tommy Kramer's "Hail Mary" pass in the final seconds. Ahmad Rashad gathered up the deflection and backed the last few yards into the end zone to secure the dramatic win and clinch a playoff berth for Minnesota.
AP/Wide World Photos

The Vikings players came running off the bench and staged a hogpile on top of Rashad. From under the humanity, Rashad screamed at his pal LeCount, "Do you like money?" in reference to the $5,000 that the players would earn automatically as a playoff team.

Those 80 yards on the last two plays pushed Kramer's passing production for the afternoon to 456 yards on 38 completions in 49 attempts.

Kramer's best day ever was followed three weeks later by his worst in a playoff game at Philadelphia.

The Eagles had buried the Vikings, 42-7, in the second game of the season in Philadelphia. Grant was angry with Philly coach Dick Vermeil for what he perceived to be running up the score.

"Vermeil isn't playing for [college football poll] ratings now, like he was when he coached at UCLA," Grant said after that game.

In the playoff game on January 3, 1981, the Vikings took a 14-0 lead over the favored Eagles. Philadelphia quarterback Ron Jaworski, who had played a miserable first half, led an 85-yard touchdown drive that cut Minnesota's lead to 14-7 with 54 seconds left in the half.

The Vikings then came out and played a historically inept second half. They committed eight turnovers in the half, including five Kramer interceptions. The final score was Eagles 31, Vikings 16. Philadelphia went on to earn

its first Super Bowl trip a week later with a victory over Dallas in the NFC title game.

For the Vikings, the loss would be followed by a six-season stretch where the only playoff appearance would come in 1982, when the playoff field was expanded to 16 teams due to a season interrupted by a players strike.

PLAYOFFS? WHAT PLAYOFFS?

From 1969 through 1977, the Minnesota Vikings posted a regular-season record of 92-29-1, and also had nine playoff victories. Over the next three seasons, from 1978 to 1980, they went 24-23-1 without a playoff victory.

This mediocrity seemed to be grating on Bud Grant. The coach criticized the local fans for leaving in the fourth quarter during the Cleveland game the previous December.

The 1981 season opened with Steve Dils at quarterback in place of the injured Kramer (knee) and with the Vikings—the team of the Purple People Eaters' front four—aligned in the now-trendy 3-4 defensive front.

Dils threw 62 passes and completed 37 of them for 361 yards in the season-opening 21-13 loss against Tampa Bay. The performance kicked off a season in which the Vikings quarterbacks would throw an NFL-record 709 passes, a mark that still stands.

Minnesota fell to 0-2 with a 36-10 loss to Oakland in a Monday-night affair at Met Stadium. Kramer was back by week three and the Vikings rallied for five straight wins. The fourth was a 33-31 victory in San Diego, and that's when Grant's indignation poured forth.

Grant said the Chargers came from the "Cadillac division" of the NFL. He said the "hotshots" (meaning, national reporters) would never believe that Joe Senser outplayed Kellen Winslow as a tight end or that Terry LeCount was such an effective receiver.

"The hotshots said, 'Joe who?'" Grant commented a couple of days after the San Diego upset. "They said, 'Terry who?' They wondered where LeCount came from. There just isn't a lot of news that goes out of here about us."

Grant also ripped the officiating in the San Diego game, despite knowing that it would lead to another fine from Commissioner Pete Rozelle.

Minnesota made a Monday-night appearance on November 3 and lost 20-19 in Denver. Tommy Kramer, a Texas boy who remembered Craig Morton from his days with the Cowboys, went into the Broncos locker room after the game and asked Morton, now the Denver quarterback, to sign a game program for him.

"You almost pulled it off again," said Morton, in reference to Kramer's growing reputation as a comeback quarterback.

The Vikings followed the loss in Denver with victories against Tampa Bay and New Orleans. They were sitting at 7-4 and had a two-game lead in the NFC Central with

The Vikings earned their fifth-straight win of 1981 in a 35-23 shootout against Philadelphia on October 18 at Met Stadium. Here Tommy Kramer delivers a pass to Terry LeCount in the face of an Eagles pass rush.
William Seaman/Star Tribune

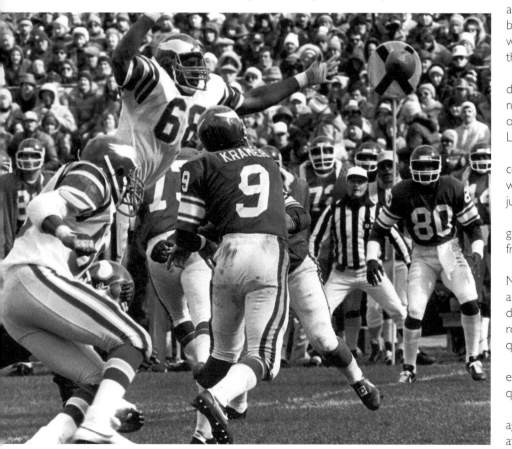

five to play. They closed the season with a five-game losing streak, which was the first suffered by Grant in his 15 seasons as the Vikings coach.

After the streak reached four, Grant came out and defended his players. "Believe me," he said, "honest to God, these guys have worked their tails off. They're not complacent. They're very concerned, more so than anybody on the street is concerned."

A few days later, the Vikings played their final game at Metropolitan Stadium. They lost to Kansas City, 10-6, in front of an announced crowd of 41,110, which was more than 6,000 below the old park's capacity.

This game was the final event held at the Met. When it was over, fans swarmed the field to take away souvenirs, hack down goalposts, tear up sod, and knock out seats with sledgehammers. An hour after the game, there was so much pounding that it sounded like a construction project.

Ted Brown, the third-year running back, had a spectacular season in 1981. He rushed for 1,063 yards and also caught 83 passes for 694 yards. Joe Senser had 79 catches for 1,004 yards as a tight end, Sammy White had 66 catches for 1,001 yards, and Ahmad Rashad had 58 catches for 884 yards.

The Minnesota Vikings played their final game in Metropolitan Stadium on a chilly December 20, 1981. They lost to Kansas City to close out a 7-9 season.
William Seaman/Star Tribune

Kramer amassed 3,912 passing yards in a season in which he missed two games with his knee injury.

Yet, all that firepower added up to a 7-9 record for Minnesota in Grant's year of "High Indignity."

A NEW HOME, AND A LEGENDARY COACH SAYS GOOD-BYE

The inaugural season of the Hubert H. Humphrey Metrodome in downtown Minneapolis didn't exactly start off as the team or the city had hoped. The opening game was a preseason matchup against the Seattle Seahawks. The crowd of 57,880 spectators quickly discovered that not having air conditioning in this indoor stadium was folly. It was a steamy August night, and for much of the game there were as many people outside, gulping for air, as there were inside watching the action. The "Sweatro-

dome," as it came to be called that first summer, would get its air conditioning a year later.

Five weeks after the sweltering preseason opener, the NFL players walked out in a league-wide strike that put the schedule on hold for two months. It was not quite what the Vikings' landlords at the Metrodome had in mind when they set the operating budget for the new building.

The long battle between league management and the NFL Players Association finally culminated in a strike after the second game of the 1982 season.

The players had managed to get the Rozelle Rule overturned with the favorable decision in John Mackey's lawsuit in December 1975. Yet, the teams did very little bidding for free agents under the new rules.

As a result, the players' union tried a new demand: 55 percent of gross revenues, which they would then

Although tight end Joe Senser couldn't get his hands on this Steve Dils pass, Senser emerged as a top passing target for the Vikings quarterbacks in 1981. Senser led the team in receiving yardage and touchdowns that season, but his career lasted only 17 more games due to injuries.
Star Tribune

distribute among the players. The owners refused and the strike continued for 57 days.

Eventually, the owners retained the right to set salaries, but they also guaranteed a total sum of money that the players would receive, which amounted to more than 50 percent of the revenues.

The Vikings were 1-1 when the strike was called following the Monday night game on September 20. They resumed play on November 21 with a 26-7 loss to the Packers in Milwaukee. The crowd in County Stadium was only 44,681, which was more than 11,000 below capacity, and there were 4,799 unsold tickets.

The Milwaukee Brewers had played in the World Series the previous month and football briefly played second-fiddle to baseball among the Wisconsin faithful.

"The caliber of play was all right," Grant commented after the game, "but I don't think the enthusiasm from either team or the crowd was what we're used to."

The NFL had set a nine-game regular-season schedule. The enthusiasm was back by the time that abbreviated schedule ended with a Monday-night game between the Vikings and the Cowboys on January 3 in the Metrodome. The crowd was 60,007 and the largest in the Dome to that point.

The Vikings were 4-4 and already had clinched a place in the Super Bowl tournament. A victory against Dallas would earn them a first-round home game.

John Turner's interception return on the first play of the fourth quarter gave the Vikings a 24-13 lead and sent the crowd into a frenzy. The noise only increased when Dallas' Tim Newsome fumbled the kickoff and recovered at his 1-yard line.

Then quarterback Danny White gave a handoff to Tony Dorsett, who squirted through the line and was gone—99 yards and the longest run from scrimmage in NFL history.

The crowd was stunned again in the middle of the fourth quarter when the Cowboys drove 64 yards to take a 27-24 lead. Then Two-Minute Tommy led the Vikings on another dramatic comeback. Their 80-yard drive was capped by a 14-yard touchdown pass to Rickey Young. Young was so open that although he fell down while catching the pass, he still got up and ran the last seven yards to the end zone.

The 31-27 win gave the Vikings a chance to play Atlanta in the first playoff game at the Dome. In front of a crowd of 60,560, Kramer again spearheaded a late touchdown drive to give Minnesota a come-from-

Ahmad Rashad and Tommy Kramer appear happy to be back in their Vikings uniforms after the 57-day players' strike came to an end in November 1982. *Bruce Bisping/Star Tribune*

behind victory. Ted Brown's 5-yard run with 1:44 to play put them ahead to stay for a final score of 30-24.

The Vikings then went to Washington to play the Redskins. This was the second season for Washington coach Joe Gibbs, who was not a widely known football figure when hired by owner Jack Kent Cooke.

Gibbs had introduced to the NFL the concept of power running out of a one-back formation. Fullback John Riggins put that strategy on full display and bulldozed through the Vikings defense for 185 yards on 37 carries. The Redskins scored two touchdowns in the first quarter, and the Vikings had trouble getting possession for their high-powered passing game. Minnesota lost 21-7.

"That's the kind of game you don't want to get into with Washington," Grant said. "That's what we didn't want to happen—them getting ahead 14-0 and being content to run the ball."

The Redskins would go on to defeat Miami 27-17 to capture the first of Gibbs' three Super Bowl championships.

Early in the 1983 season, the 1-1 Vikings were in Tampa Bay to take on the Buccaneers when Kramer suffered a knee injury in the first quarter. Although the

Vikings pulled out a 19-16 overtime win in the game, their starting quarterback would not make another start that season.

Steve Dils, who had been a backup since he was drafted out of Stanford in 1979, started 12 out of the next 13 games. Wade Wilson, a third-year player who carried the nickname "Whiskey" thanks to Kramer, got his first career start in the 1983 season finale—a 20-14 victory over Cincinnati.

The Vikings had a 6-2 record at the season's midway point, and then they reversed that record to go 2-6 in the second half of the schedule. It was the second time in three seasons that the Vikings had collapsed and missed the playoffs.

The season also saw Grant suspend Ted Brown in December for failing to show up for treatment for a separated shoulder. Grant said it was the first time he had suspended a player in his 27 years of coaching in the CFL and the NFL.

Still, there were no hints to the extent of Grant's frustration until the *Minneapolis Star and Tribune* hit doorsteps on January 28, 1984. The shocking news was revealed in the headline above Sid Hartman's byline: "Grant resigns as Vikings coach."

The Vikings defense pulled and grabbed and did all they could to thwart the progress of Washington's John Riggins, but the tough fullback was virtually unstoppable in the Redskins' playoff victory on January 15, 1983.
Bruce Bisping/Star Tribune

Grant told Hartman: "In my mind, timing is the most important thing. I decided this was time to quit. There wasn't any pressure on me. There are a lot of things I want to do while I still have my health."

Grant and Hartman were friends going back to Grant's days as a player with the Gophers. He gave the big scoop to Hartman, although only after Grant and Mike Lynn flew to Max Winter's winter home in Hawaii to give him the news.

"Bud's decision was a real shock," Winter said. "I've never thought the time would come that he would want to quit coaching. I started him as a player with the Lakers 35 years ago. In my book, he's the best football coach who ever lived."

THE SHORT-LIVED STECKEL EXPERIMENT

There was no time to speculate on Grant's replacement. The resignation came on a Friday. By Saturday, the Twin Cities newspapers were reporting that 38-year-old Les Steckel, an assistant coach since 1979, would be the new head coach.

Steckel flew to Hawaii after Grant's resignation and went through the formality of a sit-down with Winter, the team president. Lynn was running the day-to-day operations and, with consultation from Grant, decided that Steckel should be the new coach.

This decision was a considerable disappointment to Jerry Burns, who had been on Grant's staff since 1968 and had been the brains behind the Vikings' sophisticated passing game.

There had been rumors back in December that Steckel was a leading contender to replace Joe Salem as coach of the Minnesota Gophers. Steckel backed out as a candidate, and Lou Holtz was hired away from Arkansas. Lynn said that no promises had been made to Steckel about replacing Grant in order to keep him from leaving for the Gophers.

Grant himself offered assurances on Steckel's capabilities: "Les Steckel will be a great head football coach. He has the ability to teach and handle players. He has impressed me from the day he joined our staff."

Grant was right about most things as a football man, but he missed this one worse than a blocked field goal.

The Vikings held a press conference in Honolulu before the Pro Bowl, and Steckel was a guest during ABC's telecast of the game.

Steckel promoted his military background—he had been a combat officer in Vietnam—as a reason to look at him as an excellent leader. He wanted to dump Grant's coaches and bring in a young, gung-ho group of assistants.

Lynn did not allow him to get rid of Burns, John Michels, Bob Hollway, or Floyd Resse, so Steckel wound

Outgoing coach Bud Grant introduced his successor, Les Steckel, to Twin Cities reporters at a press conference on January 30, 1984.
John Croft/Star Tribune

The four contenders for the starting quarterback job enjoyed a light moment at minicamp in May 1984 (left to right): Steve Dils, Archie Manning, Tommy Kramer, and Wade Wilson. Kramer would emerge as the starter, while Wilson was the primary backup.
Darlene Pfister/Star Tribune

up with 14 assistants—a huge number for that era. He also took away Burns' control of the offense.

Grant's system always had called for a late start to training camp and a work schedule that would not beat up his players. Steckel started early and made no secret that he intended to run a "boot camp."

Punter Greg Coleman showed up for the first workout in Mankato in military fatigues and saluted Steckel. This photograph made newspapers in the Twin Cities and all over the country.

The Vikings went 1-3 in the exhibition season and lost the last one by a score of 31-0 in St. Louis. Max Winter told the *Star and Tribune*'s Doug Grow, "After that game, I am really down. We had a very poor exhibition of football."

Winter's level of angst increased when Steckel lost his regular-season opener 42-13 to San Diego in the Metrodome. The signs of trouble increased in the week that followed. First, Steckel said he was going to bench Joey Browner in favor of Carl Lee at safety, and then he decided to waive receiver Terry LeCount because of "attitude problems."

The Vikings were 2-2 after four games and then collapsed. They lost five in a row, defeated Tampa Bay, and lost the last six in increasingly emphatic fashion: 45-17 vs. Green Bay, 42-21 vs. Denver, 34-3 vs. Chicago, 51-17 at San Francisco, and finally, 38-14 to the Packers in the Dome.

In late November, Steckel had a public run-in with Ted Brown and Sammy White, two injured veterans.

They had been watching a Thursday-night game against Washington, a 31-17 loss, from the Metrodome press box, and they left at halftime.

When Steckel learned this, he flipped. The next day, he told Brown and White, in front of the team, that they would be fined and put on injured reserve. He also said he didn't want to see their faces if they showed up for treatment. Then he kicked them out of the Winter Park practice facility.

BUD'S BACK

All this defeat and dissension in the Vikings organization during the 1984 season took place at a time when Lou Holtz was filling the Gophers' long-suffering fans with optimism. He also was filling the Metrodome, while the crowds for the Vikings were slipping.

Lynn later admitted that a big reason he cut his losses and fired Steckel after a single 3-13 season was his worry that the Vikings were in danger of losing the exalted status they held among Minnesota's football fans since the Bud Grant turnaround of 1968.

What better way to get people feeling good about the Vikings than to bring back an old savior?

That's what happened. Lynn fired Steckel on December 17, one day after the season ended with a home loss to the Packers.

"It wouldn't have mattered if we won 55-0," Lynn said. "The win-loss record didn't enter in the decision. We just didn't feel that under Les and his program that this team would succeed in 1985."

White's response? "I'm really shocked about it," the veteran receiver said. "It did show a positive sign overall. I'll tell you, it does brighten the outlook."

Rickey Young said, "I just didn't think he was ready to be a head coach. Unfortunately, I was right. Les, I think, was the sort of person it was his way or no way. He refused to listen to some of the players who had been there."

Again, there was no time to speculate on a replacement. The day after Steckel was fired, the media was summoned to Twin Cities International Airport for the announcement of a new coach.

Lynn and Winter were flying in from a league meeting in New York. Among those who showed up to greet the new coach was Rudy Perpich, Minnesota's governor.

The news conference was scheduled for 10 p.m. It took another half-hour for the coach to make an appearance because he had his attorney looking over the contract before agreeing to the deal.

The cautious new coach was actually the old coach: Bud Grant.

There was relief among the athletes. "I think the players who played for Bud will be very happy," Tommy Kramer said.

Things got so bad during the Les Steckel era that some Vikings fans were ashamed to show their faces at games.
Duane Braley/Star Tribune

Mike Lynn had not done much to help Steckel in the manpower department. He had allowed defensive tackle Keith Millard, the team's first-round choice in 1984, to get away to Jacksonville of the United States Football League.

Grant understood that the team needed to right that wrong. The Vikings paid Jacksonville to allow Millard and his four-year, $1.9 million contract to come to Minnesota. They also selected Chris Doleman, a linebacker/end from Auburn, in the first round of the 1985 draft.

The Vikings were in their fifth (and last) season of a 3-4 defensive front in 1985. Doleman started 13 games as a pass-rushing linebacker. Millard didn't start but played extensively at end and nose tackle. The two wound up playing together on an excellent Vikings defensive front from 1986 through 1989.

Grant's return also came in time for the Vikings' celebration of their 25th season.

On the Saturday night before the season opener, a dinner was held to honor the playing greats from the team's first quarter-century. Grant was scheduled to speak for 10 minutes, but he made it much shorter.

After three minutes, Grant started to choke up and then said, "I wish I could take the hearts of these great players at the head table and implant them into our present players."

Grant's new team showed some of the old fire and forced seven turnovers in a 28-21 victory over San Francisco in the next day's opener. The Vikings were 5-4 after beating the old reliable, Detroit, on November 3.

Then they finished with five losses in seven games for a record of 7-9. The Vikings were out of the playoffs for a third consecutive season. One of the losses came in Atlanta, where a crowd of 14,167 showed up to see the lowly Falcons claim a 14-13 victory.

Linebacker Matt Blair, in his twelfth season with the Vikings, was emotional in the Metrodome locker room following the 37-35 loss to Philadelphia in the season finale.

"This is going to be a great Viking team," he said. "I just would like to know where I fit in, if I fit in."

Grant was asked if he intended to have a conversation with Blair about the linebacker's future. "He would have to ask," Grant said. "Really, it's something he has to decide for himself."

That might sound a bit cold, which was often Bud's style, but the coach had his own plans to worry about. On Decemeber 28, after one season of righting the Vikings from their 3-13 sinking ship to a competitive 7-9, Grant resigned again—and this time for keeps.

It was also the last season for Blair, the five-time All-Pro, as well as for receiver Sammy White, Fran Tarkenton's favorite rookie from way back in 1976.

After the team failed to sign him as a draft pick in 1984, Keith Millard came to Minnesota in 1985 and became a central piece in the formidable frontline under defensive coordinator Floyd Peters. Millard is shown here celebrating one of his eight sacks in 1988.
Brian Peterson/Star Tribune

BUD GRANT

One thing that hasn't changed in the NFL through the years is the tendency for teams to hire a head coach who is the opposite of the person he is replacing. That theory explains why offensive tackle Grady Alderman figured that new coach Bud Grant would have a different demeanor than his predecessor. Grant was hired to replace Norm Van Brocklin, who was fired following the Vikings' 4-9-1 finish in 1966.

Steely-eyed Bud Grant stares intently at the action on the field during a game against the St. Louis Cardinals in October 1981. Quarterback Tommy Kramer is in the background. *Kent Kobersteen/Star Tribune*

"Norm was volatile and up-and-down, so we knew Bud would most likely be different than that," Alderman said. "But the contrast was way more than even we had anticipated. Norm thought he was a motivational guy and he was always after the players. Bud kind of let the players prepare themselves and do what they had to do to try to win a game. That was a lot different. We didn't have nearly as much talking and yelling and screaming on the practice field."

This new approach worked just fine. Grant, a 1994 inductee into the Pro Football Hall of Fame, compiled a 168-108-5 record in 18 seasons as the Vikings coach and led the franchise to four Super Bowls.

Ron Yary played 14 of his 15 NFL seasons under Grant. In a 2001 story on Yary's induction into the Pro Football Hall of Fame, the offensive tackle praised his former coach.

"Fran Tarkenton gave the most accurate, simplest and highest accolade any head coach can receive from an active player when he stated in a conversation among teammates that if you can't play for Bud, you can't play for anyone," Yary said.

Tight end Stu Voigt spent 11 seasons (1970–1980) under Grant in Minnesota. Although he didn't get much initial feedback from the coach, Voigt soon began to understand that wasn't necessarily a negative.

"Bud was more of a delegator," Voigt said, acknowledging Grant wasn't labeled an Xs and Os type of coach. "But he had a way of handling things with little or no conflict. . . . I would say he was a minimalist as a coach. There were no tricks or gadgets or long hours or coaches sleeping in the office. I think that carried over to the rest of the team. We didn't have real high highs or low lows, and that consistency was something the players appreciated."

The visual image that many still have of Grant is that of a stoic coach standing on the sidelines. Alderman said that what many didn't realize is Grant also loved a good practical joke. "He enjoyed that as much as anything but was understated about it," Alderman said. "It was almost as though he didn't need for anybody else to laugh. As long as he knew the joke and got it, that was fine with him."

One legend about Grant that seems to grow each year is his approach to the cold-weather games the Vikings played at the old Metropolitan Stadium in Bloomington. To hear some tell it, Grant would not allow his players any means to keep warm on the sideline.

Alderman laughs at some of those stories.

"I think the myth is bigger than the truth," he said. "It's almost like an urban legend and taken on a life of its own. Talk to some of the players and you will find out they had gloves on the sideline. Players who it was really important to had ways to keep their hands warm. I can't say Bud didn't know that. The coach knows what's going on.

"What Bud didn't want was a big show of things. I remember when [Jets quarterback] Joe Namath was playing in a cold weather game in the 1960s and they made a huge deal of the fact it was cold. When he came off the field he had these huge burnt-orange mittens that went all the way up to his elbow. There he was on the sideline looking like a traffic cop. Bud just didn't like that kind of attention."

Coach Grant is all smiles in December 1984 after he agreed to return to the Vikings as head coach, taking over for Les Steckel.
David Brewster/Star Tribune

Though calm and subdued compared to Norm Van Brocklin, Bud Grant wasn't afraid to get tough with his players. Here he barks out instructions during training camp in 1985, his second stint with the team.
Bruce Bisping/Star Tribune

CHAPTER 7

REBUILDING WITH BURNSIE
1986–1991

During Jim Finks' tenure as general manager from 1964 to 1974, the Vikings had an extremely close organization, from the upper levels to the grass-roots. Finks brought in a couple of Iowa Hawkeyes, Jerry Reichow and Frank Gilliam, to be in charge of college scouting. He embraced Fred Zamberletti as the trainer for life and Stubby Eason as the equipment manager. He hired away Bill McGrane from the *Minneapolis Tribune* to be his public relations director.

Finks was tremendously popular with his employees, the public, and the Twin Cities media. His departure fol-

lowing a fall-out with team president Max Winter was lamented in all those circles.

In contrast to the experienced Finks, his successor Mike Lynn had a flimsy football pedigree. Lynn's close attachment to Winter made the fans and the media very skeptical about the team's new general manager in 1975. Yet, as the years passed, Lynn would show the same loyalty to employees as had Finks.

Reichow and Gilliam continued to run scouting under Lynn. Zamberletti and Eason remained beloved characters. Stubby died of lung cancer in 1981 and was replaced

Jerry Burns led the Vikings back to winning ways in his first season as head coach in 1986. In 1987, he took them to the playoffs after a four-year absence.
Charles Bjorgen/Star Tribune

by Dennis Ryan, who still has that job. McGrane followed Finks to the Chicago Bears, and Lynn hired Merrill Swanson—also a *Minneapolis Tribune* reporter—as the new public relations director. The office staff remained constant year after year. He also was smart enough to treat Bud Grant with proper reverence.

Finks took care of his people and Lynn was no different.

The one notable occasion on which Lynn decided not to reward loyalty was when he hired Les Steckel rather than Jerry Burns to replace Grant.

Steckel had spent five seasons on Grant's staff and was the receivers coach. Burns had spent Grant's entire 17 seasons on the staff and was the offensive coordinator.

The result of the Steckel hire was a one-year, 3-13 disaster and the return of Grant. When Bud decided to end his comeback after a single 7-9 season in 1985, Lynn corrected his earlier mistake by naming Burns as the replacement.

The announcement of the two events—Bud's second retirement and the hiring of Burns—took place simultaneously.

"We went with another person the last time," Lynn said. "That wasn't successful. You can't bat 1,000 percent in anything you do. You can't look back—you have to look forward. We think this is an excellent choice for the future."

Burns would turn 59 years old in January and was three months older than Grant. Yet, he was a professional coach and more interested in preparation than in over-the-top motivational tactics.

A couple of years later, Burns told the *Star Tribune*'s Dan Barreiro, "Les Steckel was a very talented coach from a technical standpoint. But I always felt, 'This guy is the ideal college coach.' If you're a parent and this guy walks into your house, you're going to be impressed. Every facet of his background was made for college."

Burns said that Steckel's failure as a head coach to relate to pros was similar to what Lou Holtz, Burnsie's long-time friend from their days together on the Iowa staff in the 1950s, faced when he went from North Carolina State to the New York Jets in 1976. He lasted 13 games before resigning abruptly to return to the college ranks as coach at Arkansas.

"The way Lou talks, he's great with the alumni, perfect for college," Burns said. "Lou gets with the Jets and he wants to have a Jets fight song and get them to sing in the locker room.

"What the hell? Joe Namath and those guys just wanted to go chase skirts, not sing a fight song. There's a big difference in guys in the pros."

The transition from Grant to Burns was certain to be much smoother than what had taken place two years earlier. What no longer was going smoothly was the rela-

tionship between Lynn and Winter, the man who had brought him to the organization in 1974.

BATTLE FOR CONTROL

In April 1984, Lynn had convinced Winter to give him a $1-million-per-year contract that included wide-ranging powers to run the organization. Winter had regrets about giving this control to Lynn; he decided to sell his share of stock to Irwin Jacobs and Carl Pohlad.

Winter had owned 48 percent of all the stock, but only one-third of the votes among the owners. The other votes belonged to John Skoglund and Jack Steele. They were allies of Lynn and claimed a right of first refusal if Winter's stock was put up for sale.

The internal conflict among the ownership group would continue for years. The issue first went to trial in February 1986. The trial marked the beginning of a nearly six-year legal odyssey that would not end until December 16, 1991, when an ownership group put together by Lynn bought out Jacobs and Pohlad for $50 million (twice what they had paid Winter for the stock).

During this battle, Lynn assembled a group of 10 prominent Minnesotans to buy into the Skoglund and Steele shares and also to get as much available non-voting stock as possible.

As General Manager Mike Lynn increased his control over the operation of the Vikings organization, he became embroiled in a prolonged struggle among the owners. His most memorable move, however, was the disastrous trade for Herschel Walker in 1989.
David Brewster/Star Tribune

In September 1987, Lynn's newly formed board voted 6-3 to oust Winter as team president and to replace him with Wheelock Whitney. "I'm deeply hurt," Winter said.

As the legal fight carried on, there were reversals of decisions favoring both sides in state courts. By the time Pohlad and Jacobs went away, Lynn was also gone. Lynn resigned from the Vikings on October 10, 1990, to become president of the NFL's new European project, the World League of American Football.

More than anything, Lynn was trying to escape all the heat he got from the sporting public and the media for the failed Herschel Walker trade he engineered with Dallas on October 12, 1989.

Lynn installed Roger Headrick, a former General Mills executive, as his replacement, effective January 1, 1991. Headrick was given the title of team president (replacing Whitney) and CEO. As Lynn had back in 1974, Headrick was coming to the Vikings with no football background.

This was now a completely different organization than the one that existed in January 1986 when Burns became the fourth man to serve as head coach of the Vikings.

BURNSIE TAKES CHARGE

Vikings sellouts were not automatic inside the Metrodome in the 1980s, which helped to foster Lynn's fascination with star power.

Before the 1986 draft, Lynn was passing along information that the Vikings might be on the brink of making

Shown here during a loss in 1988, Jerry Burns had many ups and downs as the Vikings' head coach from 1986 to 1991, but during his 18 seasons as offensive coordinator, he pioneered the use of running backs as pass receivers and the strategy of moving the ball up-field with short- and medium-range passes.
Brian Peterson/Star Tribune

a trade for Bo Jackson, the Heisman Trophy-winning running back from Auburn.

Lynn leaked a rumor that he had offered receiver Anthony Carter and defensive end Chris Doleman to Tampa Bay in exchange for their number-one overall pick to give the Vikings a chance to draft Jackson.

The Buccaneers said no, and the Vikings wound up with a much-less ballyhooed Auburn player: defensive end Gerald Robinson. He broke his leg during his rookie season and then suffered a knee injury in 1987, which ended his brief Vikings career.

"A year ago, we tried to get the rights to quarterback Bernie Kosar, who was the top-rated player in the draft," Lynn said. "We failed last year and also this year to get the best player. But we will continue to give it a try every year."

Any time there was a chance to attach the Vikings to a headline athlete, Lynn would go after it. He went so far, in the fall of 1988, to suggest that the Vikings might be willing to give a tryout to Ben Johnson, the Canadian sprinter who returned from the Seoul Olympics in disgrace after testing positive for steroids.

Lynn did make a large move after the 1985 season: He worked out a deal to acquire left tackle Gary Zimmerman from the USFL. Zimmerman played seven seasons in Minnesota and then had a long run in Denver. He was elected to the Pro Football Hall of Fame in February 2008.

"The addition of Zimmerman can't be underestimated," Burns said in May 1986. "The past four or five years, left tackle has been an Achilles' heel to our offense."

Lynn had added Anthony Carter and Keith Millard from the USFL a year earlier. Zimmerman, linebacker David Howard, running back Sam Harrell, and defensive backs David Evans and Mike Lush opened the 1986 season with the Vikings to give the team seven former USFLers.

Lynn said the flow of talent from the USFL was "like we're getting a lot of first-round draft choices within two years."

Lynn had a reputation for being tight-fisted for much of his time with the Vikings. He took considerable criticism for failing to sign Millard originally and for the long holdouts of number-one draft choices such as Darren Nelson and Doug Martin.

It might not be a coincidence that Lynn—in need of positive publicity—started to become much more aggressive with his spending as the legal battles over control of the team were making headlines.

The influx of USFLers and Kramer's offensive slinging brought back some optimism to Vikings' fans for the start of the 1986 season.

Jerry Burns was from Detroit and raised a Lions fan. As a member of Grant's staff, he had been part of the 13-game winning streak against the Lions.

THE WEST COAST OFFENSE IN MINNESOTA

The late Bill Walsh is widely credited with being the innovator of the so-called West Coast offense. This is in large part due to the three Super Bowls his San Francisco 49ers captured the 1980s using a system that featured high-percentage short and medium-range passes that often went to running back Roger Craig.

The 49ers had great success with an offense that allowed for ball control through the air, but they were hardly the first to utilize it. Jerry Burns, the Vikings head coach from 1986 to 1991, created a similar system during his long tenure as Bud Grant's offensive coordinator that started in 1968.

"We never tried to put any special name on the offense," said offensive tackle Grady Alderman, who played for the Vikings from 1961 to 1974. "What we were doing was the best we could at taking what the other team gave us. The easy stuff. We didn't think we had to throw the ball down the field 80 yards like Oakland. We were content to march it down, taking 3, 4, 5 yards at a time."

This strategy became even more effective after the Vikings re-acquired quarterback Fran Tarkenton from the New York Giants in 1972 and selected running back Chuck Foreman with their first-round draft choice a year later.

"Using the running back as a receiver, that was Jerry," said tight end Stu Voigt, a member of the Vikings from 1970 to 1980. "And really where the Vikings offense showed that was with Foreman. He was one of the first guys who was not just a runner but also a talented receiver. Bill Brown was a heck of a receiver, but Foreman could really utilize that offense. . . . Tarkenton, because he did not have an incredibly strong arm, was into that approach."

In a 2000 interview, Grant commented, "Throwing to the backs wasn't a big thing in NFL offense until the Vikings started doing it. The idea was to clear out the defense and get the ball to someone who could beat somebody. We did that early on, and then more with Chuck Foreman."

During his rookie season, Foreman finished second on the Vikings with 37 catches. He then led the team in receptions each of the next three years with a combined 181 catches. This included a career-high 73 receptions as the Vikings went 12-2 in 1975.

Over the next seven seasons, a running back led Minnesota in receiving four times. Rickey Young's 88 catches in 1978 still stands as the franchise's single-season mark for a running back.

Voigt was an analyst on Vikings radio broadcasts in the 1980s when the 49ers began having their success.

"I was watching all of this as a broadcaster and there was no question the 49ers were a dominant team," he said. "I was looking at it and saying, 'Yeah, it seems like kind of the same system.' Then they put the West Coast name to it and the 49ers put the Super Bowl trophies on the wall. The Vikings didn't. The ones who put it to the highest and best use was the 49ers, but it looked like the exact same thing to me."

The Tarkenton-to-Foreman Minnesota connection in the 1970s epitomized the so-called West Coast offense before Bill Walsh made it famous in San Francisco. Here Tark delivers a short pass to his running back in a game against Denver in September 1978.
Bruce Bisping/Star Tribune

The acquisition of tackle Gary Zimmerman—wearing number 65 and shown here with his fellow linemen in 1988—from the USFL did much to fortify the Vikings offensive line. He spent seven seasons of his Hall of Fame career in Minnesota.
Brian Peterson/Star Tribune

Burns' first game as head coach was a 13-10 loss to Detroit in the Metrodome. The Lions won by giving the ball to running back James Jones 36 times, which he used to gain 174 yards. They had the ball for 37½ of the 60 minutes.

This loss would prove to be something of an aberration for Burns. His Vikings would not lose again to Detroit until 1990—a seven-game winning streak.

But that 1986 opener hurt Burnsie and his players. "It's a sad day in Mudville," linebacker Scott Studwell said. "I hope we realize there are 15 games left."

They won the next game, 23-10, over Tampa Bay, despite the fact that Kramer completed only 9 of 21 passes for 130 yards and had several overthrows of open receivers.

"For us to go where we want to go, be a playoff-contending team, he has to play better," Burns said.

This struggle was the start of an ongoing quarterback saga that hounded Burns through his first four seasons: Tommy Kramer or Wade Wilson?

Kramer's injuries, along with time spent very publicly in chemical dependency treatment, would give Wilson several chances to take the job. The battle between the two generated a lot of tension. Whenever Wilson got the start, Kramer was mad about it. Then, after Wilson had his tremendous run during the playoffs following the 1987 season, he would get upset whenever Burns went back to Kramer.

Three games into Burnsie's tenure, Kramer led Minnesota to a 31-7 victory over Pittsburgh. Still angry about his head coach's comments following the Tampa Bay game, Kramer said, "I don't think he needed to say

that to the press when he could've said it to me. I think I was at that [playoff-contending] level today."

A week later, Kramer threw for six touchdowns in a 42-7 victory over Green Bay in the Metrodome. It was such a blowout that he was pulled from the game after throwing number six early in the third quarter.

Kramer said he told offensive coordinator Bob Schnelker, "Come on, I want to get the NFL record."

Schnelker said, "Save it for a bigger game."

(The record of seven touchdown passes was shared by Joe Kapp, set in a game against Baltimore in September 1969 at Met Stadium.)

The public's appreciation for Kramer took a blow a few days later. Stories had circulated widely about Kramer's fondness for late nights and malt beverages from his early days with the Vikings.

Then, on a Friday morning in early October before a game against the Bears, he went on a previously arranged interview with a Chicago radio station. The tape became infamous. The interview was at 8:30 a.m. and Kramer was slurring his words to the extent that he sounded inebriated.

Kramer and his wife, Carrie, both claimed that it was because he was "dead tired" after being up through the night with their two-year-old daughter.

Whatever the cause, the Vikings went to Soldier Field, lost 23-0, and Kramer's nocturnal habits became a public issue.

In week nine of the 1986 season, Kramer passed for four touchdowns and a team-record 490 yards, and yet the Vikings lost 44-38 in overtime to the Redskins in Washington.

Burns had changed his opinion of Kramer considerably from the second week of the season. "I can't think of a quarterback playing better," the coach said.

The Vikings were 6-4 and looking good for a playoff spot heading into a home game against the New York Giants on November 16. They lost 22-20 after Giants quarterback Phil Simms completed a 22-yard pass to Bobby Johnson on fourth-and-17 with under two minutes to play. That conversion set up a winning field goal by Raul Allegre.

Kramer had to leave the game after he got his right thumb caught in Lawrence Taylor's facemask. He missed three starts, and the Vikings finished the season at 9-7 to miss the playoffs for the fifth time in six seasons.

BURNSIE'S BOYS MAKE A RUN

The 1987 season might rate as the wackiest in Minnesota Vikings history. It started with an embarrassing run of DWI arrests involving Vikings players, which got a huge amount of attention from the media. In August, both quarterback Kramer and cornerback Issiac Holt were at the Hazelden chemical dependency facility in Center City, Minnesota.

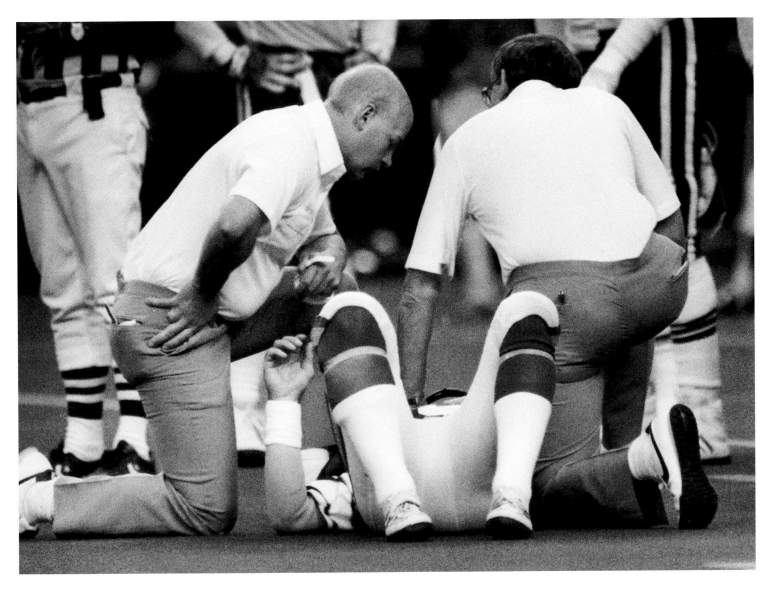

Kramer was arrested in late July in Bloomington. His lawyer released a statement saying that Kramer planned to voluntarily enter a rehabilitation program.

He had gone through treatment in Orange, California, in 1982. That time, the Vikings basically made a PR campaign out of it and held a press conference with Kramer in attendance. They encouraged fans to send messages of support to the then-young quarterback.

This time, Kramer talked to reporters on the day he headed for Hazelden. He wouldn't be rejoining the Vikings until August 23, after the second exhibition game.

Burns' second season also included a players strike that cost the Vikings three losses in replacement games. The season featured an upset run in the playoffs that put the Vikings on the cusp of a return to the Super Bowl.

It wasn't a late arrival from alcoholism treatment, but a pinched nerve in his neck that kept Kramer out of the season opener.

Wade Wilson had a horrendous first half against Detroit. He threw three interceptions and put the Vikings in a 16-10 hole. Wilson, the people's choice during Kramer's struggles in prior seasons, was now hearing the Metrodome boos.

Then, Wilson hit Anthony Carter with a 73-yard touchdown pass midway through the third quarter and triggered a 24-point explosion that gave the Vikings a 34-19 victory over the Lions.

Minnesota won again the next week, 21-16 over the Rams in Los Angeles. Then came the players strike. The NFL cancelled the games of September 27 and then resumed play with strike-breakers on October 4.

The Vikings were slow to sign these replacement players. Six days before the first scheduled strike game, Lynn asked the Vikings to return en masse to play the October 4 game against the Green Bay Packers.

A pinched nerve suffered in a preseason game sidelined Tommy Kramer for much of 1987, although he regained his job from Wade Wilson for five starts in the second half of the season.
Brian Peterson/Star Tribune

If the players wouldn't come back, Lynn asked the veterans to allow the seven rookies on the roster—including quarterback Rich Gannon and running back D. J. Dozier—to play for the strike team.

"He was looking for viable alternatives to win the game," said Steve Jordan, the Vikings tight end and union representative. "We made it clear it couldn't happen. Nobody's crossing the picket lines."

The Vikings wound up with Tony Adams, a paunchy 37-year-old who had not played since 1981 in Canada, as their quarterback for the strike games. They lost to the Packers 23-16 in front of 13,911 fans in the Metrodome and then went on the road to lose 27-7 to the pseudo-Bears and 20-10 to the pseudo-Buccaneers.

The strike ended on October 15 when the players association gave up their demand for 55 percent of gross revenues. Instead, they filed an antitrust suit against the NFL in federal court.

Dozens of players had started to return to their teams, and the strike was falling apart. The Vikings were one of the few teams to remain unified throughout the strike.

The Vikings were offering replacement football at the same time that the Twins were becoming World Series-winning heroes. It had been a couple of decades since the Vikings were in such an inferior position when it came to popularity with the Minnesota sporting public.

The real Vikings returned to competition in a Monday-night game against Denver on October 27. The Vikings won a 34-27 shootout to give Minnesota's NFLers a 3-0 record, but officially they were 3-3 in the standings.

The loudest cheer of the first half came when an announcement appeared on the Dome scoreboards congratulating the Twins on their World Series championship. There were boos for Wilson, who threw five interceptions, but big cheers for a number of explosive plays—including a 72-yard touchdown run by Darren Nelson.

A loss to Seattle followed in week seven, and Burns went back to Kramer as his starting quarterback. The Los Angeles Raiders sacked him four times early in the next game. Kramer reinjured his neck, and Wilson relieved him to spark a 31-20 victory.

Wilson and Kramer would share a musical-quarterbacks situation for the next three seasons. No matter Wilson's hot streaks, there was always the impression among Vikings' followers that Burns had more confidence in Kramer.

The Vikings of the Burnsie years were known for their erratic ways both on and off the field, yet those teams had some hard-nosed competitors. One such player was center Kirk Lowdermilk, who had spent two years as the backup to veteran Dennis Swilley before moving into the starting lineup in 1987.

On November 15, 1987, the Vikings were playing the Buccaneers in Tampa Bay. Lowdermilk sprained a ligament in his left knee early in the game and was replaced by Swilley. Then, Swilley suffered a broken leg. Lowdermilk took the ice bag off his knee and insisted on returning to the lineup.

Dave Huffman, the starting left guard, said of Lowdermilk's effort, "It was like taking out a platoon of Germans."

The Vikings put together a four-game winning streak that concluded with a 44-38 overtime victory in Dallas. Anthony Carter caught eight passes for 184 yards and two touchdowns. It was a preview of what the Vikings would see from Carter in the playoffs. The Vikings regulars were 7-1 at that time and were awaiting a visit by Mike Ditka and the Chicago Bears on December 6.

At a press conference in Chicago that week, Ditka had referred to the Metrodome as the Rollerdome. "I just don't like indoor football," he said. "Indoor domes should be used for roller rinks."

Mike Lynn couldn't pass on this opportunity, of course. He had the Vikings cheerleaders on roller skates for the game.

The Vikings were leading 24-23 in the fourth quarter when Chicago quarterback Mike Tomczak threw a 38-yard touchdown pass to Dennis Gentry with 40 seconds remaining. The win clinched a fourth-straight NFC Central Division title for the Bears.

It was also the start of a schedule-ending streak of three losses in four games for Minnesota. The Vikings lost 27-24 in overtime to Washington in a Saturday game in the final week of the regular season. That put them at 8-7 in a season that included three replacement losses and one cancelled game.

The Vikings' only chance to make the playoffs after that loss was for St. Louis to lose against Dallas. "I'm not comfortable with the Cowboys winning for us, but they're all the hope we got," Darren Nelson said.

The Cardinals did lose, 21-16, and the Vikings became indignant when media members suggested that they had backed into the playoffs. The Vikings had a point, since the record of the "real" players was 8-4.

"I've always been a Cowboys fan," Burns said, satirically. "They are America's team."

That was on Sunday night. A day later, Burns ripped into the local media with a profanity-laced tirade. "You [reporters] come up with the same [stuff] all the time," he said. "Killer instinct. Backing into the championship. You're flat.

"I told the team, 'You're 8-7 and St. Louis is 7-8. The 10 best teams got in the playoffs and we're one of them.'"

The Vikings went to New Orleans for the first-round playoff game. The Saints, now run by former Vikings general manager Jim Finks, ended their two decades of futil-

In the first-round playoff game at New Orleans on January 3, 1988, Anthony Carter's 84-yard punt return (an NFL playoff record) gave the Vikings a 10-7 first-quarter lead. Carter finished with 143 yards (also a record) on six punt returns, while gaining an additional 79 yards on pass receptions.
AP/Wide World Photos

ity with an explosive season in 1987 and their first trip to the playoffs in franchise history. The constant refrain in the Superdome was, "Who dat? Who dat say dey gonna beat dem Saints?"

Anthony Carter had an 84-yard punt return in the first quarter to give the Vikings a 10-7 lead. He finished with 143 yards on six punt returns and six receptions for 79 yards and a touchdown.

Burns used all three quarterbacks in the game—Kramer, Wilson, and Gannon—and all directed scoring drives. Wilson threw a "Hail Mary" pass that Hassan

Jones caught for a touchdown at the end of the first half. The Vikings amassed 417 yards of offense, compared to 149 for the Saints. The defense had four interceptions against Bobby Hebert.

The final score was 44-10 in the Vikings' favor. "Who dat goin' home for six months?" Carter said after the game.

The Vikings next traveled to San Francisco to play the 49ers in a Saturday game. Ditka, the division rival coach, predicted, "Minnesota will beat San Francisco. They are a better team all around."

Tight end Steve Jordan, defensive tackle Keith Millard, and quarterback Wade Wilson celebrate their 36-24 playoff win over San Francisco on January 9, 1988. Next stop, Washington for the conference championship. *Jeff Wheeler/Star Tribune*

He was correct. The Vikings whipped San Francisco, 36-24, and did so in such convincing fashion that quarterback Joe Montana, the 49ers icon, was booed off the field by the Candlestick Park crowd. He was replaced by Steve Young in the second half, but it was too late.

The Vikings had a 20-3 lead at halftime, aided by a 45-yard interception return for a touchdown by Reggie Rutland (later Najee Mustafaa). Anthony Carter was unbelievable in the game and set an NFL playoff record with 227 receiving yards on 10 catches.

A delegation of Vikings supporters was sitting low in the stands, and as the visitors headed for the locker room, the fans shouted, "Super Bowl! Super Bowl!"

Steve Jordan looked over and yelled, "Yeah, that's it! That's it!"

The remaining obstacle was the Washington Redskins, whom the Vikings would face in the NFC championship game in RFK Stadium. This Redskins team had beaten Burns' Vikings in 1986 and in the last regular season of 1987, both in overtime.

The Redskins were able to contain Minnesota's explosive offense. They had eight sacks against Wilson, the red-hot playoff quarterback.

Still, the Vikings were within a touchdown, 17-10, when they took control of the ball at their 33-yard line with

five minutes remaining. Wilson completed five passes for 49 yards, and the Vikings reached the Redskins' 6-yard line on fourth down.

Wilson swung a pass to Nelson at the goal line. Darrell Green, Washington's Hall of Fame cornerback, arrived an instant after the ball and banged into Nelson. The ball came loose.

The Vikings were 17-10 losers. Nelson's drop—even though it was more Green's hit—took its place in Vikings' infamy.

"I got hit right when I grabbed it," Nelson said. "Then, it was knocked loose."

Burns said: "We got close, but we couldn't ring the bell."

Burns was part of six Super Bowl teams—two as an assistant to Vince Lombardi in Green Bay, four with Grant in Minnesota—but this would prove to be his one real shot to get there as a head coach.

THE WILSON-KRAMER SAGA CONTINUES

The big excitement that Lynn had planned for the Vikings in 1988 was a trip to Goteborg, Sweden, to play the Bears in an exhibition game. The Vikings won that game—the first of three victories they would have over Ditka's Bears in the calendar year.

Wade Wilson (left) and Tommy Kramer both had their eyes on the starting QB job at training camp before the 1988 season.
Brian Peterson/Star Tribune

Earlier in 1988, the Vikings found a great player with the 19th pick in the first round of the draft: Randall McDaniel, a left guard from Arizona State. Years later, Vikings Coach Mike Tice would describe McDaniel as the only unbeaten football player he had ever been around—meaning, no matter a game's outcome, McDaniel always won his matchup.

Burns announced in the week before the 1988 season opener that Wilson, the hot hand from the January playoff run, would be his starting quarterback. Kramer showed his anger by saying, "All I can say is when [Wilson] screws up, that'll be the last chance he gets to play."

The Vikings lost 13-10 at Buffalo. Wilson came up with a sore shoulder and Kramer was back in the lineup. The result was consecutive victories over New England and Chicago in which the Vikings outscored those opponents by a combined 67-13.

The front four of Doug Martin, Henry Thomas, Keith Millard, and Chris Doleman had become a force of massive pressure under defensive coordinator Floyd Peters. They also had Al (Bubba) Baker as a pass-rushing specialist.

Kramer had a horrendous first half against Green Bay in week seven, and Wilson reclaimed his starting job. The Vikings responded with a 49-20 victory at Tampa Bay, a game in which Wilson threw for 249 yards and three touchdowns—in the first half.

A week later, on October 30, the Vikings lost 24-21 at San Francisco. Niners quarterback Steve Young made a game-winning, zig-zagging, 49-yard touchdown run that still can be found on NFL highlight shows.

Wade Wilson goes down hard during the 34-9 thrashing by San Francisco in the second round of the playoffs on January 1, 1989. The quarterback was sacked five times in the game.
Brian Peterson/Star Tribune

"I thought we had him sacked," Burns said. "A guy missed him fractionally here, fractionally there. Next thing you know, he's in the end zone."

The Vikings put together a five-game winning streak after that. They finished the season winning six of seven, including another victory over the Bears, 28-27, at the Metrodome in the season finale. The Bears were on the way to a winning touchdown when linebacker Walker Lee Ashley intercepted a Mike Tomczak pass and returned it 94 yards for a Vikings touchdown.

Minnesota was set to host a playoff game for the first time since January 1983. The opponents were a familiar postseason foe from the 1970s: the Los Angeles Rams.

The Rams' first two drives in the NFC Wild Card game ended with safety Joey Browner intercepting Jim Everett passes. The Vikings dominated on defense and cruised to a 28-17 victory.

Peters, the defensive coordinator, said of Browner, "I really feel I'm associated with a future Hall of Famer."

The win sent the Vikings to San Francisco for a rematch of the previous season's second-round playoff game. This time, there were only cheers for Joe Montana from the Candlestick Park crowd.

Jerry Rice caught three touchdown passes in the game. Roger Craig rushed for 135 yards. Wilson was sacked six times. The final was 34-9 for San Francisco.

Asked what the difference was from the Vikings' victory over San Francisco a year earlier, linebacker Scott Studwell said, "We got our rear ends handed to us. That was the difference."

LYNN GETS HIS SUPERSTAR

In 1989, Minnesota finally got its first Super Bowl victory. Unfortunately, it came in the spring—May 24—when the 1992 Super Bowl was awarded to the Metrodome.

Mike Lynn had steered the NFL toward a decision to play the 1992 game in the nation's northern tier, and the Twin Cities beat out Detroit (the 1982 host) and Seattle for the honors.

The efforts to get the Super Bowl in Minnesota didn't provide the only headlines of the offseason. The Vikings continued to create bad news with their off-field behavior. Keith Millard was home in the Seattle area in March when he was arrested for drunken driving.

A week later, when Millard was being charged, he told police they had the wrong guy. The cops insisted they had the right 6-foot-5, 270-pound man.

Despite the off-field problems, the Vikings were a popular choice in preseason forecasts to represent the NFC in the Super Bowl. The addition of Mike Meriweather as a pass-rushing linebacker was supposed to make the pass rush even more ferocious.

It did. The Vikings would record 71 sacks—including 21 by Doleman and 18 by Millard—for 502 yards in losses during the 1989 season.

Yet, the team started 1-2, and when Burns said of Wade Wilson, "I think he has to play better if we're going to be successful," it was Wilson (not Kramer) who was upset with the coach.

He criticized Burns for going to the press, not him.

Just to make things interesting, Browner went on ESPN—that newfangled all-sports network—in early October and accused Lynn of racism when it came to contract negotiations. Three days later, he rescinded the remark, but Lynn saw too many bad vibes around his alleged Super Bowl contenders.

He decided to take the plunge and get his superstar.

On October 12, running back Herschel Walker was acquired from the Dallas Cowboys for five players and a first-round draft choice in 1992. The Cowboys also had the option to release the five players and receive draft choices in their stead.

That was coach Jimmy Johnson's strategy all along, although Lynn tried to undersell that part of the deal to Minnesotans. In the end, the Vikings would give up first- and- second rounders in 1990 and 1991, and the first-, second-, and third-rounders in 1992. (Johnson and the Cowboys used those picks to help build a Super Bowl dynasty in the 1990s.)

There was no whining about the trade on that first Sunday in the Dome. The Packers came to town and Walker ripped them up for 148 yards on 18 carries. No Vikings running back had rushed for 100 yards in the previous 30 games.

Walker's first carry against Green Bay was the famous 47-yarder on which he lost his right shoe. Everyone was giddy after the 26-14 victory.

"Herschel Walker is the 'Running Man'," Kirk Lowdermilk said. "Unbelievable. Give him a crack and he'll go."

That would turn out to be his big game. The Vikings went 7-4 with Walker in the lineup to finish the season at 10-6. The record gave them the Central Division title for the first time since 1980.

On the day of the trade, Lynn had said, "If we don't win the Central Division, if we go to the Super Bowl and if we don't win the Super Bowl while Herschel Walker is here, then we have not made a good trade."

Lynn only got the first part of that formula right. For the third straight year, the Vikings headed to San Francisco for a playoff game. For the second time in a row, it was a 49ers blowout—41-13.

This was a Vikings team with seven Pro Bowlers, not including Walker, Lynn's new star running back.

Lynn tried to maintain a stiff upper lip in the wake of the blowout. "We're not going to judge this team by one game," he said.

LYNN STEPS ASIDE

Mike Lynn was never short of ideas. His plan to bring the Vikings together as a team—and to make them more responsible when out in public—was to take them to the Pecos River Learning Center in New Mexico before the 1990 season.

This was a new-age team-building exercise where Vikings players and officials would save one another from falling off cliffs and the like.

Herschel Walker soars over the line for extra yards against Tampa Bay on November 12, 1989. He rushed for 669 yards in 11 games during his first season with Minnesota.
Focus On Sport/Getty Images

"It was an exciting experience for us," Lynn said. "I think the experience already has helped this team."

Lynn was more aggressive in signing his veterans to lucrative contracts than he had been previously after singing around the campfire in New Mexico.

The Vikings received no significant help in the 1990 draft because of the Walker trade, but on September 4—five days before the season opener—they made a move that eventually would have tremendous impact on the franchise.

Lynn put a $100 waiver claim on Cris Carter, a fourth-year receiver who had been released by the Philadelphia Eagles. The quote from Philadelphia Coach Buddy Ryan— "All he does is catch touchdowns"—gained notoriety, although the real reason behind Carter's departure was his drug problem, as he later admitted.

The Vikings also claimed kicker Donald Igwebuike from Tampa Bay. Igwebuike was later indicted as part of a Florida drug-smuggling ring, although he was acquitted. He would kick for Minnesota for only one season before being replaced by Fuad Reveiz.

Tommy Kramer was dropped before the season and wound up as a backup in New Orleans. Wade Wilson suffered a torn ligament in his throwing hand. That left Rich Gannon, in his fourth season with the Vikings, to make 12 of the 16 starts at quarterback.

The Vikings split their first two games of the 1990 season—including a 32-3 blowout over New Orleans— then lost five in a row. The crowds in the Metrodome turned hostile.

Sports talk shows had started gaining popularity in the Twin Cities, although not with Burns.

"After a game, the host is on there, and Joe Blow from Wanamingo rips the [stuff] out of us, and we have no recourse," the coach said. "Nobody knows what this guy is talking about, but he has the soap box."

Lynn announced in early October that he planned to leave the Vikings at the end of the season to run the NFL's effort to establish American football in Europe, the World League of American Football.

When his team was sitting at 1-5, Burns was asked if he was considering retirement.

Burns said, "Yeah, maybe."

So, he might leave at season's end?

"I'm not saying nothing."

Several Vikings fans showed up with paper bags on their heads (a gimmick stolen from Saints fans) when Minnesota hosted Denver in a Sunday-night game on November 4.

The Vikings fell behind 16-0 in the first half and the boos were deafening. Then they rallied for a 27-22 victory.

The Carter duo—Cris (left) and Anthony (right)—provided a versatile and dangerous (for the opposition) receiver combination for four seasons. At training camp in 1990, the Carters were focused on mastering the offensive sets. *John Croft/Star Tribune*

The come-from-behind win over Denver was the start of a five-game winning streak that pushed the Vikings to 6-6 and in strong position for the playoffs. Five losses, five wins—now what?

Unfortunately for the Purple faithful, it was four straight losses. They closed the season at 6-10—the first non-winning record in Burns' five seasons as head coach.

One large problem was a knee injury that ruined Millard's run as a dominant player. Without him rushing from the inside, Doleman faced constant double-teams, and the Vikings' sack total dropped from 71 in 1989 to 47 in 1990.

Lynn moved out of his office and Roger Headrick moved in on January 1, 1991. Lynn had been the Vikings' lead man for getting the Metrodome built. He was the main force in landing a Super Bowl for Minnesota. He got along famously with Grant, Burns, and his front-office employees, and he was relentless in trying to maneuver the Vikings back to a Super Bowl in the 1980s.

Yet, Mike Lynn is better remembered for disasters: For the sorry outcome to the Walker trade, for announcing he was going to sign convicted rapist Mossy Cade in November 1988 (and changing his mind quickly when the outcry came), and for pushing aside team founder Max Winter at the start of the long-running ownership battle.

Headrick's first big issue as the team's new president and CEO was what to do with Herschel Walker. The running back finally signed with the Vikings in June for one season and $1.7 million.

For some people, the biggest news of the offseason was the addition of retired pro wrestler Jesse Ventura to the Vikings radio team. Jesse already was the mayor of Brooklyn Park and eventually would "shock the world" by winning the election for Minnesota governor.

Burns did make one change: He fired Floyd Peters—who had received much of the credit when the Vikings defense was overrunning quarterbacks and much of the blame when they weren't—and brought in Monte Kiffin as his new defensive coordinator.

A year earlier, Burns had put Tom Moore in charge of the offense over Bob Schnelker, the offensive coordinator that he had defended so vigorously in earlier seasons.

It was a dreary 8-8 season. The Vikings were 6-7 entering December, and Burns made a vague comment about coaching his final three games.

Reporters thought about this for a time and then contacted the public relations staff to ask if Burns was talking about the final games of the season or of his career.

"Tell them, 'Of my life,'" was Burnsie's response.

So, the two great characters of the post-Grant era—Jerry Burns and Mike Lynn—were gone and with them departed the stability that had marked the front office for more than a decade.

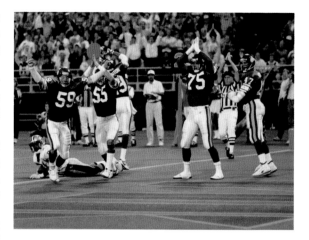

The Vikings defense celebrates after tackling New Orleans running back Dalton Hilliard in his own end zone for a safety during Minnesota's 32-3 victory in week two of the 1990 season.
John Croft/Star Tribune

Although Herschel Walker led the NFL with 2,051 all-purpose yards in 1990, it was becoming clear that the superstar wasn't going to carry the Vikings to the promised land. Here he is stopped cold by Oakland defenders during a 28-24 loss in the next-to-last game of the 1990 season. *Star Tribune*

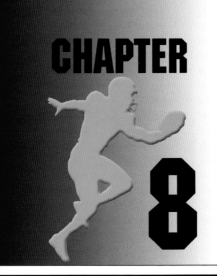

CHAPTER 8

THE SHERIFF
1992–1997

On January 10, 1992, the Vikings introduced former Northwestern and Stanford coach Dennis Green as Jerry Burns' replacement.

Green introduced himself with the statement, "There's a new sheriff in town."

That statement was in reference to what was perceived to be an undisciplined group of characters under Burns. It produced an immediate nickname for Green, "The Sheriff," and ushered in a honeymoon period during which Green would experience immediate success and popularity by turning around what was an underachieving team in 1991.

The Sheriff was chosen by Vikings president Roger Headrick from an intriguing field of candidates that included New York Jets defensive coordinator Pete Carroll, 49ers offensive coordinator Mike Holmgren, and University of Louisville coach Howard Schnellenberger.

The final decision came down to Carroll and Green, and Headrick chose to make the 42-year-old Green the second black head coach in the history of the National Football League, after Oakland's Art Shell.

Green's teams had struggled at Northwestern, but he had taken Stanford to a bowl victory and had coached Jerry Rice when Green was the 49ers' receivers coach.

The new sheriff, Dennis Green, is announced as the head coach in January 1992, with team president Roger Headrick at his side. Over the next 10 seasons, Green would lead the Vikings through their share of highs and lows.
Jeff Wheeler/Star Tribune

Known as a taskmaster in college, Green promised to rejuvenate a Vikings team filled with current and former Pro-Bowl players who had lagged in 1991.

"I know we have some tremendous talent," he said. "This franchise had some great years in the eighties, and we look forward to some championship teams in the nineties. The thing I want to do is bring some strong leadership to this team....This is not a team that has a 2-14 record."

Headrick, after making his first major decision as the Vikings' unquestioned decision-maker, said, "I'm proud. Not because of his race but because of the man."

Headrick indicated that he chose Green over Carroll because of Green's forceful personality and his head coaching experience. Headrick also said he valued the viewpoint of a coach who had never been affiliated with the Vikings. Carroll had worked as a Vikings secondary coach from 1985 to 1989. Green was the first Vikings head coach hired from outside the organization since 1967 when they brought in Bud Grant.

"He can come in here with the ability not to be bound by the past," Headrick said. "This team needed change. It needed something to give it an impetus to turn things around. He is the guy. He's a winner."

Green had a 16-18 record at Stanford and was 10-45 at Northwestern, where he was the Big Ten's first black head coach. "Those are not football factories," Headrick said. "Northwestern and Stanford are places that stress academics as well, and Dennis did a great job with that, too."

During the coaching search, Green had received support from NFL commissioner Paul Tagliabue, NFL Players Association leader Gene Upshaw, former 49ers coach Bill Walsh, and former 49ers halfback O. J. Simpson.

Green's hiring was met with positive reviews in a *Star Tribune* column: "You do not have to be a football person to make this decision. . . . Green, 42, has been a Division I-A college head coach for eight seasons. Carroll, 40, never has been a head coach. Green comes with the strong endorsement of Bill Walsh. Carroll comes with the strong endorsement of Bruce Coslet. Green will provide the objective view of an outsider to the Vikings roster. Carroll is only two seasons removed from being employed as the Vikings secondary coach. . . . If the choice is between Carroll and Green, there is no way Pete's credentials can be considered comparable."

Columnist Dan Barreiro agreed. "If you want to know the most encouraging thing about the Vikings handing over the team to Green, this is it. It was time—past time, actually—to bring in a coach who grew up in another organization and could view the Vikings with a hard, objective eye."

Green agreed to a five-year contract with the Vikings and began assembling what would become the most talented NFL coaching staff in recent history.

For his defensive coordinator, Green chose Tony Dungy, the former Steelers defensive coordinator who was then coaching the Chiefs' secondary. Monte Kiffin—who with Dungy later became known as the father of the Tampa-2 defense, and perhaps one of the great defensive coordinators of all time—became the linebackers coach. Willie Shaw, who would become a defensive coordinator with the Oakland Raiders and later the Vikings, was Green's secondary coach. John Teerlinck, who later joined Dungy's staff in Indianapolis, coached the defensive line.

From 1992 to 1995, the defense was under the guidance of defensive coordinator Tony Dungy. A former star quarterback for the University of Minnesota, Dungy helped to build the NFL's top-ranked defense with the Vikings.
Jerry Holt/Star Tribune

Linebacker Ed McDaniel was the Vikings' fifth-round draft pick in 1992. By his third season, he was a regular starter and putting fear into the eyes of opposing quarterbacks, such as Green Bay's Brett Favre.
Brian Peterson/Star Tribune

On the other side of the field, Jack Burns was Green's offensive coordinator and quarterbacks coach. Tom Moore, who had been an assistant head coach/offense under Jerry Burns, coached the receivers. (Moore later worked as Dungy's offensive coordinator for the Super Bowl champion Indianapolis Colts in 2006.) Future Notre Dame and University of Washington coach Tyrone Willingham coached the running backs. Brian Billick, who would win a Super Bowl as coach of the Baltimore Ravens, coached the tight ends.

With the Vikings, Green worked with two fellow Iowa alums: Director of Football Operations Jerry Reichow and Director of Player Personnel Frank Gilliam.

The Sheriff made a positive first impression. "Our objective in 1992 will be to make the playoffs," he said. "I don't think we need to rebuild. I'm not very happy in that kind of situation. I don't think we're in dire straits. I think we need to get back into the playoffs next year and then go every year."

Green said his new players shouldn't cringe at his forcefulness. "I come across as being aggressive," he said. "But I'm really a nice guy."

Thus began one of the most tumultuous coaching reigns in Minnesota coaching history.

REMAKING THE FRANCHISE

More than a month after Headrick hired Green, questions about Headrick's independence and authority were answered. Former general manager Mike Lynn sold his interest in the team, and the NFL approved the sale of stock owned by local business icons Carl Pohlad and Irwin Jacobs.

"It's all over," Lynn said, ending an 18-year relationship with the franchise. "The parting was fine. I would assume that everybody is delighted with the results."

Lynn sold his 10 percent interest back to the team and the nine remaining primary owners would be equal partners.

The Vikings' ownership structure and its internal disputes had caused concern in the front office of the organization and with the NFL office since 1986, when Pohlad and Jacobs purchased 51 percent of the team's stock (voting and non-voting) and challenged Lynn's authority.

Pohlad and Jacobs sued Lynn for wrongfully control-ling two-thirds of the team's voting stock through his allegiance with the Skoglund and Boyer families. In effect, he had control of the franchise. The litigation was halted only when Pohlad and Jacobs agreed in December 1991 to sell their stock to the Vikings' current ownership for $50 million.

NFL owners approved the structure of the Vikings' new ownership in 1992. The ownership group was now led by Headrick. The moves put an end to six years of turbulence in the team's front office and erased con-cerns held by some Vikings fans that Lynn would return to power and that the current ownership would remain in flux, leaving the franchise without stable leadership.

Green was making similarly meaningful changes in the way the Vikings ran their football operation on the field.

Under Jerry Burns, Vikings coaches had felt com-pelled to use Herschel Walker as a primary focus of their offense. Green, best known in the NFL for his association with the great Jerry Rice, immediately made it clear that he had more interest in the Vikings' veteran receivers: Anthony Carter, Cris Carter, and Hassan Jones.

In his first venture in Plan B free agency, Green made a killing. He signed Cowboys linebacker Jack Del Rio, Raiders running back Roger Craig, and Seahawks tight end Mike Tice.

Del Rio immediately became the starting middle line-backer. Craig became a locker-room leader and backup, and Tice became a key H-back in a system based on the Washington Redskins' popular offense.

Green traded dynamic defensive tackle Keith Millard to Seattle for two high draft picks, and he released starting quarterback Wade Wilson and thus made Rich Gannon the de facto starter. The Vikings also released popular safety Joey Browner, who had refused to attend a mini-camp.

Then, in a move that put even more distance between the new head coach and the previous regime, Green and the front office relinquished the rights to Herschel Walker and allowed him to become a free agent.

"I think it's time to move on—for the Vikings, and for Herschel," said Vikings executive Jeff Diamond.

The Vikings had a record of 27-17 in the 44 games preceding the Walker deal; they went 21-23 in the 44 games after the deal.

The team capitalized on Green's popularity and the roster turnover with a couple of television ads. The first began with a receptionist sitting in the Vikings offices and answering phone calls from fans.

"Mr. Walker is no longer with us," she said to one caller.

"Mr. Millard is pursuing opportunities in Seattle," she said to another.

"Coach Green thought he could use a change of scenery," she said.

Then, taking a final call, she said, "No, we booted his butt, too."

In the other ad, the viewer, from a peering-through-the-facemask player's perspective, sees an actor por-traying Coach Dennis Green approaching on a practice field. Green grabs the player's helmet and twists until the player is facing the goalpost. Green points at the goalpost and the player obediently nods his head.

The point: The Vikings players had not had their heads screwed on straight until Green arrived.

That might have seemed presumptuous, but the Vikings did outscore their opponents 140-6 in the pre-season without allowing a touchdown or throwing an interception. "We're a better team than we were last year, that's for sure," Gannon said.

Even before coaching his first regular-season game, the Sheriff was in control.

Under Coach Green's tutelage, Cris Carter led the league in receiving touchdowns three times and surpassed 1,000 receiving yards in every season from 1993 to 2000. He also was named to the Pro Bowl in all eight of those seasons.
Brian Peterson/Star Tribune

GREEN ERA BEGINS

Green quickly got a taste of life in the NFC Central. His first game as an NFL head coach was on a rainy Sunday at Lambeau Field. The Packers immediately drove for a touchdown.

Running back Terry Allen, who replaced Walker as the Vikings' featured back, rushed 12 times for 140 yards and caught five passes for 53 yards. His 45-yard run in overtime set up Fuad Reveiz's game-winning field goal in overtime. Vikings 23, Packers 20.

After the game, Green hinted at what would become a habit of making puzzling comments, saying, "We can't go out on the field, and I think you guys know what I'm talking about."

Dungy clarified. "We won, on the road, in a regular-season game, in the rain," he said. "We made a lot of bad plays, and we had several terrible calls go against us, and we still won."

The 1992 Vikings also hinted at what would become a trademark of Green teams: starting fast. After a loss at Detroit in week two, the Vikings won four in a row. Green received much praise for running a more disciplined operation than Burns had. The team's most dramatic victory of the season came in week five against Mike Ditka's Bears.

The Bears were up 20-0 in the fourth quarter when quarterback Jim Harbaugh threw an interception that safety Todd Scott returned for a touchdown, inciting a 21-20 Vikings victory and producing the indelible image of Ditka screaming at Harbaugh on the sidelines.

"In the past, when things got tough, we would turn on each other," said offensive tackle Tim Irwin. "Today, we turned on the Bears."

The Vikings were 7-3 when Green faced the first major in-season decision of his tenure. History shows he chose wrong.

With Gannon struggling at halftime against the Browns at the Metrodome, Green inserted Sean Salisbury, who helped lead the Vikings to a 17-13, come-from-behind win. Green handed the starting job to Salisbury that week.

Salisbury went 3-2 as a starter during the remainder of the regular season, including wins in the final two games to clinch the Central Division title, but the quarterback flopped in the playoffs against Washington.

The Vikings lost that game 24-7 at the Metrodome against a battered Redskins team. Salisbury would never again be considered a number-one quarterback in the NFL, although he remained with the Vikings for two more years and played occasionally as a backup.

Coach Green earns a Gatorade shower following the victory over Green Bay in the final week of the 1992 season. The 27-7 win gave the team an 11-5 record and the Central Division crown.
Brian Peterson/Star Tribune

Green, with that game, began a trend of losing playoff games, even when his team was favored. Gannon, who would later become an NFL MVP while with the Raiders, had his Vikings' tenure effectively ended.

"It was probably one of my least favorite years in football," Gannon said years later. "Denny had come in and wanted to put his own stamp on things, and I just think he was inexperienced and a somewhat immature head coach.

"He turned out to have a pretty good run for a number of years with some players he inherited. I just think he handled the whole situation poorly. We had a lot of talent that year; we should have gone farther in the play-offs. The way he sat me down when we were 8-3 was as bad as it gets. It was disruptive in the locker room because of the way it was handled.

"We were never able to recover as a football team. We had Jack Burns as our offensive coordinator, and he had his own agenda. Our talent really was kind of wasted. We had a lot of talented players—Terry Allen, Roger Craig, Jack (del Rio) was playing well defensively, and a pretty good offensive line, and Steve Jordan, and we lost close games. It was a shame."

DENNY SETTLES IN

Green's honeymoon continued in Minnesota following his playoff ouster. Green was named the NFC coach of the year by one wire service, and the *Star Tribune* even published a feature on Green's hobby—playing the drums—shortly after the 1992 season.

Green's second season also proved representative of his early years with the Vikings. He tried out a new quarterback (former Bears star Jim McMahon), started fast (4-2), hit a lull (lost four of five during the middle of the season), surged enough to make the playoffs (with a 9-7 record), and suffered a disappointing playoff loss (17-10 to the Giants in New Jersey). He also initiated another trend: treating core players as if they were expendable. Green traded Gannon and tackle Gary Zimmerman and lost offensive linemen Kirk Lowdermilk and Brian Habib and linebacker Mike Merriweather in free agency.

Green was hired by the Vikings the same year that the Green Bay Packers hired Mike Holmgren. Holmgren would win a Super Bowl following the 1996 season, but Green won the first four games between the coaches. Green also didn't mind needling his rival as widespread free agency became a factor in the NFL.

Veteran Jim McMahon was signed to be the new quarterback for 1993. Here he jokes during minicamp at Winter Park with his top receiver, Cris Carter. McMahon's tenure with the team lasted only 12 games. *Bruce Bisping/Star Tribune*

Two games into the 1993 season, Brian Billick was promoted from tight ends coach to offensive coordinator, a position he held for six years. Under Billick, the Vikings would become an offensive powerhouse, including setting an NFL record with 556 points in 1998.

Judy Griesedieck/Star Tribune

"Our plan is different than Green Bay's," he said. "Clearly, Green Bay thinks free agency is their way. We don't."

When that quote was repeated to Packers General Manager Ron Wolf, he said, "It's good that Dennis Green knew our plan. But Green is wrong. Our plan wasn't to win through free agency."

Wolf pointed out that the Vikings and Packers both added six free agents before the 1993 season.

"You can improve by developing players, using the draft and trades, and now free agency gives you another tool," Holmgren said. "If you choose not to use that tool, that doesn't make sense to me . . . for Denny to say that."

In 1993, Cris Carter established himself as a true number-one receiver by catching 86 passes for 1,071 yards and nine touchdowns, hinting at what would become a Hall of Fame-caliber career. McMahon threw just nine touchdown passes, along with eight interceptions, and was hardly the savior Green had hoped he would be. A running game led by journeyman Scottie Graham went nowhere.

After the team scored just 17 combined points in the first two games of the 1993 season, Green fired offensive coordinator Jack Burns and replaced him with tight ends coach Brian Billick. Green used a few of his favorite words in explaining the move.

"This is our style," Green said. "I don't have to justify it to anybody. I can explain it, but I won't justify it. . . . I've been around here long enough for people to understand what I'm about. I don't think there's any doubt about who's in charge. We're two games into the 1993 season and I think we can do better offensively. That's what we intend to do."

Employing a stealth receiver must have been part of the new plan. In week three, McMahon enjoyed his biggest moment as a Viking: He found receiver Eric Guliford strangely uncovered for a 45-yard pass. The pass set up the game-winning field goal in Minnesota's 15-13 victory over the Packers at the Metrodome.

It was Guliford's first offensive play of the season, and it left Packer fans wondering if he came straight off the sideline.

After a 15-0 shutout win over Tampa Bay in the fifth game of the season, the Vikings lost the next four home games. They broke that streak with a victory against Kansas City at the Metrodome, which proved to be the centerpiece of a three-game winning streak that closed the season and put Green in the playoffs again.

McMahon dealt with injuries all season, and Salisbury was less than impressive in relief. In December, 61.7 percent of respondents to a *Star Tribune* poll said that third-stringer Gino Torretta should be the Vikings' quarterback for the rest of the season.

McMahon played better toward the end of the season and helped the Vikings to a 14-9 victory at Washington in the season finale to earn a wild-card spot in the playoffs.

The Vikings headed to the Meadowlands to take on the New York Giants in the opening round of the playoffs. In the second quarter, McMahon hit Cris Carter with a 40-yard touchdown pass to help the Vikings to a 10-3 halftime lead. The Giants scored two touchdowns in the third quarter to go ahead by seven. Salisbury took over after McMahon again got injured, and in the fourth quarter, he hit Carter for a 38-yard pass. Carter fumbled at the Giants' 15-yard line while trying to extend the run, and the Vikings lost the game, 17-10.

In 1994, Green maintained his modus operandi. He brought in a new quarterback: veteran Warren Moon, whom the Vikings signed before the season. Among the other changes, the team watched Anthony Carter leave for Detroit, and John Randle replaced Chris Doleman (who had departed for the Falcons) as the Vikings' dominant pass rusher, registering 13.5 sacks.

Bud Grant was enshrined in the Hall of Fame in July, with the *Star Tribune*'s Sid Hartman providing the induction speech. As the *Star Tribune* wrote of the noted stoic Grant, "Hundreds of enshrinement onlookers will squint, trying to figure out which one is the bust and which one is Grant."

Seen here celebrating a sack of Detroit's Rodney Peete in December 1993, John Randle tormented opposing quarterbacks for more than a decade. His 137.5 career sacks rank him sixth on the all-time NFL list. *Brian Peterson/Star Tribune*

The Vikings started the season with a 7-2 record before losing three straight. The streak ended on December 1 with a win over Chicago at the Metrodome, which proved to be the key game of the season.

The Vikings went into overtime against the Bears, and Moon hit Carter with a game-winning 65-yard touchdown pass to secure a 33-27 victory. Victories against Buffalo and San Francisco in the last three games gave the Vikings a 10-6 record for the season and Green his third playoff berth in three years.

"This one is at the top of my memories," Carter said after the Bears game. "A lot of people had given up on us. We couldn't do this and we couldn't do that."

Carter finished with 122 receptions, an NFL single-season record, and 1,256 yards. Again, he could not help the Vikings prevent a first-round loss. The Vikings lost 35-18 at home to the Bears—a team that featured zero Pro Bowl players and quarterbacked by St. Paul native Steve Walsh, and a team that Green had beaten in his previous six encounters. Suddenly, the coach was facing a new level of scrutiny.

Green was a successful regular-season coach stuck in a playoff rut.

GREEN HITS A LULL

Early in the 1995 offseason, the *Star Tribune* ran an investigative report on the high rate of player, employee, and coach turnover under Green. It also reported accusations of sexual harassment regarding secondary coach Richard Solomon, a longtime friend of Green's.

The story read: "The problems [facing the Vikings] include a $150,000 payment by the team to settle a sexual harassment claim against Solomon by a former secretarial intern, an age discrimination suit filed last year by longtime assistant coach and team executive Bob Hollway, and an exodus of assistant coaches inconsistent with the notion that the Vikings are on the verge of excellence. One result has been widespread grumbling from players about how the team is run.

"There is no question that the atmosphere does carry over into wins and losses," said Carl Lee, an 11-year veteran who was cut by the team. "If you get kicked around enough—like they are now—you go to practice and then you want to go home."

The report was indicative of questions surrounding Green's operation, which had received mostly praise during his first three years on the job.

"A newspaper has printed an article about certain claims allegedly against me by an unnamed woman two years ago," Green said in the statement prepared by the team's video department. "I want to say here and now that those claims are not true."

Green would win many more games as the Vikings' coach, but he would never again have a friendly relationship with many members of the Twin Cities media.

Dennis Green faced some criticism during his first few seasons as head coach, and the 8-8 finish in 1995 did not help to quiet the skeptics. The team returned to the playoffs in 1996 and in each of the next four seasons. *Brian Peterson/Star Tribune*

Warren Moon led the league in pass completions in 1995, but on this play against his former team, the Houston Oilers, he opts to run for the first down. He threw two touchdown passes in the game, contributing to his impressive season total of 33 passing TDs.
Brian Peterson/Star Tribune

Quarterback Warren Moon's reputation was sullied as well when his wife accused him of hitting and choking her.

On the field, the Vikings fell to 8-8 for the 1995 season and missed the playoffs for the first time during Green's tenure.

The season ended with a 27-24 loss at Cincinnati. Star receiver Cris Carter was angry that the Vikings hadn't thrown him one more pass in that game, which would have allowed him to break the NFL record, set by Carter the previous year, for receptions in a season. Carter finished with 122 catches for the second year in a row, while Lions receiver Herman Moore surpassed him with 123 receptions in 1995.

BACK TO THE PLAYOFFS

For all the turmoil surrounding the Vikings coach, Green did produce a playoff team in 1996. He also lost another playoff game.

Renowned defensive coordinator Tony Dungy left during the offseason to become the head coach of the Tampa Bay Buccaneers and was replaced by Foge Fazio. Defense wasn't the team's problem, though.

With receivers Cris Carter and Jake Reed leading the offense—that year they became the first receiving tandem

The Vikings' talented receiving corps received another boost with the emergence of Jake Reed in the mid 1990s. He led the team in receiving yardage in 1996 and 1997. This grab against Tampa Bay on September 14, 1997, led to a 56-yard gain in a losing effort at the Metrodome.
Jeff Wheeler/Star Tribune

Robert Smith emerged as Minnesota's top rusher in 1995 and held that role until 2000. Here he stretches for a touchdown against the Detroit Lions, a team against which he posted seven 100-yard games during his career. *Brian Peterson/Star Tribune*

in NFL history to amass more than 1,000 yards each in three consecutive seasons—Green again found his team in a transition period at the quarterback position.

Moon returned to help the Vikings to a 4-0 start, but injuries to the 40-year-old quarterback gave longtime backup Brad Johnson a chance to win the job. In his first start, Johnson secured a 23-17 victory at Atlanta, and then he led the team on a three-game winning streak in December that clinched a playoff berth.

Unfortunately for the Vikings, the playoff berth forced them to play the still-proud Cowboys in Texas Stadium, and they were crushed. The 40-15 loss left Green's playoff record at 0-4.

During the season, Green's job was rumored to be in trouble, and he admitted that he would consider coaching elsewhere. But he kept his job and entered 1997 with

Johnson as his quarterback, a healthier Robert Smith as his star back, and Carter and Reed in place as the team's leading receivers.

The 1997 Vikings produced another fast start for Dennis Green. Moon had departed for Seattle before the season, leaving Johnson as the starting quarterback when the season got underway. Minnesota won its first two games, both on the road, and used a six-game winning streak to get to 8-2 and a tie for the division lead with the Packers.

Right in the middle of the winning streak, Green published a book in which he threatened to sue the Vikings owners if they refused to sell a large share of stock to him. The book was titled *No Room for Crybabies*.

The self-published threat to his bosses stemmed from the previous season, when Green felt that Vikings

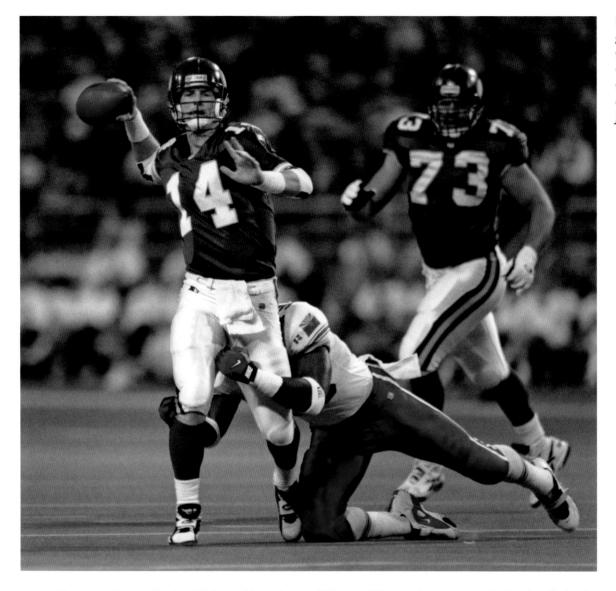

Brad Johnson started eight games in 1996, including this 41-17 thrashing of the Cardinals. In 1997, he became the regular starter with the departure of Warren Moon. *Jeff Wheeler/Star Tribune*

ownership was trying to hire Lou Holtz as his replacement. By owning a piece of the team, Green would have greater job security

Also in October, part-owner Philip Maas revealed that the Vikings were for sale, and thus began the process that would lead to the purchase of the team by Texas billionaire Red McCombs the following offseason.

On the field, Green made another quarterback change, this one forced by Johnson's season-ending neck surgery. Randall Cunningham, who had signed prior to the season as Johnson's backup, started the final three games of the 1997 season, his first starts in more than two years.

Cunningham presided over consecutive losses; then a season-ending victory against Indianapolis gave the

Vikings a 9-7 record to put them in the playoffs for the fifth time in six seasons.

"It felt like we were riding on a flat tire," Green said. "Many days in my youth I felt like I was riding on a rim. I did the best I could to fix the tire. That's what we did."

Thanks to a comeback led by Green's fifth different starting quarterback on five playoff teams, the Vikings beat the Giants, 23-22, on the road. Green expressed his pride following the win. "There aren't many games where you get the chance to show your stuff as a coach," he said.

The next week the Vikings lost, 38-22, at San Francisco.

Three months later, they drafted Randy Moss, and Coach Green would really get a chance to show his stuff.

CHAPTER 9

SO CLOSE, THEN SO FAR
1998–2001

The situation surrounding the Vikings could not have been more chaotic early in 1998. Roger Headrick, the team president and CEO, was upset both with Coach Dennis Green and with his partners in the ownership group.

Green basically had declared war on Headrick and the other owners by suggesting in his book from the previous fall, *No Room for Crybabies*, that he would sue

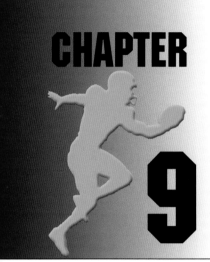

Coach Dennis Green had several run-ins with the team owners heading into the 1998 season, but it didn't interfere with the Vikings' performance on the field. Here Green celebrates a playoff win against Arizona on January 10, 1999. *Jerry Holt/Star Tribune*

if they did not allow him to purchase 30 percent of the franchise.

Green was right about one thing—the team was for sale—but ridiculing his bosses was not the way to earn a position as a serious bidder.

The problem between Headrick and his partners stemmed from the fact that Headrick was trying to put together a group to buy the team, but the other owners were unwilling to give him any preferential treatment in the process.

As for Green, there was only one season remaining on his contract. He told Headrick either to give him a contract extension or to let him go. Headrick was unwilling to offer the extension, or to negotiate a buyout of the $900,000 still owed to Green.

On January 22, Headrick said that the split between him and Green might be "irreconcilable." At the same time, Green said his plan was to "resign and look for opportunities during the year, then maybe get back into football at a later point in my life."

Four days later, Headrick and Green finally had a meeting in San Diego. Headrick gave Green an assurance that he would coach the team in 1998, no matter who became the new owner. Green agreed to come back without the extension he had demanded.

"I decided I'm going to working this year," Green told the *Star Tribune*'s Don Banks. "I'm going to be the coach for the entire year, whether it's new ownership that buys the team or Roger that buys the team."

Earlier, when Green's status was up in the air, Headrick had refused to allow the Vikings' coordinators—Brian Billick (offense) and Foge Fazio (defense)—to move to other jobs. Dallas Cowboys owner Jerry Jones wanted Billick and offered him a huge salary increase. Fazio was a

The Vikings faithful were pumped up for a big season under Coach Green in 1998. At the season opener, these face-painted fans show their support for All-Pro defensive lineman John Randle.
Brian Peterson/Star Tribune

candidate to be the defensive coordinator in Indianapolis for new coach Jim Mora.

The coolness of his relationship with Green and the coaching staff soon became the least of Headrick's problems. On February 3, it was announced that the board had accepted a $200 million bid from a group headed by author Tom Clancy. In order to be the lead partner, Clancy was required by NFL rules to own 30 percent—meaning he had to come up with $60 million.

One day later, Headrick submitted a bid for $205 million and said that under the team's partnership agreement, he had the right of first refusal to match any offer.

Headrick told the *Star Tribune*, "I've upped my [previous] offer by $20 million. I asserted my right of first refusal. The Vikings co-owners are screwed. I put these guys in heaven

Local product Matt Birk worked hard during his first Vikings training camp, and it paid off for the rookie. The 22-year-old Harvard grad earned a roster spot in 1998, and by 2000 he was the everyday starting center.
Jeff Wheeler/Star Tribune

Team President Roger Headrick presents Red McCombs with a personalized jersey at the press conference introducing McCombs as the new owner of the Vikings in July 1998. McCombs' purchase ended several tumultuous months of disputes among the previous ownership group. *Jeff Wheeler/Star Tribune*

Headrick until the ownership situation was resolved. In late March, he ruled that Headrick's claim of a right of first refusal did not apply to the board's deal with Clancy and that the author could proceed with the purchase.

Three days after this ruling, a league meeting was held in Florida. When the paperwork was submitted for league approval, it was discovered there were financial gaps in the Clancy proposal.

In mid-April, Tagliabue told the *Washington Post* that he had serious concerns about Clancy's finances and the structure of the deal. By May 19, a Vikings board member told the *Star Tribune* that Clancy's deal to buy the team was "deader than a doornail."

A week later, the team was back on the selling block. Headrick said he intended to put his group back together. Other bidders mentioned were Twins owner Carl Pohlad, Timberwolves owner Glen Taylor, and San Antonio businessman Red McCombs.

Mike Lynn told the *Star Tribune*, "I'm lurking"—as in, putting together a group of his own to regain the control of the team that he had relinquished in 1990.

When push came to shove, Headrick did not submit a bid. On July 3, the board announced that it had accepted McCombs' bid. The sale was announced at $205 million, although board members later would say it had a cash value of $240 million.

The NFL gave its official blessing to McCombs as the team's new owner on August 20. Headrick soon was gone, as were numerous employees in the business part of the operation.

McCombs appointed Gary Woods, a trusted assistant from his Texas businesses, as his team president. On August 31, he appointed Jeff Diamond, aged 45 and a career employee of the Vikings, as senior vice president for football operations.

Diamond became the boss over everyone in football, including Green. Five days later, Green was given a three-year extension. The extension was in direct contrast to what McCombs had been saying he planned to do, which was let Green coach the season and see what happened.

MOSS BRINGS A NEW OUTLOOK

The fans might have exchanged a few head shakes during the Headrick-Green feud and the Clancy debacle, but the overall outlook had changed quickly in mid-April when they seized the chance to take Randy Moss with the 21st selection in the 1998 NFL Draft.

Moss came from Marshall University, a program not located in one of the major conferences, and he kept dropping through the first round because of the notorious "character issues."

But even Minnesotans knew of his extraordinary speed and skills; the vision of putting him in tandem with Cris Carter generated immediate optimism.

and now they're licking their chops with all the money in Clancy's bid. They got their money, but they don't like me.

"Clancy is coming in for a press conference tomorrow and he has zero rights. He doesn't own the team. Nothing is signed and they all know it."

Clancy arrived for his press conference the next day and put on an over-the-top display of arrogance. "This guy Headrick, what he's doing doesn't matter," Clancy said. "It's like caring about what Saddam Hussein thinks about the Minnesota Vikings. It doesn't count.

"The best legal advice I'm getting is he's dead in the ground with a wooden stake in his heart."

This was on February 5. The Vikings' other board members planned to meet the next day to vote out Headrick as CEO and president.

"I don't think Roger's got a leg to stand on," Board Chairman John Skoglund said. "He's just cut himself off from everyone. I had no idea he was capable of this, but he's proven that he's a bad loser."

Commissioner Paul Tagliabue was brought in to mediate the dispute. He told the board that it couldn't depose

Moss was a lanky 6-foot, 5-inches tall and was timed in 4.28 seconds for 40 yards. Talent-wise, he was a top-five pick, but he had earned a misdemeanor charge of battery in high school and a marijuana possession charge in college. The offense in high school led Notre Dame to withdraw a scholarship offer, and the marijuana charge got him booted from the Florida State team as a redshirt freshman.

"This is a young man who made some mistakes in his past," Green said. "He was 18 and 19 years old. He is still only a 21-year-old young man. We think his life is ahead of him, and we're taking the high road.

"We're saying we got a full glass of water here and we've got a player whose going to help us win a championship."

Moss echoed those sentiments in a conference call with Twin Cities reporters. "Coach Green took a lot of heat for this, but he just caught a steal," he said.

The combination of Moss making acrobatic catches and McCombs running hither and yon, shaking hands, slap-

Wearing number 18 (before he donned the now-familiar 84 jersey), Moss stands tall among his teammates at training camp in August 1998. The first-round draft choice would generate a lot of attention during his seven seasons with the Vikings.
Jeff Wheeler/Star Tribune

Robert Smith takes the handoff from quarterback Brad Johnson and adds to his career-best 179 yards carried against St. Louis on September 13, 1998.
Brian Peterson/Star Tribune

ping backs, and shouting "purple pride," made for the best-attended training camp in quite some time in Mankato.

McCombs planned to get sellout crowds for the Vikings' two home exhibitions. It seemed preposterous, but with corporate assistance, the Vikings were able to announce a crowd of 60,995 for a 34-0 victory over Kansas City and 62,127 for a 42-28 victory over San Diego.

The Vikings were 4-0 in exhibitions. Moss finished with 14 catches for 223 yards and four touchdowns—huge numbers considering the limited time a regular gets in exhibition games.

"It's amazing, man," quarterback Randall Cunningham said. "It's amazing the talent that man is blessed with."

The season opener was a 31-7 blowout of Tampa Bay in the Metrodome. Starting quarterback Brad Johnson threw touchdown passes of 48 and 31 yards to Moss, and of 18 and 1 yard to Carter.

"That 84 [Moss] is going to make a big difference in that offense," said Monte Kiffin, Tampa Bay's defensive coordinator. "We wanted to keep the ball in front of us, and we didn't do that. When they put those three wide-outs—Cris Carter, Jake Reed, and Moss—on the field, they can really stretch it out."

The Vikings' next game was in St. Louis. Robert Smith rushed for a career-high 179 yards, and Minnesota hung on for a 38-31 victory. They also lost starting quarterback Johnson to a broken fibula in the fourth quarter.

CARTER AND MOSS: A PHENOMENAL TANDEM

The Vikings had routed Tampa Bay, 31-7, in their 1998 regular-season opener a few days before an interview with Cris Carter appeared in the *Star Tribune*. The Pro-Bowl receiver had caught touchdown passes of 1 and 18 yards in the victory; rookie Randy Moss had scoring receptions of 48 and 31 yards.

Carter, who had 21 more receptions than the Vikings' second-leading receiver in 1997, acknowledged that Moss' presence meant life would never be the same. "For this to go well this year, there has to be a great deal of unselfishness, starting with me and [running back] Robert Smith," Carter said. "I know that."

Carter also knew this wasn't a bad thing.

At age 32, he went from being the receiver that opponents singled out as their top priority to being part of a twosome that gave Minnesota an every-down threat both short (Carter) and deep (Moss). The Carter-Moss tandem would become among the NFL's most prolific over the next three years, during which the Vikings went a combined 36-12 (.750) in the regular season and made the playoffs each season.

Those 1998 Vikings finished with a franchise-best 15-1 record—a heartbreaking overtime loss to Atlanta in the NFC Championship Game cost them a Super Bowl berth—as Carter and Moss combined for 147 receptions, 2,324 yards, and 29 touchdowns. Carter had 78 of those catches, while Moss had 1,313 of the yards and 17 touchdowns.

Carter, who played with the Vikings through the 2001 season, also developed a reputation as a mentor to the often-petulant Moss during this time. The relationship eventually matured to a point where the two were on equal footing.

"In meetings, if Cris says something that Randy doesn't agree with or if Randy says something that Cris doesn't agree with, they will respond to each other," Receivers Coach Charlie Baggett said. "But it's in a way that you know Randy respects Cris' opinion. And Cris respects the fact that Randy has so much talent but can still draw from Cris' experience. It's so interesting to me, because every day you go in there, you don't know what's going to be said."

On Sundays, though, one thing was pretty clear. These two were going to produce.

In their four seasons as teammates, Carter and Moss caught a combined 645 passes for 9,793 yards and 93 touchdowns. Their top output from a reception standpoint came in 2000, when they totaled 173 catches for 2,711 yards and 24 TDs. The yardage established a team record, breaking the mark of 2,654 yards they had set in 1999. The latter figure had made the Carter-Moss tandem the fourth-most productive receiving duo in NFL history for one season.

To give this achievement some perspective, the 49ers' receiving tandem of Jerry Rice and John Taylor played together for nine seasons. The most passes that the two caught between them in a single season was 154 in 1993.

"The kind of relationship that they have established is very unique, especially for two guys like that," Baggett said of Carter and Moss in August 2000. "One's a Hall of Famer and the other is working his way towards that.

"Normally what happens is you get egos coming into play: 'Don't tell me what to do. You do your job, I'll do my job.' You see none of that."

Randy Moss and Randall Cunningham connected on all cylinders during the Vikings' impressive run in 1998.
Judy Griesedieck/Star Tribune

CUNNINGHAM TAKES OVER, AND MOSS CONTINUES TO AMAZE

Johnson's injury put 35-year-old Cunningham in the starting lineup. The veteran quarterback, a former star in Philadelphia, seized the opportunity, to say the least. He was named the NFL's Offensive Player of the Year by *Pro Football Weekly* and NFC Player of the Year by the *Football News*.

The Vikings defeated the Lions, 29-6, in Cunningham's first start, and they were 4-0 after beating Chicago 31-28 in Soldier Field the following week. Cunningham threw four touchdowns in the Bears game, including a screen pass to Smith that the running back turned into a 67-yard touchdown.

The victory set up a duel of unbeatens in a game against Green Bay at Lambeau Field. It was on Monday night, October 5, and the Packers—the reigning NFC champs—were favored.

The Monday-night game was the first demonstration that Moss, as good as he was with a noon kickoff on a routine Sunday, was a genuine "Super Freak" when under the national television spotlight.

Moss caught four passes of over 40 yards, including 52- and 44-yarders for touchdowns. Jake Reed had a 56-

Randy Moss gets a lift from right tackle Korey Stringer after Moss scored a second-quarter touchdown against the Packers on national television on Monday, October 5.
Jerry Holt/Star Tribune

yard touchdown reception. Cunningham threw for 442 yards and four touchdowns.

The numbers could have been even more impressive, if Moss did not have a 75-yard reception called back by penalty. "When that got wiped out," he said after the game, "I just thought, 'Then I'll get another one.'"

Cunningham said, "It was the greatest night of my football career."

Randall Cunningham celebrates a 49-yard touchdown pass to Moss against Green Bay at home on November 22, 1998. It was one of Cunningham's career-high 34 TDs on the year. *Jerry Holt/Star Tribune*

With spectacular catches like this, Moss outran his opponents all season long, in this case Green Bay defensive backs Darren Sharper (42) and Tyrone Williams (37). *Jeff Wheeler/Star Tribune*

It was also the greatest three-and-a-half hours that Vikings fans had spent in more than a decade—going back to the playoff run after the 1987 season.

Victories over Washington and Detroit gave the Vikings a record of 7-0 when they headed to Tampa Bay on November 1. Minnesota lost, 27-24. The Buccaneers won with a rushing game that featured 128 yards from fullback Mike Alstott and 115 yards from tailback Warrick Dunn.

It would be the only loss of the regular season. The Vikings' 15-1 record surpassed the previous franchise best of 12-2, which had been accomplished four times under Bud Grant (1969, 1970, 1973, 1975).

The team suffered a different kind of loss in late November. Dave Huffman, a Vikings offensive lineman for 11 seasons and then a member of their radio announcing team, was killed in a car accident. He was traveling to Notre Dame to watch his alma mater play football.

A few days after Huffman's death, the Vikings went to Dallas to play in the Thanksgiving Day game. Moss caught three passes for 163 yards and all three went for touchdowns.

Moss had expected to be drafted by Dallas with the eighth overall pick in the draft prior to the season. The Cowboys called Moss to say they would take him, and then they reneged. The Thanksgiving Day performance was his first act of revenge on "America's Team."

Yet, when the national media descended on him after the Vikings' 46-36 victory, Moss barked out a couple of obscenities and refused to talk.

Down the corridor at Texas Stadium, Dallas' star receiver Michael Irvin took responsibility for Moss not being in a Cowboys uniform. He said he had called Moss during the week to apologize.

"With everything I'd been involved in [mostly cocaine], we couldn't draft Randy Moss," Irvin said. "I apologized to Randy because I knew he really wanted to be in Dallas. I told him all my stuff is what prevented that."

The 15-1 Vikings finished the season with 556 points and a single-season NFL record that stood until the 16-0 New England Patriots (with Randy Moss) scored 589 points in 2007.

Cunningham amassed 259 completions in 425 attempts (60.9 percent), 3,704 yards passing, and 34 passing touchdowns. Considering he didn't play the first seven quarters of the season, these were amazing numbers. His quarterback rating was a sparkling 106.0, which was tops in the NFL.

Moss caught 69 passes for 1,313 yards and 17 touchdowns. Carter also had more than 1,000 yards (1,011) on 78 catches and 12 touchdowns. Smith rushed for 1,187 yards on 249 carries. He scored eight touchdowns (six rushing), and short-yardage specialist Leroy Hoard plunged for nine touchdowns.

Kicker Gary Anderson also was flawless. He did not miss a kick in 16 games, going 59-for-59 on extra points and a record-breaking 35-for-35 on field goals.

HOME FOR THE PLAYOFFS

The Vikings clinched home field through the NFL playoffs with a 50-10 victory over Jacksonville in the 15th game of the season. They also earned a first-round bye.

Arizona upset Dallas in the wild-card round—the Cardinals' first (still only) playoff victory since 1948, when they were in Chicago. The win sent Arizona to the Dome, where it was a huge underdog.

The Vikings opened with a 13-play, 80-yard touchdown drive and rolled to a 41-21 victory. Moss' only touchdown was on a 2-yard pass, but Cunningham added a 15-yarder to tight end Andrew Glover and a 16-yarder to Hoard (of all people). Along with his one-yard touch-

down run on the opening drive and his six-yard score in the final quarter, Hoard set a franchise playoff record with three touchdowns in the game. Although he didn't contribute to the scoreboard, Robert Smith's 124 yards rushing also established a Vikings postseason record.

"Let's face it," Arizona defensive coordinator Dave McGinniss said. "Their quiver has a lot of arrows."

The Vikings had a worthy opponent coming to Minneapolis for the NFC title game. The Atlanta Falcons were 15-2 on the year (including the playoffs), compared to Minnesota's 16-1 record. But this game was being played in the howling Dome. Could anyone imagine the Vikings, 9-0 with 275 points scored on their home surface, losing in this environment?

"We're just on a quest," safety Robert Griffith said after the Arizona victory. "Today, we got another piece of the puzzle. We're just going to keep marching."

Against Arizona in the 1998 playoffs, Robert Smith gained 124 yards rushing—the most in franchise postseason history. Smith provided a dangerous ground attack to complement the aerial assault of Cunningham to Moss, Carter, Reed, and Glover. *Jeff Wheeler/Star Tribune*

Oh, one more thing: Gary Anderson was 2-for-2 on field goals and 5-for-5 extra points against the Cardinals. Still perfect.

MORE DIFFICULT PATH

The unhappy details of what occurred on January 17, 1999, to prevent a return to the Super Bowl for the Vikings can be found in this book's Introduction. Any Minnesotan who follows the Vikings, even casually, can recall Gary Anderson's lone missed kick of the season in that NFC title game. The media sure didn't allow the memory to fade.

When the Vikings first reported to training camp in Mankato that July, Joe Schmit, a sports anchor for KSTP television in the Twin Cities, was occupied conducting an interview when he spotted Anderson pulling his vehicle into the parking lot outside Gage Hall, the dormitory occupied by the Vikings.

Schmit told one of his minions, "Get a sound bite from Anderson," and the fellow went sprinting toward the Vikings placekicker.

Anderson's left foot was out of the car. His kicking foot was not when Schmit's understudy blurted, "Have you gotten over missing that kick, or does it still haunt you?"

The fallout from the explosive season with the disappointing end had started just two days after the game, when offensive coordinator Brian Billick was introduced as the new coach of the Baltimore Ravens.

The postmortems of the Vikings' loss to the Falcons included this suggestion: Billick was already out the door, thinking about what he had going for him in Baltimore, and not fully involved in preparing the Minnesota offense for the NFC title game.

It was a lousy excuse, and about as cheap a shot as could be made at a dedicated football coach. Billick would get to hold the Super Bowl trophy two years later by winning it with the Ravens' record-breaking defense.

The Vikings had another quarterback decision to make heading into the 1999 campaign. Brad Johnson had vacated his starting job with a broken leg suffered early in the previous season, and Cunningham had stepped in and produced a fabulous season.

Johnson made it clear that he would be an unhappy backup. So, on February 15, the Vikings traded Johnson to the Washington Redskins for draft choices, which they turned into quarterback Daunte Culpepper in 1999 and nose tackle Fred Robbins in 2000.

The Vikings never seem to be far from an emotional jolt, and this time it came in late February, when Offensive

Although kicker Gary Anderson had a perfect regular season in 1998—making 35 of 35 field goals and 59 of 59 extra points—his miss in the NFC Championship is the one that he, and an entire generation of Vikings fans, will never be able to forget.
Brian Peterson/Star Tribune

Coordinator Chip Myers died of a heart attack at age 53. Less than a month earlier, Green had promoted Meyers as a replacement for Billick.

The Johnson trade left the Vikings in need of another quarterback to back up Cunningham. Green came up with a shocking solution: He signed nine-year-veteran Jeff George, the talented but enigmatic quarterback who had worn out his welcome with Indianapolis, Atlanta, and Oakland. George's star had fallen so far that the Vikings were able to get him for close to the minimum salary of $400,000.

Two weeks after signing George, the Vikings used the 11th pick in the draft to take Culpepper, the 6-foot, 4-inch, 260-pound quarterback from Central Florida.

The consensus had been that the Vikings needed defensive help, but Green responded, "We had [Culpepper] rated as the highest of the quarterbacks in this draft. His rating was about as high as you can get. Good teams rarely have a chance to pick the number-one quarterback."

Behind the scenes, some of that good old-fashioned infighting was taking place again in the Vikings front office.

Jeff Diamond, who had been promoted to football boss before the 1998 season, was honored as the NFL Executive of the Year in mid-March of 1999. Green was in attendance at the function. He did not bother to seek out Diamond and congratulate him.

Instead, Green was taking advantage of the clout he had gained with McCombs by coaching the Vikings to that 15-1 season. Diamond quit at McCombs' behest on May 3, and Green was given control of the football operation.

Tim Connolly, in title the team's general manager but employed to run the day-to-day business operations, had been ordered to stay out of football matters after a run-in with Green during the 1998 season. Now, with Diamond gone, Green, for the first time in his eight years, was fully in charge.

On the surface, it couldn't have looked better for him. The Las Vegas sports books were listing the 1999 Minnesota Vikings as 6-5 favorites to win the NFC and 3-1 to win the Super Bowl. No other team had shorter odds than 6-1.

A VERY STRANGE CASE

The first glitch in the smooth sailing toward a Super Bowl took place on the opening day of practice. Dimitrius Underwood, the Vikings' second first-rounder, had arrived the night before wearing army fatigues to demonstrate that he was ready for battle.

Underwood, a defensive end from Michigan State, arrived for morning practice. He was involved in a drill where Korey Stringer, the outstanding right tackle, pushed him all over the field on several occasions.

During Minnesota's 35-27 win over San Diego on November 28, 1999, Cris Carter pulled in his 900th career reception on this 4-yard touchdown pass from Jeff George. Carter would go on to accumulate 1,101 receptions, second only to Jerry Rice on the all-time NFL list.
Brian Peterson/Star Tribune

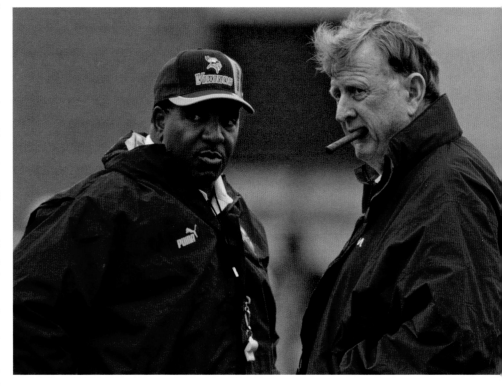

When afternoon practice started, Underwood was nowhere to be found. He had hitchhiked back to the Twin Cities and flown out of town.

A day later, Underwood called his agent and said he wanted to come back. The Vikings already had wired Underwood's signing bonus of $862,500 (minus taxes) to a bank in Milwaukee. They went to Federal court to put a freeze on what was a $543,561 deposit.

Paul McEnroe, an investigative reporter for the *Star Tribune*, finally found Underwood six days later in a Philadelphia hotel. He was sitting in the lobby with a Bible on his lap and $8 in his pocket.

Owner Red McCombs confers with his head coach at the first day of training camp in August 1999. Coach Green assumed greater control of football operations on the heels of the stellar 1998 campaign.
Jerry Holt/Star Tribune

"I wish I was man enough to confront Coach Green and look him in the eyes and tell him what I've been going through," Underwood told McEnroe.

The Vikings released Underwood. He signed with Miami, and later Dallas, where he played for part of two seasons. He was diagnosed with bipolar disorder and never had a significant NFL career.

Quarterback Jeff George holds his head in his hands in the final minutes of the 49-37 playoff loss to St. Louis on January 16, 2000. George completed 29 of 50 passes for 423 yards and threw 4 touchdowns, but his fumbled snap in the second half proved costly.
Judy Griesedieck/Star Tribune

The worst part of the Underwood selection was that the next player chosen in the draft was Patrick Kerney, a defensive end from Virginia, who was taken by the Falcons. He was rated higher than Underwood on most every draft list (other than the Vikings') and remains an NFL star a decade later.

REVENGE, SORT OF

Way back in 1970, the Vikings had claimed revenge for their upset loss in the Super Bowl when they defeated Kansas City 27-10 in the opening game of the following season. They did some of the same on September 12, 1999, when they went to Atlanta and squeezed out a 17-14 victory over the Falcons.

It was a victory over the team that ruined a great season the previous January, but it was also an indication that the magic Cunningham carried in those long swings of his right arm in 1998 had gone missing.

The Vikings went to Detroit with a record of 2-3 and then were shutout in the first half. Green benched Cunningham and brought in Jeff George. The Vikings immediately went 80 yards in five plays.

On the next possession, the Vikings went 60 yards. They actually took a 20-19 lead early in the fourth quarter, before Detroit came back for a 25-23 victory.

Reporters rushed to the visitors' locker room at the Pontiac Silverdome to quiz Green on the identity of his

Moss takes a drink from his water bottle during the playoff game against the Rams. He would later use the water bottle to less innocent ends in an incident involving an official.
Judy Griesedieck/Star Tribune

quarterback. The coach took all the fun out of the inquisition by opening with the statement, "George is going to start."

The Vikings and George scored 40 points the next week against San Francisco. It was the start of a five-game winning streak. They would go 8-2 with George as a starter and claim a wild-card spot at 10-6.

The regular-season finale was a 24-17 victory over Detroit. Chris Doleman, who had returned to the Vikings after a five-season absence, recorded his 150th career sack in that game. He joined Reggie White, Bruce Smith, and Kevin Greene as the only players to have 150 sacks at that time.

The Vikings' wild-card opponent was Dallas in the Metrodome. Robert Smith rushed for 140 yards and the Vikings overcame a sluggish start to win 27-10.

That victory sent them to St. Louis, where the Rams had put together the "Greatest Show on Turf."

The underdog Vikings led 17-14 at halftime. Then the Rams scored 35 straight points over the next 23 minutes. George did some slinging in the last few minutes, but the final score was 49-37 for the Rams.

At one point during the game, George fumbled a snap. Rather than dive toward the football, he stepped away from it. On a day of much more embarrassment than the final score indicated, George's move was the lowest moment.

It would be the last game that George played for the Vikings—great arm, but always the enigma.

He wasn't the only one to depart the Vikings' scene after the end of the season. Green got rid of five assistants, including defensive coordinator Foge Fazio and offensive coordinator Ray Sherman. General Manager Tim Connolly turned in his resignation on January 24.

A month later, Mike Kelly, a lawyer who had worked with the Vikings, was named to replace Connolly as general manager. His main task was to create political momentum for a new Vikings stadium.

CHANGE AT QUARTERBACK

The Vikings had thrown 530 passes in 1999. George and Cunningham threw 529 of those passes and the other was a touchdown pass from Randy Moss to Cris Carter.

Green made an early decision to drop Cunningham, although it did not officially happen until early June of 2000 to lessen the salary cap hit. He also rejected the contract demands of George, who ended up signing with Washington and played in only eight more NFL games.

That left Daunte Culpepper, the second-year player who had not thrown a pass as a rookie, as the only viable quarterback.

Dan Marino was out of a job in Miami after 17 seasons. Green decided to make a serious run at him in March. When it seemed that he had interest in signing with Minnesota, Dolphins owner Wayne Huizenga became

embarrassed by the idea of Marino playing somewhere other than Miami and offered him a chance to return.

This went on for a while, and then Marino made it official: He was going to retire.

In early April, Green made his decision. He signed veteran Bubby Brister and announced that Culpepper would be his starting quarterback.

Randy Moss created a minor stir during the summer when he played a couple of games in the summer pro basketball league in Los Angeles. Green said Moss was doing this with his permission.

"He's an athlete and he plays hard," NBA player Bo Outlaw told the *Los Angeles Times*. "I don't know if he could play in the NBA, but that doesn't really matter because he's great at what he does [football]."

Culpepper's official tenure as the starting quarterback began on September 3, 2000, in the home opener against Chicago. Standing in front of the Metrodome before the game, a gentleman named Adam Thronson was wearing a purple robe and offering a pregame "sermon" to arriving Vikings fans.

"Can I get an amen for Daunte Culpepper?" he would ask the crowd, and they would respond with a rousing "Amen."

A few hours later, it was a "Hallelujah," as Culpepper ran for three second-half touchdowns in a 30-27 victory. Culpepper rumbled out of the pocket with his combination of size and speed to gain 73 yards in 13 carries. He

In the 2000 season opener, Randy Moss pulls down a long pass from new quarterback Daunte Culpepper. The victory over Chicago kicked off a seven-game winning streak to start the season. *Jerry Holt/Star Tribune*

also completed 13 of 23 passes for 190 yards, including a 66-yard completion to Moss.

With Culpepper at quarterback, the Vikings stormed out of the gate with a 7-0 record. The seventh victory came in Buffalo, 31-27. Culpepper hit Moss in the back of the end zone for a 39-yard, go-ahead touchdown with four minutes left.

Later, Gary Anderson kicked a 21-yard field goal to replace George Blanda as the NFL's all-time leading scorer.

Culpepper completed 13 of his last 17 passes and finished with 251 yards. After seven victories, he was "Mr. Clutch" and boasted an enormous quarterback rating of 140.5 in the fourth quarters.

The winning streak ended with a 41-13 drubbing at Tampa Bay. Two years earlier, the Vikings also had opened

the season 7-0 before losing at Tampa Bay. The 1998 Vikings followed by winning their last eight regular-season games.

It wasn't as smooth sailing this time around. After the loss to the Buccaneers, Minnesota fell again a week later in Green Bay, but then the team rattled off a four-game winning streak—outscoring opponents 113-63 in the four games—to sit atop the division with an 11-2 record.

The Vikings closed out the season with a three-game losing streak. The defense that had only once allowed more than 30 points in the previous 13 games yielded an average of 35 points to St. Louis, Green Bay, and Indianapolis. After a 7-1 start, Minnesota went 4-4 in the second half of the schedule.

Still, the Vikings' 11-5 record was good enough to earn them the NFC Central Division title and a first-round bye in the playoffs.

Culpepper used his feet as well as his hands to lead the Vikes to an 11-5 record in his first season as the team's starting quarterback. Here he scrambles in the pocket during a 31-14 win over Arizona in week 11.
Carlos Gonzalez/Star Tribune

Culpepper had been playing with a sprained ankle that was covered by a brace in the final weeks of the season. The week off gave him some healing time.

Minnesota hosted New Orleans in a second-round playoff game on January 6, 2001. On the Vikings' first series, Culpepper hit Moss on a slant and the receiver turned it into a 53-yard touchdown.

The Metrodome let out an explosive roar that seemed to signal the slump was over. The Vikings rolled to a 34-16 victory, their first win since November 30.

The win sent the Vikings to the Meadowlands in New Jersey to play the New York Giants in the NFC title game. Despite being on the road, the Vikings were 2-point favorites. In the days before the game, Green and his coaches were filled with confidence—expressing their belief that they had too much offense for the Giants to handle.

Final: Giants 41, Vikings 0.

The score was 34-0 at halftime. Kerry Collins, a quarterback of modest reputation, went 28-for-39 for 381 yards and five touchdowns against the Vikings' meek pass rush and woeful cornerbacks.

Moss issued his now-legendary "41-doughnut" comment when asked about the game, then made further statements that created the first real rift between him and some of the team's fan base:

"I'm going to have a Super Bowl ring. I'm not worried about that. I doubt if it's in Minnesota. I can't really say I'm going to be a Minnesota Viking in a couple of years.

In one of many frustrating moments during the 41-0 thumping by the Giants in the NFC championship game, New York defensive back Emmanuel McDaniel pulls a pass away from Cris Carter in the end zone for a first-quarter interception.
Jeff Wheeler/Star Tribune

The looks on the faces of (left to right) Daunte Culpepper, Cris Carter, Randy Moss, and tight end Andrew Jordan says it all: 41-doughnut.
Jeff Wheeler/Star Tribune

Hopefully, I would like to win one for Coach Green, but I can't really tell the future.

"I don't want to say anything I might regret. It's going to be hard for us to win a Super Bowl in Minnesota. I believe that. It's going to be hard."

Then Moss made things worse when he said that he hoped Cris Carter would return, rather than retire, but that Carter should not "have his hopes set on winning a Super Bowl."

In the next day's *Star Tribune*, columnist Dan Barreiro addressed Moss' attitude before and after the game:

"[CBS broadcaster Howard] David reportedly observed Moss melting down after a Giants Stadium security guard refused to allow some buddies of the wide receiver to hang out on the field. The CBS [radio] crew reported that Moss then let loose with a string of expletives.

"So let's see if we have this straight: The guy who [after the game] is hammering away at the pregame mindset and commitment of his teammates apparently was focused mainly on getting his cronies on the field in the hour or two before kickoff.

The affable Robert Smith surprised many when he announced he was hanging up the cleats prior to the 2001 season. Coming off a career year in 2000, the 28-year-old Smith retired with a franchise-record 6,818 rushing yards for his career.
Judy Griesedieck/Star Tribune

"That's where Moss' head was, not long before the biggest game of his career."

One person not offended by Moss' postgame comments about the Vikings not having a Super Bowl in their future was McCombs. The owner was back in his San Antonio office on the day after the 41-0 humiliation and told the *Star Tribune* by phone:

"I liked what Randy said. Randy speaks what he feels, and frankly I wish I had fifty Randy Mosses. He's a very competitive athlete, and he wants to win."

Whatever Moss' loyalties to receiving partner Carter and Coach Green, that 41-0 loss was the beginning of the end for both of those gentlemen in Minnesota.

SHOCK AND TRAGEDY

The first shock of the 2001 offseason came when running back Robert Smith announced on February 7 that he was going to retire. It was a month before his 29th birthday, and Smith was coming off a season in which he had posted career highs in rushing yards (1,521), carries (295), receiving yards (348), receptions (36), and touchdowns (10).

He had struggled with injuries in the first four seasons of his career, then put together four seasons in which he averaged nearly 1,250 yards. He had played the full schedule for the first time in 2000 and was starting to challenge Chuck Foreman for the title of greatest running back in Vikings history.

Smith also was intellectual and unpredictable. Once he announced he was quitting, there was no talking him out of it. Smith's departure put the Vikings in desperate need of a running back, so they took Wisconsin's Michael Bennett with the 27th overall selection in the 2001 draft.

"We got a gift," said Green, in reference to Bennett still being available so late in the first round.

Bennett was a 5-foot, 10-inch, 210-pounder, and a national contender as a sprinter in track.

The Vikings made some big news at the start of training camp, when it was announced that McCombs had decided to take the plunge on a new contract for Moss: $75 million over eight years with a $18 million signing bonus.

It was the fourth-richest contract in the NFL history, behind only the contracts of three quarterbacks: New England's Drew Bledsoe, Green Bay's Brett Favre, and Dallas' retired Troy Aikman.

In a twist of logic that made sense only to Moss, he said the reason he eventually focused on $18 million as the number for his signing bonus was this: He wore the number 18 in his first training camp, before a receiver named Tony Bland was cut and Randy could take his preferred 84.

"I felt comfortable with 18," he said—which is very comfortable when there are six zeroes behind it.

The Vikings were greeted at camp with sizzling heat in Mankato. The temperature was in the 90s and it was humid on the morning of July 31. The Vikings worked out in full pads.

Korey Stringer, the 27-year-old, massive right tackle, had not completed the morning practice the previous day. He was determined to get through this one. He did so and then was involved in post-practice conditioning with his fellow offensive linemen.

Stringer summoned trainer Chuck Barta and told him to meet him at the air-conditioned trailer that the Vikings kept alongside the field. Once there, Stringer collapsed. Barta called an ambulance, and the 6-foot, 4-inch, 335-pound lineman was rushed to a Mankato hospital.

Word spread through camp that it was a very serious situation, and teammates went to the hospital to maintain a vigil. The doctors never could lower Stringer's body temperature to a tolerable level. He was pronounced dead during the long night.

Lawsuits were later filed by Kelci Stringer, Korey's widow, but the Vikings, their coaches, and their medical staff were exonerated from any liability. It was heatstroke on a very hot morning for football practice—plain, simple, and tragic.

(That same week, Northwestern safety Rashidi Wheeler, 22, collapsed during a preseason conditioning drill and died an hour later in an Evanston, Illinois, hospital.)

Robert Smith and Korey Stringer had been teammates at Ohio State. Smith said there was a special bond between a running back and his offensive linemen, and that he "especially felt that kinship" with Stringer.

"This is a guy who had pretty much been there with me for all but something like 500 of my yards in my career," Smith said. "There was this big guy, always there to put out his hand and pull me up. This is a loss that for me is really very hard to describe."

On July 31, 2001—the hottest day of the year—offensive tackle Korey Stringer works out at training camp in Mankato. The practice in the intense heat would have fatal consequences later that day. *Carlos Gonzalez/Star Tribune*

Vikings players and coaches huddle together for a moment of silence at practice on August 2, 2001, after Korey Stringer's death. *Carlos Gonzalez/Star Tribune*

IRRETRIEVABLE SEASON

Stringer was always like a big kid in the Vikings' locker room and very popular with his teammates. His death tore at the hearts of most everyone in the organization, including Green. After the tragedy, the coach did not strut around with the same defiance. An air of the inevitable—that this would be his last season in Minnesota—seemed to fall over Green and then his locker room.

The 41-0 drubbing against the Giants, one of four losses in the 2000 Vikings' last five games, had exposed defensive flaws that could not be patched rapidly.

The offensive line became decimated, first when left tackle Todd Steussie was allowed to leave for Carolina as a free agent and then with the death of Stringer.

The Vikings had gone 15-1 with a tremendous offensive line in 1998: Steussie, Randall McDaniel, Jeff Christy, David Dixon, and Stringer, from left to right.

McDaniel and Christy both left for Tampa Bay as free agents after 1999. Matt Birk came along to replace (and surpass) Christy as a center. Yet, by the start of the 2001 season, only Birk and Dixon were anything more than journeymen.

The rushing game desperately missed Smith, despite Green's optimism when he drafted Bennett. The rookie topped the Vikings rushers in 2001 with a meager 682 yards, followed by Culpepper with 416.

On the defensive side, John Randle also was gone after a wonderful decade on the defensive line. He finished his career with three seasons in Seattle. Left in his wake was the unimpressive foursome of Stalin Colinet, Chris Hovan, Fred Robbins, and Talance Sawyer.

The 2001 season opened with Carolina rookie Steve Smith returning the opening kickoff 93 yards for a touchdown. The Panthers left the Metrodome with a 24-13 victory and proceeded to lose their next 15 games.

Wins against division rivals Tampa Bay, Detroit, and Green Bay carried the Vikings to a 3-3 record by mid-

Stringer's tragic death was felt by his fellow players and fans alike. He was honored by many fans at the first preseason home game on August 16. Stringer's 77 jersey number was retired by the team that November.
Judy Griesedieck/Star Tribune

In a preemptive move, Dennis Green announced at a press conference before the final game of the 2001 season that he was leaving the Vikings. He departed with a career record of 101 wins and 70 losses, including the postseason.
Richard Sennott/Star Tribune

Mike Tice had just three days to prepare for his head-coaching debut against the Baltimore Ravens on January 7, 2002. He shed the "interim" label three days later when Red McCombs named him the permanent head coach.
Brian Peterson/Star Tribune

October, but then they lost four of the next five. The last of those came in Pittsburgh on December 2. Culpepper entered the game with a protective brace on an injured left knee. He moved well initially, but wound up hobbling in frightful fashion and was replaced by Todd Bouman, a rookie out of St. Cloud State.

Bouman played well and Bennett scored on an 80-yard swing pass, but the Vikings lost 21-16 to fall to 4-7 and to give up any hopes of the playoffs. They won the next week against Tennessee, then lost three in a row.

When Bouman was also injured, the inexperienced third-stringer Spergon Wynn was forced to lead the offense, which resulted in a 24-13 loss at Green Bay in the second-to-last game of the season.

The Vikings were 5-10 with one game remaining when ESPN's Chris Mortenson reported at mid-week that McCombs planned to fire Green after the season.

Green and his agent Ray Anderson had hostile discussions with McCombs and his representatives on Thursday. The early hours on Friday were spent negotiating a settlement on the two years that remained on Green's contract.

McCombs was at Winter Park and planned to announce Green's firing.

Green beat him to it, announcing at an afternoon news conference that he and the Vikings had "mutually agreed on a contract fulfillment." He was due almost $5 million.

The 52-year-old Green said that he planned to take no shots at the Vikings organization—that he could be found on the "high road."

McCombs would not describe Green's departure as a firing, stating only, "Green is no longer with the Vikings organization."

Mike Tice, the offensive line coach, was named as the interim head coach. The 19-3 loss in Baltimore in the final game of 2001, with the hapless Wynn at quarterback, wound up on Tice's record.

The 5-10 mark in 2001 was Green's only losing record in 10 seasons in Minnesota. The Vikings were in the playoffs eight times in those 10 seasons, but they had a record of only 4-8 in those postseason appearances.

McCombs did not bother with an extensive search for a replacement. Tice was named as the permanent head coach on January 10, only four days after the Vikings' worst season since 1984 had come to an end.

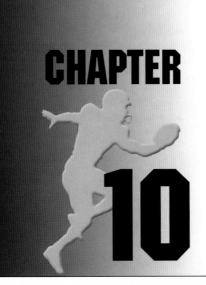

INTO THE GREAT UNKNOWN

10 2002–

During his seven seasons in Minnesota, "Super Freak" Randy Moss earned headlines both for his on-the-field accomplishments and his off-the-field indiscretions.
Carlos Gonzalez/Star Tribune

Randy Moss was fined $25,000 by the NFL for squirting an official with a water bottle in the playoff loss to St. Louis on January 16, 2000. He was fined another $25,000 for touching an official during a regular-season game in November of 2000. He was fined $15,000 by the Vikings for verbally abusing corporate sponsors on a team bus in 2001.

Then in November 2001, following a 28-16 victory over the New York Giants in the Metrodome, Moss recited those infamous words into Sid Hartman's ancient tape recorder:

"I play when I want to play."

Those seven little words continue to plague Moss to this day, even though the context in which they were spoken was considerably different than the short version suggests. Moss was speaking immediately after a game in which he caught 10 passes for 171 yards and three touchdowns, and the night on which the jersey of Korey Stringer was retired.

Here's the fuller extent of what Moss told Hartman, and what Sid wrote, after the receiver was asked if playing in the spotlight of Monday Night Football was extra motivation for his dynamic performance against the Giants:

> "I think that I got more emotional over them retiring Big K's jersey," Moss said. "Monday night had nothing to do with it. I think if it had been a regular game, retiring his jersey would have been just as emotional."
>
> Moss has been criticized by some media members for not giving 100 percent all of the time. His veteran teammate, Cris Carter, will tell you there is not a player who goes 100 percent all of the time.
>
> "I play when I want to play," Moss said. "Do I play up to my top performance, my ability every time? Maybe not. I just keep doing what I do and that is playing football. When I make my mind up, I am going out there to tear somebody's head off.
>
> "When I go out there and play football, man, it's not anybody telling me to play or how I should play. I play when I want to play, case closed."

The brouhaha over that quote was more baggage for Mike Tice to inherit in January 2002 when he replaced Dennis Green as head coach of the Vikings. He also was inheriting an immense talent who had 308 receptions and 53 touchdowns in four regular seasons.

Newly named Head Coach Mike Tice and President Gary Woods are all smiles at the press conference announcing Tice's hiring. The coach's wife and two children are in the background.
Mike Zerby/Star Tribune

Tice responded to the two sides of his superstar—explosive in both talent and temperament—by announcing he would institute a "Randy Ratio" for the 2002 season. The idea was that a minimum of 40 percent of the pass plays would be thrown toward Moss.

To institute this, Tice went through a search process for a new offensive coordinator. He hired Scott Linehan, who had that job at the University of Louisville.

When asked about the Randy Ratio, Linehan said, "I think that might have been one of the smartest things Mike did was make that a priority. The offensive systems I've been involved in always have been able to get the ball to a featured receiver."

Moss lost his receiving partner when Cris Carter retired. Carter returned during the 2002 season with Miami, in one last (failed) attempt to make it a Super Bowl.

Another, much-larger problem than Carter's departure was lurking in the shadows for Tice: owner Red McCombs, having gotten so close to reaching the Super Bowl, had grown disenchanted. His team had gone from 15-1 in 1998 to 5-11 in 2001. His attempts to get the taxpayers to fork over a new stadium and increase his profits were going nowhere.

The main reason that McCombs quickly hired Tice rather than conduct a search for Green's replacement was that he wasn't going to pay the salary for a big name. Red was miffed that it would cost him nearly $5 million to pay off Green. He gave Tice a chance, but only if he accepted a lowball four-year contract that started in the $600,000 range.

McCombs also considerably reduced the budget for assistant coaches. That's why Tice was giving opportunities to coaches with college backgrounds—Linehan, Steve Loney, and George O'Leary—rather than established NFL assistants.

O'Leary had been Tice's high school coach on Long Island. He had been named as the new coach at Notre Dame, then was forced to resign because of inaccuracies on his resume. Coming to the Vikings was his chance to get back into coaching.

After dumping Green, McCombs gave Frank Gilliam the title of vice president of player personnel. He had been an important figure in college scouting for the organization for 32 years and he was given full control of the 2002 draft.

The first player the Vikings selected was Bryant McKinnie, a much-needed left tackle from the University of Miami, who they took with the seventh overall selection. The Vikings were late getting the selection to the podium, and Kansas City slipped in front to take Ryan Sims, a defensive tackle from Texas.

The Vikings received considerable ridicule for the draft-day slip, but McKinnie turned out to be a much more effective NFL player than Sims, who suffered a significant knee injury.

A week after the draft, it was announced that Gilliam was fired and the title of vice president for football operations was going to 32-year-old Rob Brzezinski, who had been in charge of the Vikings' salary cap. His main strength was saving McCombs money, which was priority number one with Red as the Vikings entered the fifth season of his ownership.

Gilliam was allowed to remain with the organization as a consultant. McCombs said the plan had never been to give Gilliam any long-term power in the operation—merely to get them a boss for the draft now that Green was gone.

In late May, McCombs announced that he had hired J.P. Morgan Securities Inc. to explore possibilities for selling the franchise. He also said that moving the team was a possibility.

"We're going to explore every option," he said.

So, that was Tice's situation—a superstar he was trying to mollify and get the most out of, while the owner was so upset over his stadium situation that he was threatening to move the team, and was refusing to pay to get McKinnie into training camp and help to shore up a porous offensive line.

The Vikings did find a lineman that they liked in camp in Lewis Kelly, an unsigned second-year player out of South Carolina State. Kelly was going to get a chance to start at left tackle; however, on August 25, Kelly's wife, Rakiva, died in childbirth.

These types of tensions and tragedies were no way for a rookie coach to start the season.

WAITING FOR A WIN

The Vikings season opener was played in Champaign, Illinois. Chicago's Soldier Field was being rebuilt, and Memorial Stadium on the University of Illinois campus served as the Bears' home for the 2002 season.

A Doug Brien field goal in the fourth quarter gave the Vikings a 23-13 lead with 9:07 remaining. On the Bears' first play from scrimmage after that field goal, Jim Miller threw a 54-yard pass to Marty Booker. That pass set up a 1-yard TD plunge by Anthony Thomas.

The Vikings followed with a time-consuming drive, but the drive came to an end when Daunte Culpepper's pass was intercepted by Bears safety Mike Brown. Miller then threw a 9-yard touchdown pass with 35 seconds left in the game to give the Bears a 27-23 victory.

"That was a very bad decision by me," Culpepper said of the interception.

Tice went to 0-2 the next week following another gut-wrenching loss: 45-39 to Buffalo at the Metrodome. The Bills sent the game into overtime when Mike Hollis' 54-yard field goal on the last play of regulation hit the crossbar and then hopped forward for a 39-39 tie.

In the game, Buffalo quarterback Drew Bledsoe went 35-of-49 for 463 yards passing and three touchdowns. And yet, if not for two missed extra points by Brien, Tice would have had his first victory in regulation.

"We're going to win as a team and lose as a team," Moss said. "Our kicker missing those extra points—I wasn't really down on him."

Tice was. More than an hour after the game, he called into a postgame radio show and ripped Brien. One day later, the Vikings brought back Gary Anderson to be the kicker of field goals and extra points.

Comically, they also kept Brien, supposedly as a kickoff specialist. The real reason was that McCombs was upset that he was stuck with Brien's signing bonus and salary, so he made Tice keep a second kicker.

Coach Tice had to wait patiently for his team to win its first game under his leadership in 2002. At Detroit in September 2003, he looks on as the Vikings defeat the Lions 23-13, their third victory in what would be a six-game streak to open that season.
Jerry Holt/Star Tribune

The Vikings opened the season 0-4, and in middle of the streak, there was this sidelight: Moss was charged with running into a traffic control agent with his slow-moving vehicle. He wound up pleading guilty in December to the misdemeanor of careless driving and paid a $1,200 fine.

Tice's first victory finally came on October 15 at the Metrodome with a 31-24 win against Detroit. The Vikings had fallen behind by two touchdowns in the first quarter. Culpepper completed 15 of 18 passes in the second half for 193 yards to lead the winning comeback.

The players staged a hogpile in the Vikings' end zone when safety Corey Chavous intercepted a pass on the game's final play to guarantee the victory. Tice was given a Gatorade shower that dislodged the ever-present pencil from its location snug above his ear.

This win was the start of Tice's domination of Detroit. In his four seasons as the Vikings' head coach, he was 8-0 against the Lions and 24-32 against the rest of the NFL.

The Vikings were on another losing streak (three games) and sitting at 3-10 when they went to New Orleans on December 15. The Vikings were also in the midst of a 17-game road losing streak that dated back to Thanksgiving Day in Dallas in 2000.

They were trailing the Saints 31-24 and appeared headed for another loss with five minutes left, but then Culpepper marshaled a 13-play, 73-yard drive. He connected with Moss on a touchdown pass to make it 31-30 with five seconds left in the game. Suddenly, there was Tice on the sideline holding up two fingers and signaling the offense to try for a game-winning, two-point conversion.

"Honestly, we were a 3-10 team," Tice said. "What did you have to lose? Let's go for the win. Why not?"

Because, in the nine seasons that the two-point conversion had been an option in the NFL, only twice had a team gone for two in the final two minutes when a kick would tie the game. Both times, the two-point try failed.

Tice said the Vikings had practiced the play regularly. He also said that he told his coaches halfway through the last drive to get ready for a two-point conversion.

The Vikings put Culpepper in a shotgun formation with an empty backfield. The play was a quarterback trap, not a draw. The idea was to spread the Saints defense to cover Moss and the other receivers, and then use six blockers to take on the four-man defensive front.

Culpepper was so anxious that he dropped the snap. He reached down quickly, and fortunately there were no rushing Saints to make him pay. He picked up the ball, saw the large hole in front of him, and went crashing into the end zone.

Daunte Culpepper has trouble fielding the snap on a two-point conversion attempt against New Orleans on December 15, 2002, but he recovered and scrambled into the end zone to secure a 32-31 victory.
Jerry Holt/Star Tribune

Gus Frerotte got a chance to show his stuff following a back injury to Culpepper in 2003. On September 28, the veteran threw four touchdowns and led the Vikes to a 35-7 blowout over San Francisco.
Jerry Holt/Star Tribune

The Vikings running game got a boost from their fourth-round draft pick in 2003, Onterrio Smith, who was also the team's top kick returner. Here he breaks free from the line of scrimmage in Atlanta on October 5.
Judy Griesedieck/Star Tribune

This was the start of a season-ending three-game winning streak. The final game was a 38-36 victory in Detroit. The Lions scored late but quarterback Mike McMahon misfired on a two-point conversion pass.

"We stuck together when a lot of teams fall apart," said Culpepper, pointing out that the Vikings had closed with four victories in five games.

And the Randy Ratio? Tice would declare that it was a bad idea—to tip off defenses that the Vikings were going to concentrate on getting the ball to Moss. He declared it dead for 2003, saying only that the Vikings would try to take full advantage of Moss' talents and the double-teams that his explosiveness always attracted.

Unfortunately for Tice, his postmortem as the Vikings' coach always includes mentions of the "Randy Ratio" as a failure that helped limit him to four seasons.

FAST START AND A FADE

The Vikings became the subjects of some embarrassing headlines in February 2003, when an annual charitable fundraiser at Mille Lacs Lake—the Arctic Blast—ended with allegations of sexual assault against Vikings players.

The snowmobile rally had degenerated into a boozy, hard-partying weekend where football players met ladies. Backup quarterback Todd Bouman was accused of assaulting a woman, but he was never charged. Former Viking Ted Brown ended up facing assault charges.

The incident cost Bouman his career in Minnesota. He was traded to New Orleans for a sixth-round draft choice before the 2003 season.

The Vikings targeted veteran Gus Frerotte to be the backup for Culpepper. Frerotte wanted a better deal than the Vikings were willing to offer. In an attempt to get him to budge, the Vikings brought back Jeff George—the enigmatic quarterback allowed to depart after the 1999 season—to discuss his return as a backup.

The actual purpose was to make Frerotte think that he might lose his chance at the job and get him to take the deal, which is what happened. It was a clever move by Tice, and he later admitted to some reporters that the meeting with George was strictly a ruse.

The Vikings again found themselves the subject of ridicule on draft day, when they failed to reach the podium in time to make the seventh overall pick. Two teams beat them before the Vikings finally selected Kevin Williams, a defensive tackle from Oklahoma State.

What wasn't known by the public was that the Vikings had been set to go with the Williams pick several minutes before the 15-minute period between choices expired, but team president Gary Woods was in the draft room ordering Tice, scouting director Scott Studwell, and Brzezinski to keep trying to trade down.

Again, the purported gaffe didn't hurt the Vikings, and Williams remains one of the top handful of defensive tackles in the NFL in 2008.

In May, a news conference was held at Winter Park that went against all the frugality that McCombs had previously displayed. The Vikings signed quarterback Culpepper to a contract that was advertised as being worth $102 million over 10 years.

The guaranteed money was much more modest: $16 million. The cash value would become a huge barrier in Culpepper's relationship with the team in later years and ultimately led to Daunte's acrimonious departure.

McCombs also agreed to a contract with Williams that got the number-one draft choice to Mankato for the start of training camp.

The Vikings opened the 2003 season with a 30-25 victory over the Packers at Lambeau Field that started them on a six-game winning streak. The sixth of those victories came by a 28-20 score over Denver in the Metrodome.

Moss caught 10 passes for 151 yards against the Broncos. The most memorable one came on the last play

Daunte Culpepper eludes Detroit linebacker Boss Bailey during a game on September 21, 2003. It was Minnesota's third-straight win to start the season, but Culpepper left at halftime with an injury and would miss the next three games.
Brian Peterson/Star Tribune

Running back Moe Williams races to the end zone after receiving a lateral from Randy Moss (on the turf in the background) in a game against the Broncos on October 19, 2003.
Brian Peterson/Star Tribune

At the end of the heartbreaking loss to Arizona at Sun Devil Stadium on December 28, Vikings Chris Hovan (99), Kenny Mixon (79), and Chuck Wiley (94) are in disbelief after being eliminated from the playoffs.
Jeff Wheeler/Star Tribune

of the first half. Culpepper—who was back in the lineup after fracturing several small bones in his back a month earlier—broke from the pocket and threw toward Moss, who went above two defenders at the 15-yard line, caught the ball, and then tossed it over his head toward Moe Williams. The veteran running back took the lateral and ran into the end zone.

"Right now, I would be telling you a lie to say we're not looking for a Super Bowl ring," Moss said.

Then the New York Giants came to the Metrodome and defeated the Vikings 29-17. It would start a four-game losing streak, including a loss to Green Bay at home.

The Vikings had lost six of nine as they headed to Arizona for the season finale. A victory against the Cardinals meant that they were NFC North champions; a loss left them out of the playoffs.

The Vikings held a 17-6 lead with less than two minutes remaining. The Cardinals converted twice on fourth downs, the second one coming on a 2-yard touchdown pass from Josh McCown to tight end Steve Bush with 1:54 left.

Arizona missed the two-point conversion, so it was 17-12 and the Cardinals would need a touchdown to win. After regaining possession on an onsides kick, they were fourth-down-and-25 at the Vikings' 28-yard line, with time for one play.

McCown threw a pass toward the right corner of the end zone, where Nate Poole—a deep reserve as a receiver—was covered by both cornerback Denard

Walker and safety Brian Russell. As he went up, Poole managed to get his hands on the football and then came down out of bounds.

He held onto the ball. The officials ruled it was a forceout and a catch.

Final: Cardinals 18, Vikings 17.

Tice was incensed on the field that the officials had ruled a forceout, but he later said that to blame the officials was a "loser's lament."

With the loss, the Vikings became the second team in NFL history to start a season 6-0 and then miss the playoffs. They joined the 1978 Washington Redskins in that unhappy company.

The Packers were finishing off a 31-3 throttling of Denver in Lambeau Field when the final score came in from Arizona. This set off a wild celebration in the Green Bay stands, since it put the Packers in the playoffs as division champions.

The Packers hosted Seattle in the opening round of the playoffs. Nate Poole and his wife were invited to the game by Green Bay Mayor Jim Schmitt, who said, "Nate Poole is my favorite non-Packer player."

When the Vikings were 6-0, Red McCombs told the *Star Tribune*'s Sid Hartman that Tice was the best coach in the NFL. After the 9-7 finish and the heart-breaking loss in Arizona, McCombs refused to say whether Tice would be back for the 2004 season.

He maintained that silence for two days before announcing that Tice would return for a third season.

BACKING IN, RANDY STYLE

The Vikings and their fans were in need of some good news after that devastating loss to Arizona. It came at the end of January, when Carl Eller finally was voted into the Pro Football Hall of Fame after 20 years of eligibility.

Eller was the ferocious pass rusher on the Vikings' four Super Bowl teams. He was on the defensive line every week with Alan Page and Jim Marshall, his fellow Purple People Eaters.

"Carl called and I hollered so loud I didn't hear most of what he said," said Ernestine Eller, Carl's 78-year-old mother. "But I heard enough. He was a finalist for so many years that I wanted them to quit putting his name in the paper and just let it go. It was so hard."

Eller became the fifth Vikings player to reach the shrine in Canton, Ohio, following Page, Fran Tarkenton, Paul Krause, and Ron Yary. Gary Zimmerman, a member of the Vikings for seven years, was part of the 2008 induction class. Bud Grant is in as a coach and Jim Finks as an administrator.

Randy Moss also will be there eventually, but in March 2004 rumors were spreading in the NFL's national media that the Vikings were considering a trade of the mercurial receiver.

The alleged reason was a rift between Tice and Moss. This rumor was based on a report by Larry Fitzgerald Sr., a columnist for the *Minneapolis Spokesman*, that Moss was unhappy because of Tice's comment that Randy was a "tough nut to crack."

Moss' agent, Dante DiTrapano, denied the rumors, saying, "Randy is happy. Nobody likes to win more than Randy. He might have been mad during those games [Minnesota's 3-7 finish], but it wasn't anything personal with Tice. Randy loves Tice."

Tice was able to pull off a bit of a coup in March, when he convinced free-agent cornerback Antoine Winfield to sign with the Vikings rather than the New York Jets. He was given a $10.8 million signing bonus on a six-year contract, a move that went against owner McCombs' previous tight-fisted approach to free agency.

As an additional effort to improve the defense, Tice hired Ted Cottrell as his coordinator. He was the fifth defensive coordinator in six seasons following Foge Fazio, Emmitt Thomas, Willie Shaw, and George O'Leary.

The sidebar in training camp was the appearance of Brock Lesnar as a defensive line candidate. Lesnar had been an NCAA heavyweight wrestling champion at the University of Minnesota and then a superstar attraction in the World Wrestling Federation.

Lesnar had not played football since 1995 at Webster (S.D.) High School, but this did not prevent numerous Vikings fans from hitting the Internet to speculate on Lesnar as a star tackle.

The rawness showed immediately and Lesnar was an early cut in the 2004 training camp.

Cornerback Antoine Winfield was a key acquisition for Minnesota before the 2004 season, and the move paid off. Winfield led the team with three interceptions, including this game-ending grab against the Lions on November 21.
Brian Peterson/Star Tribune

The Vikings opened the exhibition season on August 14 in the Metrodome against the Arizona Cardinals and their new coach, Dennis Green. When the preseason schedule was announced, Green said, "They must have a sense of humor in the league office."

Green faced booing that was more indifferent than hostile from the Dome crowd. The Vikings won 23-6.

The regular season opened with a 35-17 victory over Dallas in the Metrodome. Daunte Culpepper was tremendous and led the Vikings to 415 yards of total offense.

The Cowboys had the NFL's top-rated defense in 2003. "We went from number 1 to number 32 in one day," said Dallas coach Bill Parcells.

This was the beginning of another fast start for the Vikings. They reached a record of 5-1 with a 20-3 victory over Tennessee in the Dome on October 24. Moss played only briefly because of a pulled hamstring, although he did continue his streak of not missing a game in his six-season career.

Moss was hobbled the next week, and the Vikings were hammered, 34-13, by the New York Giants. The Giants had started the Vikings' skid a year earlier, and now they did it again.

Defensive tackle Chris Hovan (lower left) and linebacker Dontarrious Thomas take down Deuce McAllister in a game against the Saints on October 17, 2004. The Vikings defense held the former All-Pro running back to 73 yards in the 38-31 win.
Jim Gehrz/Star Tribune

The Vikings lost five of eight, and they were 8-6 when they hosted Green Bay on Christmas Eve. A victory would clinch the NFC North for the home team.

The Vikings led 31-24 after linebacker Chris Claiborne intercepted Brett Favre and returned it for a touchdown midway through the fourth quarter. Favre tied the score on a 3-yard TD pass to Donald Driver and then Green Bay's Ryan Longwell kicked a 29-yard field goal on the game's last play to secure a 34-31 Packers victory.

Team employees hurriedly put away T-shirts that read, "Minnesota Vikings: NFC North Champions," which had been readied for use a half-hour earlier.

"It takes your insides out," Tice said. "When you've worked as hard as we've worked—it rips out part of your insides that doesn't grow back."

There was another side drama taking place as well. Tice's contract called for McCombs to pick up his option for the following season by January 1, 2005. The Vikings'

last regular-season game was scheduled in Washington on January 2.

There was some thought that Tice could use this for leverage, but by mid-week McCombs and Tice agreed that the decision would come after the Washington game.

The Vikings lost 21-18 to fall to 8-8. Moss left the bench a few seconds before the end of the game. His departure was caught on national television and became a large story. Center Matt Birk confronted Moss after the game.

"I didn't like it," Birk said. "I made sure to get to the locker room quick to talk to him about it."

And then, a half-hour after the Vikings had lost, Carolina lost 21-18 to New Orleans, and Tice's team backed into the NFC playoffs as a wild-card team. The incomprehensible defeat in Arizona that kept them out of the playoffs in the 2003 season had been followed by

During the 2004 season, Nate Burleson led the team with 1,006 receiving yards, including this spectacular touchdown grab against Chicago cornerback Charles Tillman. It wasn't enough on this December afternoon, however, as the Bears won the game, 24-14.
Jim Gehrz/Star Tribune

an incomprehensible opportunity to continue the 2004 season.

McCombs picked up Tice's option, and the Vikings went to Green Bay to play the Packers in the first round of the playoffs. It was the first time the fierce border rivals ever met in the postseason.

During the week, Moss gave an interview to ESPN's Andrea Kremer and said that Birk's opinions about his behavior in Washington—or any future behavior—were meaningless.

There didn't seem to be much reason for optimism when the Vikings went into Lambeau Field on January 9. The team had suffered two regular-season losses to the Packers—both by a score of 34-31 and both on last-second scores by Green Bay.

Moss was booed vociferously by the Packers crowd throughout the playoff game. In the fourth quarter, he caught a 34-yard touchdown pass that put the Vikings up 31-17. After making the catch, Moss ran to the goal

Randy Moss heads off the field before the final seconds tick off the clock during the final game of the 2004 season, a 21-18 loss to Washington. Moss' action created a stir in the newspapers and in the Vikings locker room.
Evan Vucci/AP/Wide World Photos

Left: Moss beats cornerback Al Harris in the end zone to grab Culpepper's 34-yard pass and give the Vikings a 31-17 lead in the final quarter against Green Bay on January 9, 2005. *Jeff Wheeler/Star Tribune*

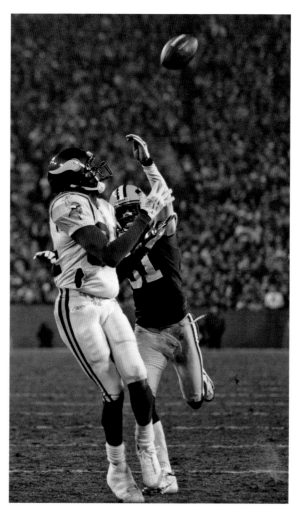

Left: Moss beats cornerback Al Harris in the end zone to grab Culpepper's 34-yard pass and give the Vikings a 31-17 lead in the final quarter against Green Bay on January 9, 2005. *Jeff Wheeler/Star Tribune*

Right: Moss greets the Packer faithful with a simulated moon following his touchdown. *Jeff Wheeler/Star Tribune*

post and then pantomimed as if he were pulling down his uniform to moon the Green Bay fans.

Joe Buck was outraged in the Fox television booth, screaming that Moss' actions were "disgusting."

Tice did not share that view of his superstar, not immediately after what would be the biggest victory of his four-year tenure as coach.

"Come on over here and give me a hug," Tice shouted at Moss at game's end, and Randy obliged.

The NFL gave Moss another fine—$10,000—for the fake moon. When asked by a reporter how he intended to pay the ten grand, Moss responded, "Straight cash, homey."

TROUBLE WITHOUT MOSS

The Vikings went to Philadelphia after the upset victory in Green Bay. The Vikings weren't much of a challenge to the Eagles, losing 27-14.

Immediately, stories in the local and the national media were reporting what was now the NFL's worst-kept secret: The Vikings intended to trade Moss.

When looked at individually, Moss' indiscretions were more annoying than horrendous, but they just kept com-

ing, until the question at Winter Park became, "Is Randy more trouble than he's worth?"

There were other questions as well. From McCombs, back to his frugal ways: "How much money can I save by trading him?" From the football department: "Are this season's leg injuries—first a hamstring, then a knee—the start of a decline in Moss' physical abilities?"

The question the Vikings did not ask often enough was this: "How much has it meant to our offense—and specifically to Culpepper—to have a receiver with career totals of 574 receptions, 9,142 yards, and 90 touchdowns in 109 career games?"

The Vikings agreed on February 23, 2005, to trade Moss to Oakland for the number-seven overall selection in the 2005 draft and linebacker Napoleon Harris.

A new wave of Vikings fans had arisen in 1998 when Moss came to Minnesota and helped to turn a team that was having trouble selling out the Dome into a 15-1 phenomenon. These people loved Moss—still do a decade later—and they were extremely upset at the trade.

The trade could not become official until March 1 because of league rules. The Vikings refused to comment, until McCombs finally came out two days after it was official and tried to blame it all on problems between Tice and Moss.

McCombs said he had considered firing Tice in order to get Moss to stay. One problem with that claim: Tice had called McCombs before the trade was made and said, "Let's not do this. I can work out any problems with Randy."

What Red really wanted was to save $8 million in payroll in 2005, just in case he wasn't able to complete the sale of the team.

Tice had a larger problem—from a personal standpoint, anyway—within two weeks of the Moss trade. Allegedly, a former Vikings player contacted the NFL office and said that Tice had lobbied with players to purchase the Super Bowl tickets available to them, with the promise he would have them sold and they would split the profits.

Tice had run this operation during his time as an assistant coach and then continued it with assistant coach Dean Dalton as a middle man after he became the head coach.

This ticket scalping was said to be a popular way for assistant coaches to make some extra bucks across the NFL. Two things were different this time: Tice was now a head coach, and he got caught.

After originally denying involvement, Tice came clean with the NFL a couple of days later. He was fined $100,000, which was a sizable hunk for a coach earning $800,000 per year.

As if this wasn't embarrassing enough, on May 11 the *Star Tribune*'s Kevin Seifert reported that running back Onterrio Smith had been detained at Minneapolis-St. Paul International Airport after trying to sneak an "Original Whizzinator"—an instrument used to try to beat a drug test—through security in a carry-on bag.

Smith, a fourth-round draft choice in 2003, was placed in the NFL substance abuse program when he came into the league because of problems at the University of Tennessee. He then was suspended for the first four games of 2004 because of a violation of the program.

This time, Smith was scheduled for another drug test when he was caught with the device on April 21. The NFL treated this as if it was another positive test and suspended Smith for the 2005 season.

WILF TAKES CHARGE

Red McCombs had made a tentative deal in February 2005 to sell the Vikings to Reggie Fowler, an Arizona businessman. He agreed to a sale price of $625 million—a number that would allow McCombs to leave Minnesota with a profit of roughly a half-billion dollars (when expansion fees and annual profits were added) for his seven years as the Vikings owner.

A dejected Moss watches from the sidelines as the Vikings' 2004 season comes to an end with a loss in Philadelphia. It would be the receiver's last game in a Vikings uniform.
Brian Peterson/Star Tribune

173

STADIUM STRUGGLES

The Vikings followed the Twins into Metropolitan Stadium as tenants in the late summer of 1961. They had to haggle with the Twins, the Metropolitan Sports Commission, and the city of Bloomington in their attempts to get better bleachers along the left-field line and to build a two-deck pavilion behind the left-field fence.

Eventually, the capacity of the ballpark was increased to 49,784 for an NFL game, but the Vikings began expressing the need for a new facility as early as 1970.

General Manager Jim Finks and several city of Minneapolis officials announced early in 1972 a plan to build a domed,

Though it was built originally to host baseball, Metropolitan Stadium in Bloomington served as the home of the Vikings for 21 seasons and regularly attracted capacity crowds. *Star Tribune*

football-only stadium on the northwest edge of downtown. The deal died early in 1973.

Vikings President Max Winter was upset over the opposition to the downtown dome. In May 1973, he told Twin Cities reporters that he had received "favorable offers" for relocation from seven cities: Seattle, Phoenix, Memphis, Birmingham, Tampa, Orlando, and Jacksonville.

Two days later, Bernie Ridder, a member of the Vikings' ownership group, took away Winter's thunder by saying, "The National Football League wouldn't permit a transfer of the Minnesota franchise under any circumstance even if we wanted to move—and we don't."

Finks had a falling out with Winter and resigned in May 1974. Ridder, a tremendous admirer of Finks, sold his shares to Winter and the Boyer and Skoglund families.

Winter hired Mike Lynn, a man who had been trying to get an expansion franchise for Memphis, as an assistant a couple of months later. During the winter of 1974–75, Lynn and owner H. P. Skoglund went to Phoenix to discuss relocation and stadium possibilities.

Lynn was appointed as Vikings general manager in July 1975. Stories kept popping up that Lynn was traveling hither and yon to discuss relocation. This was intended to intimidate Minnesota politicians into providing a satisfactory stadium for the Vikings.

After a long battle, a stadium bill made it through the Minnesota State Legislature, and construction on the Hubert H. Humphrey Metrodome started in December 1979. The local business community put heavy pressure on Twins owner Calvin Griffith, and he also signed on as a tenant for the domed stadium that opened in 1982.

The Twins started expressing their need for a new ballpark in the mid-1990s. Their new outdoor stadium will open in 2010, and it is located only a couple of blocks from where Finks had envisioned building the football-only dome 38 years earlier.

Red McCombs purchased the Vikings in the summer of 1998. Even though he got the team at the bargain price of $240 million (estimated cash value), it didn't take long for Red to start beating the drum for a new Vikings stadium.

Before the start of the 1999 season, McCombs was making a speech to a local business group and said, "We need a new stadium or the Vikings won't be here five years from now."

This became a constant drumbeat with McCombs. When the State Legislature failed to take any action during its 2002 session, McCombs said he was either going to sell the team or relocate the franchise.

In October 2004, he told Mike Silver from *Sports Illustrated:* "Let's face it. I would like to be in Los Angeles. But I can't just pick up and go to L.A.; that is a league issue."

Finally, in June 2005, McCombs closed a deal to sell the Vikings to New Jersey real estate developer Zygi Wilf and his family. The purchase price was $600 million, which was basically the price for a team with a new stadium, not one with seven seasons remaining on the lease to play in the low-revenue Metrodome.

Wilf agreed to try to partner with Anoka County for a new stadium in Blaine, then he backed away. The vision in 2008 was for a retractable-roof stadium that would replace the Metrodome.

Pricetag: Roughly $1 billion, and growing daily.

Outlook: Stay tuned, folks. By now, we should be old hands at stadium battles involving the Vikings, Minnesota's most popular sports team.

Even in the "nosebleed" seats, fans have been coming to the Metrodome in droves since 1982, despite years of debate and discussion about building a new stadium for the Vikings. *Carlos Gonzalez/Star Tribune*

Even after the controversial Moss was shipped out of town, Mike Tice's troubles didn't end. The Vikings posted a winning record in 2005, but it proved to be the coach's last season on the job.
Brian Peterson/Star Tribune

Zygmunt "Zygi" Wilf, seen here with his brother Mark, took over the ownership of a team in turmoil in May 2005.
Jennifer Hulshizer/Star-Ledger

As it turned out, Fowler could not come up with enough money to become the primary owner. He had tied in with the Wilf family, real estate developers from New Jersey, as partners.

Eventually, Zygi Wilf emerged as the lead investor, and Fowler was reduced to a small piece of the ownership. Zygi and his family received NFL approval as the new owners on May 25.

Wilf would show a willingness to spend for assistant coaches and free agents, but it was too late for Tice to keep his staff intact. McCombs had refused to pay competitive salaries during the months when the sale was uncertain.

Offensive Coordinator Scott Linehan left for Miami and a big raise. Red didn't allow Tice to hire a replacement, so Steve Loney was promoted from offensive line coach.

The departure of Linehan would prove to be as much of a loss to Culpepper as the trade of Moss. Linehan had been very successful as a mentor to Culpepper when it came to reading defenses and changing plays. They had worked together for weeks in the offseason to eliminate plays that didn't work, and Culpepper's interceptions had gone from 23 in 2002 to 11 in 2003 and again in 2004.

RALLYING FROM SCANDAL

Culpepper was fabulous during the 2005 exhibition schedule as the Vikings went 3-1. It appeared that he was more than ready to succeed without Moss—with targets such as Jermaine Wiggins, Nate Burleson, Marcus Robinson, Travis Taylor, and Troy Williamson, the rookie speedster taken with the number-seven overall selection in the draft.

The Vikings opened the regular season with considerable optimism against Tampa Bay in the Metrodome. Monte Kiffin, the Bucs' crafty defensive coordinator, came up with some schemes that seemed to confuse Culpepper.

Culpepper threw three interceptions and lost two fumbles; the Buccaneers beat the Vikings 24-13. The postgame talk shows—affectionately known as the Viking Whine Line shows—were filled with calls ripping Culpepper.

A week later, the Vikings went to Cincinnati and the offense was completely hapless in a 37-8 loss. The Vikings had seven turnovers, and Culpepper again was responsible for five.

This time, Tice joined in the criticism of Culpepper. He said that the quarterback had received "better than solid" protection against the Bengals.

The Vikings returned to the Metrodome to face New Orleans in the season's third game. It had taken only two losses—accompanied by 10 large turnovers—for the fans to turn hostile toward Culpepper.

Tice was fully aware of the loss of fan favor, so he went against tradition. His defense, not the offense, was introduced before the game. He was protecting his quarterback against the boos.

Culpepper threw for 300 yards and three touchdowns (with no interceptions) in the game, and the Vikings beat the Saints with a 33-16 victory.

Turnaround? In week four, the Vikings went to Atlanta and were smothered 30-10. Culpepper was sacked a career-high nine times and had another three turnovers.

"We're just not very good," said Tice, and admitted he was looking forward to his team's bye week.

Be careful what you wish for.

On October 11, it hit the local media that two nights earlier numerous Vikings had rented two yachts from Al and Alma's Charter Cruises on Lake Minnetonka and then engaged in a wild sex party that involved women who had been brought in from Atlanta, among other locations.

This became known in Vikings' lore as the "Love Boat scandal." Among those implicated was Culpepper, which served to increase the heat he already was facing from Minnesota's Vikings-mad public.

Eventually, charges against Culpepper were dropped. A couple of players would pay small fines. But it was a national story—and fodder for the Jay Leno and David Letterman monologues—for weeks.

Wilf met with his team to deliver an angry tirade about the off-field embarrassment and vowed to produce a manifesto that would demand proper personal conduct. He delivered on that later in the season, a 73-page tome that appeared to forbid everything from sex cruises to spitting on the sidewalk.

Wilf and Tice promised a "new era" for this team, and then they went to Chicago and lost 28-3. The Vikings were 1-4 with Green Bay coming to town, and it was beginning to appear that Tice might not make it through October, much less the season.

Bears fans at Soldier Field taunt the embattled Vikings during a 28-3 blowout by Chicago on October 16, 2005. *Jeff Wheeler/Star Tribune*

Which proves: You never know, especially with your beloved Purple.

The Vikings came back from a 17-point halftime deficit to the Packers and won, 23-20, when Paul Edinger kicked a career-best 56-yard field goal as time expired. The *Star Tribune* headline the next morning described Edinger's kick as the "Love Boot."

The Vikings celebrated as if they finally had won the Super Bowl.

"Just an extremely beautiful, chaotic moment," said receiver Burleson.

The next week was only chaotic when the Vikings visited Carolina. Culpepper suffered a devastating knee injury and was replaced by Brad Johnson, who had come back in the offseason to serve as Daunte's backup.

Steve Smith, Carolina's outstanding receiver, worked over the single coverage of Fred Smoot—a major figure in the Love Boat reports—for 11 catches and 211 yards. Worst of all, after catching a touchdown pass, Smith sat in the end zone and pretended to row a boat. You couldn't turn on ESPN's SportsCenter for the next week without seeing Smith rowing the Vikings' Love Boat.

What next? Johnson was in, Culpepper was headed for surgery, the Vikings were 2-5, and it had been a season featuring Tice's ticket scalping, Onterrio's Whizzinator, and cruisin' with the ladies on Lake Minnetonka.

This was next: A six-game winning streak sparked by Johnson's solid play and a much-improved defense.

The scandals were in the rearview mirror, and the 8-5 Vikings were staring at the playoffs. They were one game behind Chicago in the NFC North and tied for the final playoff spot.

The Pittsburgh Steelers came to the Metrodome on December 18 and ended the winning streak with a 18-3 thumping of the Vikings. This was a Pittsburgh team that would go on the road as an AFC wild-card team, win three games, and then go into Detroit and beat Seattle to win the Super Bowl.

The Vikings lost again, 30-23, at Baltimore to drop them to 8-7 and out of the playoffs. The Johnson-led offense cooled considerably when it ran into a pair of strong AFC defenses.

The season ended with a 34-10 victory in the Metrodome over a Chicago team that already had

Daunte Culpepper is carted off the field after suffering a season-ending knee injury against the Carolina Panthers on October 3, 2005.
Jerry Holt/Star Tribune

clinched the NFC North. Tice had taken a team with an underfinanced roster, an underfinanced coaching staff, and a series of scandals to a 9-7 record.

His reward was to be fired by owner Zygi Wilf within a half-hour after the win over Chicago.

"I didn't get a chance to savor the victory very long," Tice said. "I've been the one saying [let me know] sooner than later. I guess he took that to mean, 'As soon as possible. ASAP.'"

He added, "It's a shame that I'm not going to be able to coach for the Wilfs. I think they're going to be great owners."

In four seasons (plus one game with Green's team at the end of the 2001 season) as head coach, Mike Tice had a record of 32-33 in the regular season and 1-1 in the playoffs. That 9-7 record in his final campaign would look pretty good a year later, but as Wilf would say, it was all the off-field problems that got Tice fired, more than wins and losses.

MAKING A QUICK DECISION

Tice was fired on January 1, 2006. Five days later, the Vikings called a news conference to introduce Wilf's first coaching hire: Brad Childress, 49, the offensive coordinator from the Philadelphia Eagles.

Childress' name had been bandied about for other NFL openings over the previous several seasons. He was scheduled to go to Green Bay for an interview, where

Brad Johnson stepped in for the injured Culpepper and responded by leading the Vikings on a six-game winning streak, including a 21-16 victory over the Lions on December 4.
Brian Peterson/Star Tribune

Mike Tice waves farewell to the Metrodome crowd following a 34-10 win over the Bears in the 2005 season finale. Less than half an hour later, Tice was fired as the Vikings head coach.
Jerry Holt/Star Tribune

Minnesota's new head coach, Brad Childress, addresses his charges during training camp in Mankato on July 31, 2006.
Jerry Holt/Star Tribune

the Packers were replacing Mike Sherman, but the Wilfs convinced him to stay in a Minneapolis hotel while they raced through a couple of other interviews.

Childress talked about the Vikings being the best of the available NFL jobs because he was inheriting a 9-7 team and not a rebuilding project. It didn't turn out that way.

Culpepper had $6 million in cash added to his contract before training camp in 2005. He was starting to figure out how little of the $102 million in his 10-year deal was guaranteed, and there were indications that he might boycott training camp without more money.

Now, he was rehabilitating from knee surgery, but he still was focused on getting more guaranteed money out of that contract. He came to Minnesota from his Florida home, ostensibly to meet with Childress, but wouldn't walk down the corridor to have a conversation after he learned that there would be no more money in the contract before the 2006 season.

Culpepper came back on February 1 and did meet with Wilf and Childress. The coach and the quarterback never were able to make a connection. Culpepper started the bizarre practice of sending e-mails to reporters, rather than answering media questions.

It took until March 14 and then the Vikings traded Culpepper to the Miami Dolphins for a second-round draft choice. The player turned out to be Ryan Cook, the Vikings' starting right tackle as a second-year player in 2007.

Childress had criticized Culpepper for being unwilling to come to Winter Park to do his rehabilitation. He suggested that Culpepper was rehabbing in an ill-equipped facility in a strip mall in Florida.

"A quarterback and head coach have got to be in lockstep," Childress said on the day of the trade. "Somewhere, there has to be a buy-in factor. I just didn't think that was the case, right from the beginning.

"I never had a conversation with him about this football team. It was always about what he needed financially and money. I never heard team. I always heard 'me' and 'I need $10 million.'"

The Culpepper trade came only two days after the Vikings made a move that shook up the NFL: They made a free-agent offer to Steve Hutchinson, Seattle's All-Pro left guard, that would have forced the Seahawks to guarantee an entire $49 million to match.

After a week of fuming over this tactic and appealing to the NFL arbitrator, the Seahawks allowed Hutchinson to come to Minnesota. The Seahawks then made a similar move to get receiver Nate Burleson away from the Vikings—but getting Hutchinson, in effect, for Burleson was a trade any NFL team would make.

The Vikings' exhibition opener came against Moss and the Raiders. There were more cheers than boos for Moss while he played briefly. The Raiders won 16-13 in the Monday-night game.

The players were supposed to be back in Mankato by 11 p.m. the next night. Koren Robinson, a troubled wide receiver, had been signed by the Vikings six games into the 2005 season. He returned kicks well enough to make the Pro Bowl, and he also had an 80-yard touchdown catch as a wide receiver.

The new Vikings regime was impressed enough to give Robinson a three-year contract. The contract included language that allowed the Vikings to void the deal if Robinson were to get in trouble.

And he did: On his way back to Mankato the night after the Raiders game, Robinson was arrested following a 15-mile police chase. He was clocked driving 104 miles per hour in St. Peter at 10:46 p.m., and that's where the chase started. It finished at the Minnesota State Mankato campus, where Robinson was hoping to beat curfew and stay out of Childress' doghouse.

Instead, Robinson registered a blood alcohol level of 0.09, just over the legal limit, and spent 15 hours in jail before posting a $50,000 bail. He was cut by the Vikings and wound up serving a 20-day jail sentence a year later in St. Peter.

Robinson's sudden departure left the Vikings hurting for receivers. Still, they opened Childress' tenure with a 19-16 victory in Washington on a Monday night. It would have been an easier win, but Williamson dropped three passes from quarterback Brad Johnson. It was becoming clear that Williamson shared Moss' blazing speed, but the hands and the ability to adjust to the ball that made Moss a superstar were not among Williamson's skills.

The Vikings had a 4-2 record after a 31-13 win in Seattle that included a 95-yard run by Chester Taylor, another free agent who had been signed through Wilf's more generous spending policies.

Running back Chester Taylor is off to the races with a 95-yard touchdown run against the Seahawks on October 22, 2006.
Carlos Gonzalez/Star Tribune

Brad Johnson (14) was hardly thrilled to be benched during a 31-7 loss to New England on Monday Night Football in October. Coach Childress put backup Brooks Bollinger (9) in the game after Johnson threw three interceptions.
Jim Gehrz/Star Tribune

Then, the Patriots came to the Metrodome for a Monday-night game. New England opened with Tom Brady operating a five-receiver formation, and they went on to rip up the Vikings, 31-7. Brady threw for 372 yards and four touchdowns, while Brad Johnson threw three interceptions and finished with a woeful quarterback rating of 38.1.

The Patriots game was the start of a four-game losing streak and a 2-8 finish to the season. A definite coolness developed between Johnson, often a hero to Vikings fans, and Childress. Rookie Tarvaris Jackson started the last two games of the season: a 9-7 loss in Green Bay and a 41-21 loss to St. Louis in the Dome.

Childress had talked of inheriting the NFL's best coaching vacancy. He had a roster reinforced with well-paid free agents and the staff of assistants that he wanted. Still, the 9-7 record of 2005 turned into 6-10 in Childress' first season.

A NEW STAR ARRIVES

The Vikings had no trouble selling out the Metrodome after Moss brought his unique excitement to town in 1998. The team featured additional star power with Cris Carter and then quarterback Daunte Culpepper.

Carter left after 2001, Moss was traded after 2004, and when Culpepper fell out of favor in 2005 he was also traded away.

The Vikings were without star power and needed corporate help to keep the sellout streak alive in 2007. Then Adrian Peterson, the running back from the University of Oklahoma and the seventh overall selection in the 2007 draft, turned out to be everything the Vikings had hoped, and then some.

Johnson was gone, and Jackson, the second-year player from Division I-AA Alabama State, was installed as the starting quarterback. Kelly Holcomb was acquired from Philadelphia to join Brooks Bollinger as veteran backup assistance for the young quarterback.

The Vikings went 1-3 in the first month of the 2007 season. Jackson got hurt in the second game, which was a loss in Detroit. Childress tried Holcomb, who was ineffective in losses to Kansas City and Green Bay.

Following a bye week, Jackson returned to the lineup for an October 14 game in Chicago. It was the official coming-out party for Peterson, who had gotten only two carries in the second half of the loss in Green Bay.

This time, Peterson had the reasonable workload of 20 carries, and he turned them into 224 yards, a Vikings record. He had touchdown runs of 67, 73, and 35 yards. With 1:30 left in the game, Peterson contributed a 53-yard kickoff return that gave the Vikings' Ryan Longwell a chance to kick the game-winning field goal for a final score of Vikings 34, Bears 31.

"He can bounce outside, he can cut back, he can leave guys behind," center Matt Birk said of Peterson. "He might be all right."

The Vikings followed with two more losses, to fall to 2-5. San Diego, which was rallying from a slow start, came to the Metrodome on November 9.

Peterson had 13 carries for 43 yards at halftime and the Vikings trailed 14-7.

In the first game of the 2007 season, quarterback Tarvaris Jackson held up under pressure and led the Vikings to a 24-3 win against the Falcons. It would be an up-and-down year for the young QB.
Brian Peterson/Star Tribune

Rookie Adrian Peterson's coming-out party occurred on October 14, 2007, when he rushed for 224 yards and scored three touchdowns against Chicago. In the final minutes of the game, he returned a kickoff 53 yards to set up the winning field goal.
Jeff Wheeler/Star Tribune

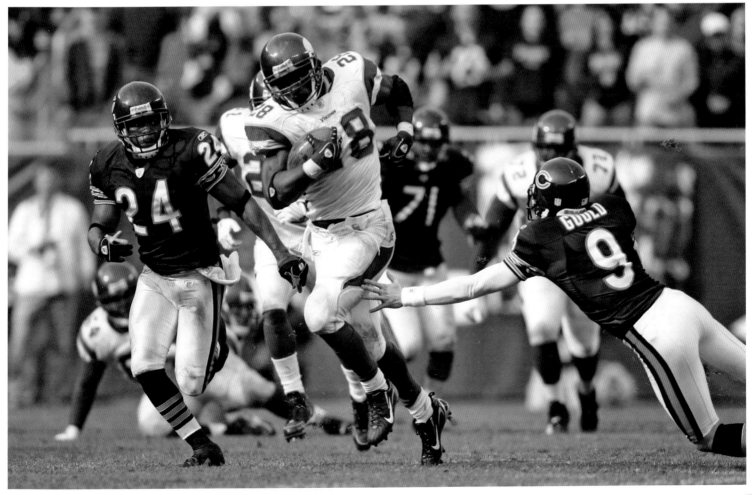

He started the second half with a 6-yard run, then on third-and-2 from the Vikings' 36, he went 64 yards for a touchdown. He had 107 yards on eight carries in the third quarter.

He scored again on a 46-yard run in the fourth quarter. He also had runs of 16, 19, and 35 yards—a total of nine rushes in the final quarter for 146 yards. In 30 carries on the game, Peterson totaled 296 yards rushing—an NFL record. He also helped secure a 35-17 victory for the Vikings.

"Even this year as a rookie, you don't know what the kid is going to do next," safety Darren Sharper said. "Every time he touches the ball you don't know. It could be the play of all time."

A week later, Peterson suffered a tear of the non-weight bearing ligament in his right knee in a 34-0 loss at Green Bay. He missed two weeks, which turned out to be victories over Oakland and the New York Giants.

Against the Giants on November 25, the Vikings intercepted four Eli Manning passes and returned three for touchdowns in a 41-17 drubbing at the Meadowlands in New Jersey. (Amazingly, 10 weeks later, the Giants would upset New England, 17-14, in the Super Bowl to end the Patriots' quest for perfection—and Manning was the game's MVP.)

The Vikings extended the winning streak to five games with wins over Detroit, San Francisco, and Chicago. They had a record of 8-6 and needed only a victory over Washington at home to clinch a playoff berth.

The Vikings were beaten 32-21 in the Metrodome. The Redskins put themselves in position to clinch the wild-card spot—and deny Childress a playoff trip in his second season—with a victory over Dallas in the season's final week.

Washington did just that and rendered the Vikings' finale—a 22-19 overtime loss in Denver—irrelevant.

The good news was that Jackson, after an erratic season in which he had three injuries, played his best football of the season in the season finale. He led a fourth-quarter comeback that forced the overtime session.

The better news was that Peterson finished with the season 1,341 rushing yards and an average of 5.6 yards. Star power was back in Minnesota.

Just to remind everyone of his talent and to remind people that he might be on his way to being the Randy Moss of Vikings' runners, the rookie was named the Most Valuable Player in the Pro Bowl in Hawaii. He rushed 16 times for 129 yards and two touchdowns, which left the Purple zealots back on the mainland to let out their eternal exclamation: "This could be our year!"

And one of these years, it will be.

Peterson leaped into the record books when he ran for a total of 296 yards against San Diego on November 4. This fourth-quarter touchdown came on a 46-yard run.
Carlos Gonzalez/Star Tribune

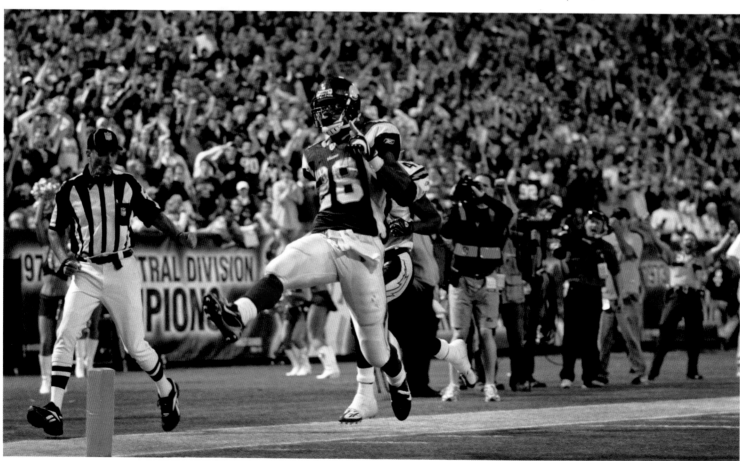

The young quarterback confers with his coach during the final game of the 2007 season. Jackson sparked the team in a fourth-quarter comeback but ultimately lost to Denver in overtime. *Jerry Holt/Star Tribune*

Adrian Peterson takes a breather after one of his many long runs during the 2007 season. He was named Offensive Rookie of the Year by the Associated Press, among other honors. *Jeff Wheeler/Star Tribune*

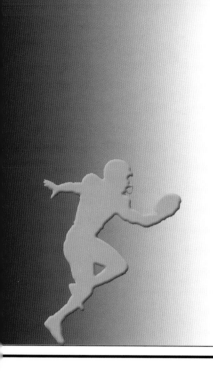

AFTERWORD
BY SENATOR AMY KLOBUCHAR

On September 18, 2007, the Commerce Committee of the United States Senate convened a hearing slightly more glamorous than the typical deputy-secretary confirmation or agency reauthorization. Television cameras were there in abundance, and the still cameras ferociously clicked as the star witness entered the room.

The topic? Disability and health benefits for retired NFL players.

The witness? Former NFL player and coach Mike Ditka.

As the junior Senator from Minnesota and the least senior member of the committee, I was at the tail-end for questions. But I had a connection to football that no other elected member of the Senate had.

"Coach Ditka," I said. "I grew up with football. My dad covered football, including the Bears and the Vikings. One of my earliest memories from that rough-and-tumble era of the NFL was of my dad getting into a brawl with then-Vikings coach Norm Van Brocklin in a hotel room. I also remember that the only thing that got broken was the television."

"Senator," Coach Ditka responded. "Let the record reflect that I too have gotten into a brawl with Norm Van Brocklin in my living room."

No one was under oath that day.

America's founders designed our democracy without patrician requirements; our elected representatives would truly be of the people. As James Madison explained in The Federalist Papers, the door of American government is "open to merit of every description" regardless of a person's background. But Madison probably had not imagined the background I would bring to our nation's capital.

I grew up on play-by-plays and Monday Night Football at a time when the Vikings were the Purple People Eaters and the team practiced in a park that doubled as a livestock showing ground. Early memories included evening calls from the stoic Coach Bud Grant, who would scare any fifth grader with his brevity. I would answer the phone: "Klobuchar residence, Amy speaking." An icy "JIM" is all I would hear.

Growing up, I would watch Monday Night Football with my dad, and he always seized on the games as an educational opportunity.

One night, one of the players was hurt. The trainers worked on him and then helped him off the field. The announcers weren't sure what happened, but at age 13, I was feeling pretty knowledgeable about the world. "It looks to me like a groin injury," I said to my dad. Sure enough, 15 minutes later, they announced the player had been felled by a serious groin injury.

My father always prided himself on writing all the news worth printing. The next day he wrote about our session watching pro football. I hadn't read the paper yet but one of the guys at school stopped me in the hallway. "Hey," he said, "great headline about you watching football." I smiled modestly and quickly grabbed a newspaper. The headline was spread across four columns: "Daughter, 13, Spots Groin Injury."

I got to go to many Vikings games with my dad at the old Met Stadium in Bloomington. Sometimes I would even get to bring a junior high friend. We would huddle in the stands in our snowmobile suits and blankets. At the end of each game, we would go down to meet my dad outside the locker room. We would see all the players as they left: Alan Page, Gary Larsen, Jim Marshall, Carl Eller, Joe Kapp, Mick Tingelhoff, Paul Krause, and more. Finally, when we'd leave the stadium, we'd inevitably come upon some very cold and very drunk fans still lagging behind. "Great game," they would say to my dad, patting him on the back. The fact that my dad is only five-foot-eight never seemed to deter their hopes that they had met an actual Viking. My dad would not even pause before saying, "Hey, thanks. It was a team effort."

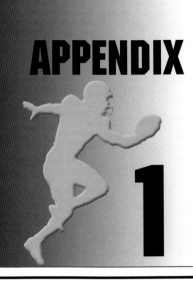

THE MINNESOTA VIKINGS, YEAR 1 BY YEAR

Year	Record	Finish	How the Season is Remembered
Head Coach Norm Van Brocklin (6 seasons, 29-51-4 combined record)			
1961	3-11	7th West	Tarkenton leads blowout of Bears in first game
1962	2-11-1	6th	Defense surrenders 410 points
1963	5-8-1	Tied 4th	RB Tommy Mason is team's first All-Pro
1964	8-5-1	Tied 2nd	First winning season; "Wrong-way" Marshall
1965	7-7	Tied 5th	Van Brocklin resigns, then returns
1966	4-9-1	Tied 6th	Dutchman, Fran feud, both depart
Head Coach Bud Grant (17 seasons, 149-87-5, 10-12 in playoffs)			
1967	3-8-3	4th Central	Finks trades bring Alan Page, much more
1968	8-6	1st	Sweep of Packers; first playoff season
1969	12-2	1st	Kapp rejects MVP, declares "40 for 60"
1970	12-2	1st	Kapp holds out, leaves hole at QB
1971	11-3	1st	QB shuffle with Cuozzo, Lee, Snead
1972	7-7	3rd	Tark returns; Vikes fall to .500
1973	12-2	1st	Rookie Foreman sparks offense
1974	10-4	1st	Sutherland becomes fourth People Eater
1975	12-2	1st	10-0 start ends with 31-30 loss to Redskins
1976	11-2-1	1st	White, Rashad provide Tark targets
1977	9-5	1st	Last season for Purple People Eaters
1978	8-7-1	1st	Tark's last season; Grant waives Page
1979	7-9	3rd	Tommy Kramer takes over at QB
1980	9-7	1st	6-2 second half means playoff return
1981	7-9	4th	Season ends with 5 straight losses
1982	5-4	N/A	Dorsett goes 99; Vikes still win
1983	8-8	4th	Kramer hurt; Grant resigns
Head Coach Les Seckel (one season, 3-13)			
1984	3-13	5th	Les: One and done; Bud returns
Head Coach Bud Grant II (one season, 7-9)			
1985	7-9	3rd	Bud ends chaos, then quits
Head Coach Jerry Burns (6 seasons, 52-43, 3-3 in playoffs)			
1986	9-7	2nd	A.C., Zimmerman arrive from USFL
1987	8-7	2nd	0-3 with strike-breakers; 8-4 in reality
1988	11-5	2nd	Wilson, Kramer QB controversy
1989	10-6	1st	Lynn gives away farm for Herschel
1990	6-10	5th	Trade's a flop and Lynn quits
1991	8-8	3rd	Cris Carter emerges; Burns bails
Head Coach Dennis Green (10 seasons, 97-62, 4-8 in playoffs)			
1992	11-5	1st	Sheriff Green arrives; wins division
1993	9-7	2nd	Ex-Bear Jim McMahon is number-one QB
1994	10-6	1st	Cris Carter catches 122 with Moon as QB

Year	Record	Finish	How the Season is Remembered
1995	8-8	4th	Another 122 plus 17 TDS for Carter
1996	9-7	2nd	Fans want QB Brad Johnson, get him
1997	9-7	4th	Healthy Smith rushes for 1,266 yards
1998	15-1	1st	Randy Moss explodes in Green Bay
1999	10-6	2nd	QB Cunningham abdicates to Jeff George
2000	11-5	1st	Young QB Culpepper debuts in style
2001	5-11	4th	Green fired; Tice coaches final game
Head Coach Mike Tice (4 seasons, 32-33, 1-1 in playoffs)			
2002	6-10	2nd North	Cris Carter gone; Moss catches 106
2003	9-7	2nd	Moss: 111 catches, 1,632 yards, 17 TDs
2004	8-8	2nd	Moss: Walkoff, a moon, then a trade
2005	9-7	2nd	Ticket scalping, "Love Boat" scandals sink Tice
Head Coach Brad Childress (2 seasons, 14-18)			
2006	6-10	3rd	2-8 finish as offense crawls along
2007	8-8	2nd	Surge ends with Redskins flop

The Playoffs

Year		How the Season is Remembered
1968	0-1	loss at Baltimore
1969	2-1	first two playoff wins, then upset loss to Kansas City in Super Bowl IV
1970	0-1	upset loss at Met Stadium against San Francisco
1971	0-1	loss at Met Stadium to Dallas
1973	2-1	upset win in Dallas, then Super Bowl loss to mighty Dolphins
1974	2-1	fierce win over Rams at Met, then Super Bowl loss to Pittsburgh's Steel Curtain
1975	0-1	Vikings scream Pearson push-off in loss to Dallas at Met
1976	2-1	Rams, 'Skins fall at Met; Oakland puts Vikings at 0-4 in Super Bowls
1977	1-1	upset win in mud at Los Angeles, then loss at Dallas
1978	0-1	Rams get revenge with blowout in LA
1980	0-1	turnovers destroy Vikings in Philadelphia
1982	1-1	Vikings split two games in post-strike, 16-team Super Bowl tourney
1987	2-1	great January runs ends with narrow loss in Washington
1988	1-1	49ers get payback with blowout in Candlestick
1989	0-1	49ers get more payback with blowout in Candlestick
1992	0-1	squashed in Dome by Redskins' running game
1993	0-1	offense fails in windy Giants Stadium
1994	0-1	Steve Walsh leads Bears upset in Dome
1996	0-1	confident going in, Vikes get stomped by Cowboys
1997	1-1	Denny Green finally gets playoff win with unlikely comeback vs. Giants
1998	1-1	painful overtime loss to Atlanta in NFC title game at Dome
1999	1-1	Randy Moss squirts his water bottle in loss to Rams in St. Louis
2000	1-1	Vikings, favored by 2, lose "41-doughnut" to Giants in NFC title game
2004	1-1	upset win in Green Bay, no match for Eagles in Philadelphia
Total	18-24	4-4 in conference title games, 0-4 in Super Bowls

187

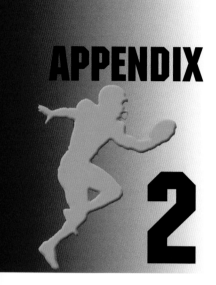

THE ALL-TIME MINNESOTA 2 VIKINGS TEAM

The Vikings will be marking their 50th season in Minnesota in 2010. No doubt, the team will run a promotion and ask fans to vote for an all-time team. Here is one ballot.

Offense

Wide Receiver	Cris Carter (1990–2001)	He came to Minnesota for the waiver price of $100 and wound up catching 1,004 passes for 12,383 yards and 110 touchdowns in 12 seasons.
Wide Receiver	Randy Moss (1998–2004)	Fell to number 21 in the 1998 draft because of checkered history, then caught 574 passes for 9,142 yards and 90 touchdowns in seven seasons with Minnesota.
Wide Receiver	Anthony Carter (1985–1993)	Magnificent play led Vikings to NFC title game after 1987 season. Explosive as receiver and punt returner.
Left Tackle	Grady Alderman (1961–1973)	Gary Zimmerman, a Viking from 1986 through 1992, is a Hall of Famer, but we'll go with Alderman, who didn't miss a game in 13 seasons and went to five Pro Bowls.
Left Guard	Randall McDaniel (1988–1999)	Called by Mike Tice the only "unbeaten football player he ever coached," meaning McDaniel always won his head-to-head matchup.
Center	Mick Tingelhoff (1962–1978)	Took over at center as an undrafted rookie for the 1962 season opener and didn't miss a start in 17 seasons. Six Pro Bowls.
Right Guard	Ed White (1969–1977)	Played left side at start of the career, then moved alongside Ron Yary in 1975 to make for a ferocious right side of the line.
Right Tackle	Ron Yary (1968–1981)	The Giants were given a bonus choice at the top of the draft as part of the NFL-AFL merger. They gave it to the Vikings in the first Fran Tarkenton trade, and the Vikings turned it into Yary. Hall of Famer, seven Pro Bowls.
Tight End	Steve Jordan (1982–1994)	The Vikings had a history of exceptional tight ends for their first three decades, including Stu Voigt and Joe Senser. Jordan was a tremendous threat, collecting 498 receptions and 28 touchdowns.

Quarterback	Fran Tarkenton (1961–1966, 1972–1978)	He was the team's first star, was involved in its first major feud with Coach Norm Van Brocklin, and returned from New York to lead Minnesota to three Super Bowls.
Running Back	Chuck Foreman (1973–1979)	Great runner, great receiver. He was the missing ingredient in the offense that got the Vikings back on the Super Bowl track.
Fullback	Bill Brown (1962–1974)	The relentless "Boom Boom" came from the Bears with little buildup and soon was fitting the Vikings' mold of a dual running and receiving threat out of the backfield.
Kicker	Fred Cox (1963–1977)	He comes from the age of the straight-ahead kickers. Freddie was good enough for Bud Grant for over a decade, so he's good enough for us.

Defense

End	Carl Eller (1964–1978)	We called him "Moose," even though he usually carried around 250 pounds on his 6-foot, 5-inch frame. He had 130 sacks and made the Hall of Fame in 2004 in his 20th year of eligibility.
End	Jim Marshall (1961–1979)	The NFL's all-time ironman among position players with 282 consecutive games, all starts, with 270 coming for the Vikings.
Tackle	Alan Page (1967–1978)	Perhaps the greatest defensive tackle in NFL history and the first defensive player to be named as the league's MVP in 1971. He was the NFC's Defensive Player of the Year four times.
Tackle	John Randle (1990–2000)	An undrafted free agent out of Texas A&I, he served an apprenticeship in 1990, then emerged with 9-1/2 sacks in 1991. Led team in sacks nine times and finished with 114 as a Viking.
Left Linebacker	Matt Blair (1974–1985)	Outstanding tackler, had the speed to pass-cover backs and is the Vikings' all-time leader with 20 blocked kicks.
Middle Linebacker	Jeff Siemon (1972–1982) and Scott Studwell (1977–1990)	Impossible to choose between these two, who overlapped for six seasons—three apiece as the starter. Siemon had club record with 229 tackles in 1978, until Studwell broke it with 230 in 1981.
Right Linebacker	Wally Hilgenberg (1968–1979)	He was on his way home after getting cut by Pittsburgh in 1968 when the Vikings called and asked him to come to Minnesota for the season opener. Reliable, feisty, and big in the clutch.
Cornerback	Bobby Bryant (1968–1980)	A case also could be made for Ed Sharockman (1962–1972) and Carl Lee (1983–1993), but the preference here is Bryant for his big-play ability and Wright for his talent as a coverman.
Cornerback	Nate Wright (1971–1980)	Wright had 32 interceptions and was an ironman from 1973 through 1978, starting 85 of 86 games.
Free Safety	Paul Krause (1968–1979)	NFL's all-time interception leader with 81 (53 in Minnesota), and a Hall of Famer.
Strong Safety	Joey Browner (1983–1991)	When it came to all-around athletic talent, not many Vikings have topped Browner. His hands were so strong he could reach out and grab a ball-carrier one-handed and bring him to a screeching halt.
Punter	Greg Coleman (1978–1987)	Easy choice here, since Coleman had a 10-season run in a role where the Vikings have had 16 other regular punters in the 37 non-Coleman seasons.

INDEX